CHICKEN DEVIL ™

VOLUME ONE
UNDER PRESSURE

BRIAN BUCCELLATO

HAYDEN SHERMAN

HASSAN OTSMANE-ELHAOU

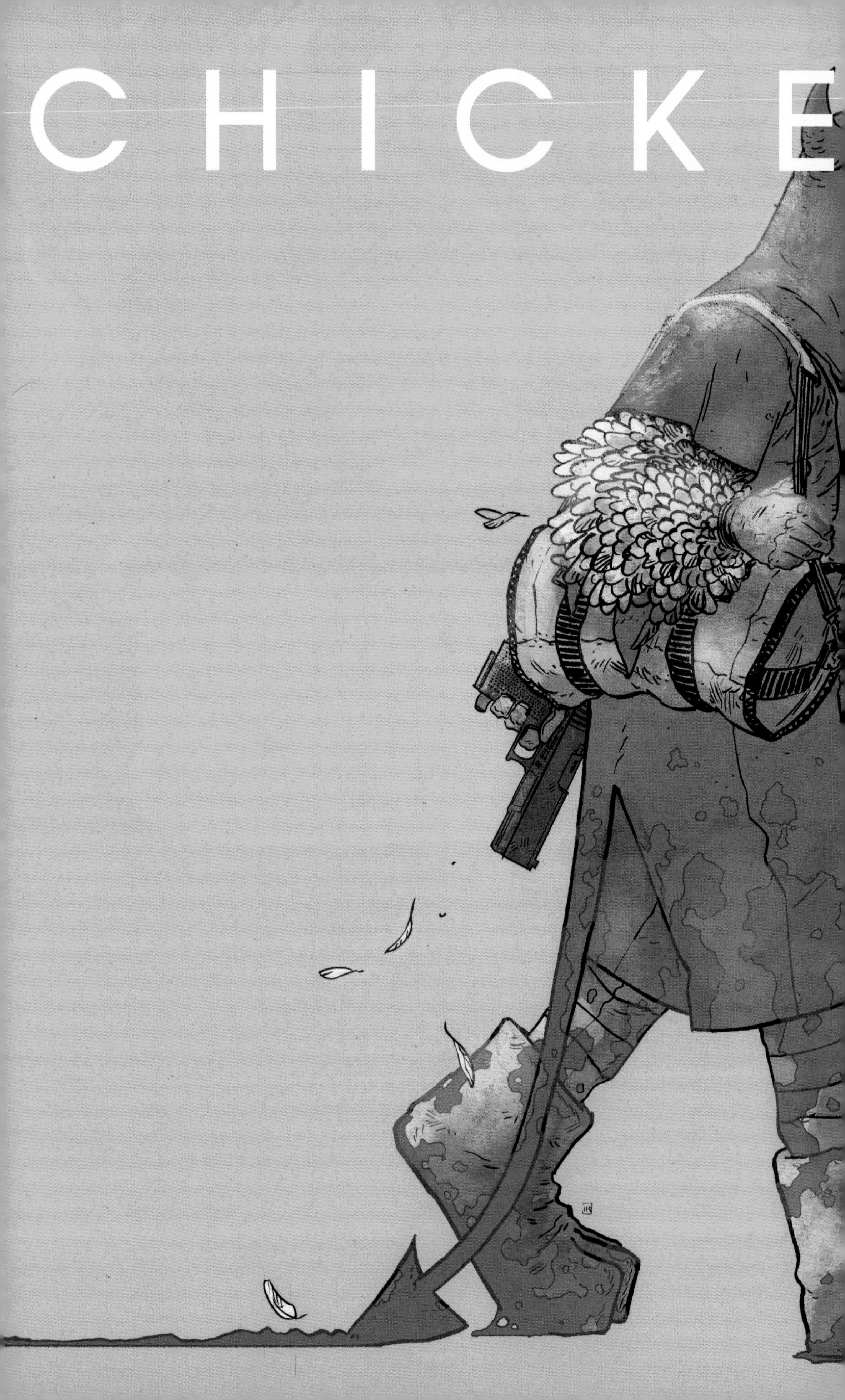
CHICKE

N DEVIL

VOLUME 1: UNDER PRESSURE

BRIAN BUCCELLATO writer

HAYDEN SHERMAN artist

HASSAN OTSMANE-ELHAOU letterer

HAYDEN SHERMAN front, original & mask covers

DAVID LOPEZ incentive cover

MIKE ROOTH Happy Hour cover

MIKE McKONE w/ CHRIS O'HALLORAN ambassador cover

DAN PANOSIAN NYCC & Baltimore Comic Con exclusive covers

ROB CSIKI, AMANDA DUFRESNE, GODTAIL, CHINH POTTER & **HUGH ROOKWOOD** variant covers

DAVE SHARPE logo designer

CHARLES PRITCHETT issue #1 backmatter designer

COREY BREEN book designer

MIKE MARTS editor

created by **BRIAN BUCCELLATO** & **HAYDEN SHERMAN**

AFTERSHOCK™

MIKE MARTS - Editor-in-Chief • JOE PRUETT - Publisher/CCO • LEE KRAMER - President • JON KRAMER - Chief Executive Officer
STEVE ROTTERDAM - SVP, Sales & Marketing • DAN SHIRES - VP, Film & Television UK • CHRISTINA HARRINGTON - Managing Editor
MARC HAMMOND - Sr. Retail Sales Development Manager • RUTHANN THOMPSON - Communications Specialist
KATHERINE JAMISON - Marketing Manager • KELLY DIODATI - Ambassador Outreach Manager • BLAKE STOCKER - VP, Finance
AARON MARION - Publicist • LISA MOODY - Finance • RYAN CARROLL - Director, Comics/Film/TV Liaison • JAWAD QURESHI - Technology Advisor/Strategist
RACHEL PINNELAS - Social Community Manager • CHARLES PRITCHETT - Design & Production Manager • COREY BREEN - Collections Production
TEODORO LEO - Associate Editor • SARAH PRUETT & GIGI WILLIAMS - Publishing Assistants

AfterShock Logo Design by COMICRAFT
Publicity: contact AARON MARION (aaron@publichausagency.com) & RYAN CROY (ryan@publichausagency.com) at PUBLICHAUS
Special thanks to: ATOM! FREEMAN, IRA KURGAN, MARINE KSADZHIKYAN, KEITH MANZELLA, ANTHONY MILITANO, ANTONIA LIANOS, STEPHAN NILSON & ED ZAREMBA

AFTERSHOCKCOMICS.COM Follow us on social media 🐦 📷 f

I N T R O D U C T I O N

Write what you know.

That's what they say. Moving past who THEY are, it's still good advice. When not taken literally. Because let's be honest, most people's lives are mind-numbingly average...with the occasional meme-worthy event. Myself included. So, YES...I admit up front that I never have, nor do I ever hope to, go on a kill-crazy rampage to avenge my family.

And, yet, CHICKEN DEVIL is STILL writing what you know — with a twist. Our protagonist Mitch is a regular guy with a monotonous life and a normal (somewhat challenging) family dynamic. He also makes really good Hot Chicken. At first blush, it's not the recipe for an exciting comic. Not until you get to the secret sauce — the extraordinary, kind of meta, weirdly funny, REALLY dark and violent circumstances that Mitchell is thrust into. Without giving away the entire plot, I will double-down and say this book has a lot of me in it. Weirdly, it's an attempt to answer the question:

What would boring-ass Brian (with no military training or killing skills) do if he had to become the Punisher, John Wick, or any Liam Neeson character bent on bloody revenge?

It would be a train wreck.

What you're holding in your hands is the most ME comic I've ever written. And even if I didn't write what I know...I DID write what would probably happen if my *very particular set of skills* were applied to taking on the Eastern European mob. I hope you enjoy. A bazillion thanks to Hayden and Hassan, my partners in this endeavor...

...and to the lovely folks at AfterShock, who co-signed this bizarre idea.

BRIAN BUCCELLATO
February 2022

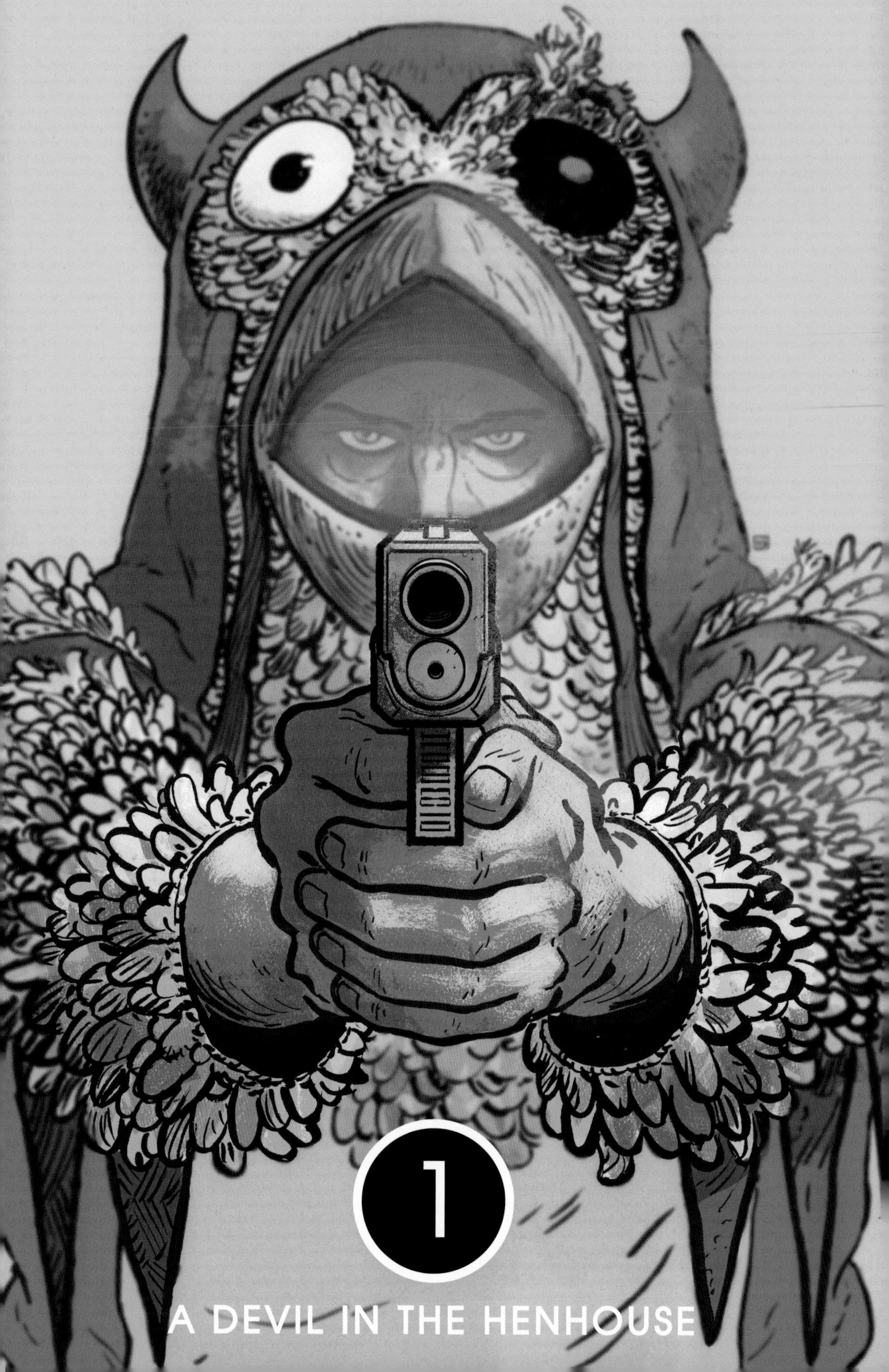

1

A DEVIL IN THE HENHOUSE

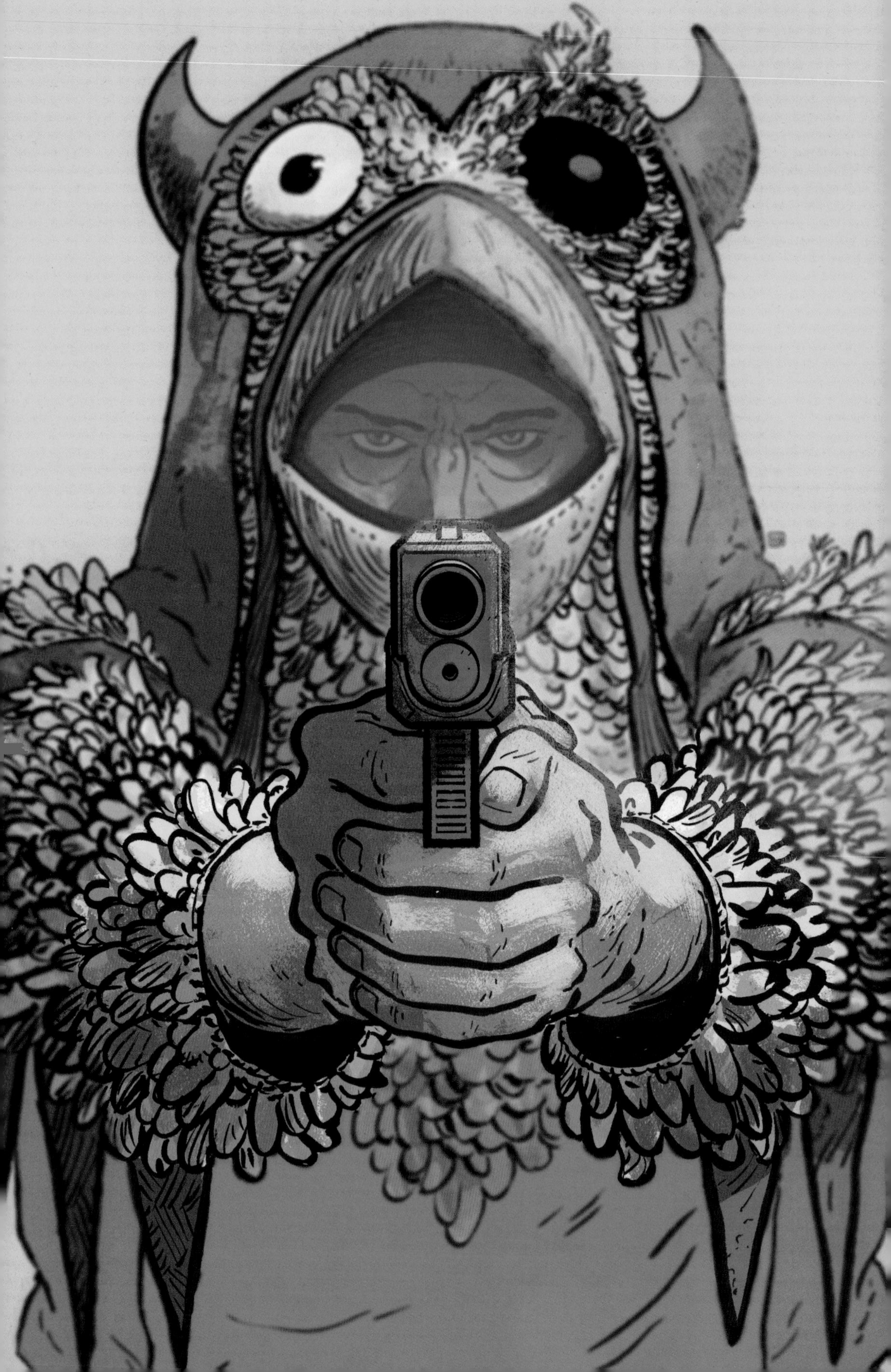

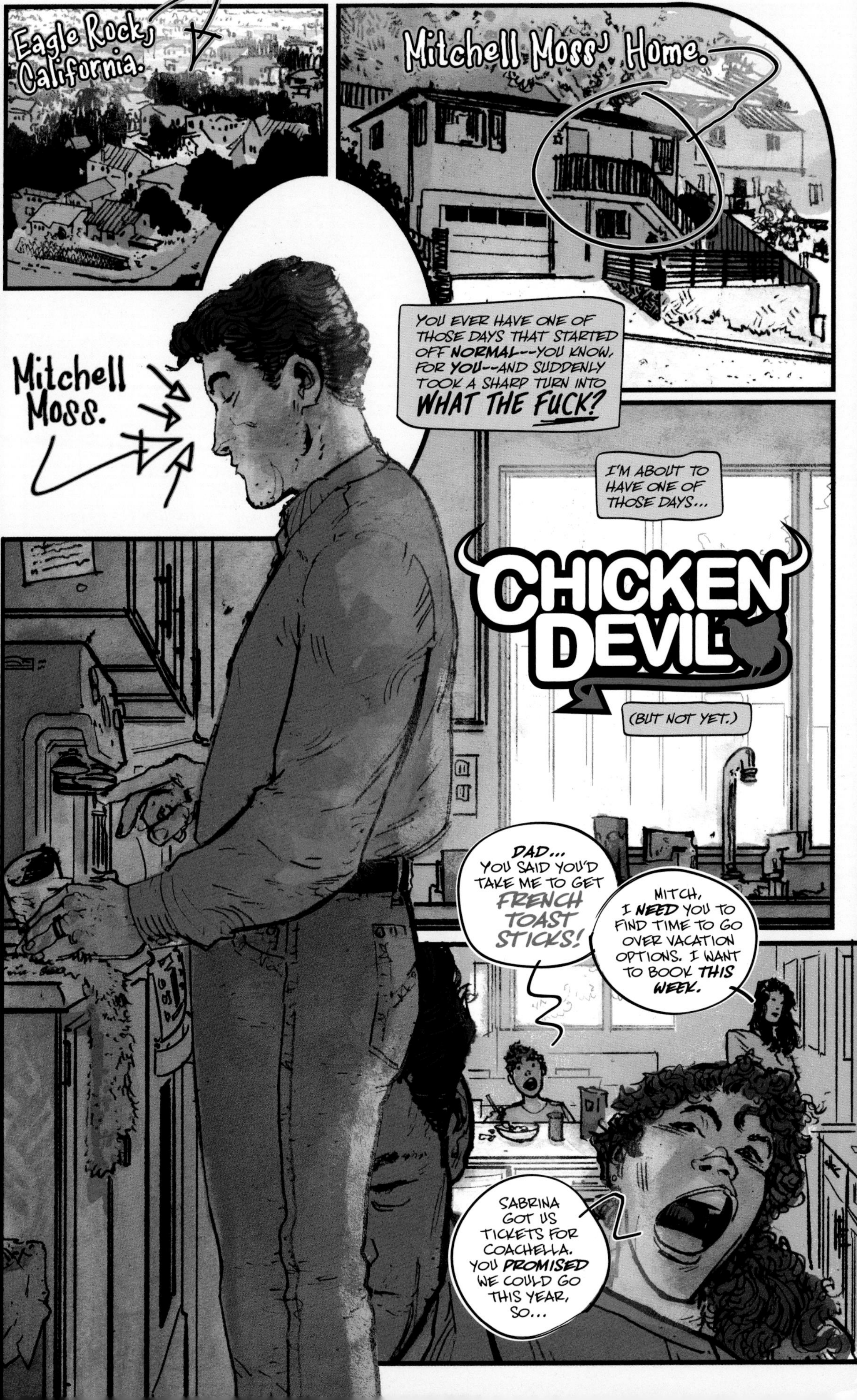
Eagle Rock, California.
Mitchell Moss' Home.
YOU EVER HAVE ONE OF THOSE DAYS THAT STARTED OFF NORMAL--YOU KNOW, FOR YOU--AND SUDDENLY TOOK A SHARP TURN INTO WHAT THE FUCK?
Mitchell Moss.
I'M ABOUT TO HAVE ONE OF THOSE DAYS...
CHICKEN DEVIL
(BUT NOT YET.)
DAD... YOU SAID YOU'D TAKE ME TO GET FRENCH TOAST STICKS!
MITCH, I NEED YOU TO FIND TIME TO GO OVER VACATION OPTIONS. I WANT TO BOOK THIS WEEK.
SABRINA GOT US TICKETS FOR COACHELLA. YOU PROMISED WE COULD GO THIS YEAR, SO...

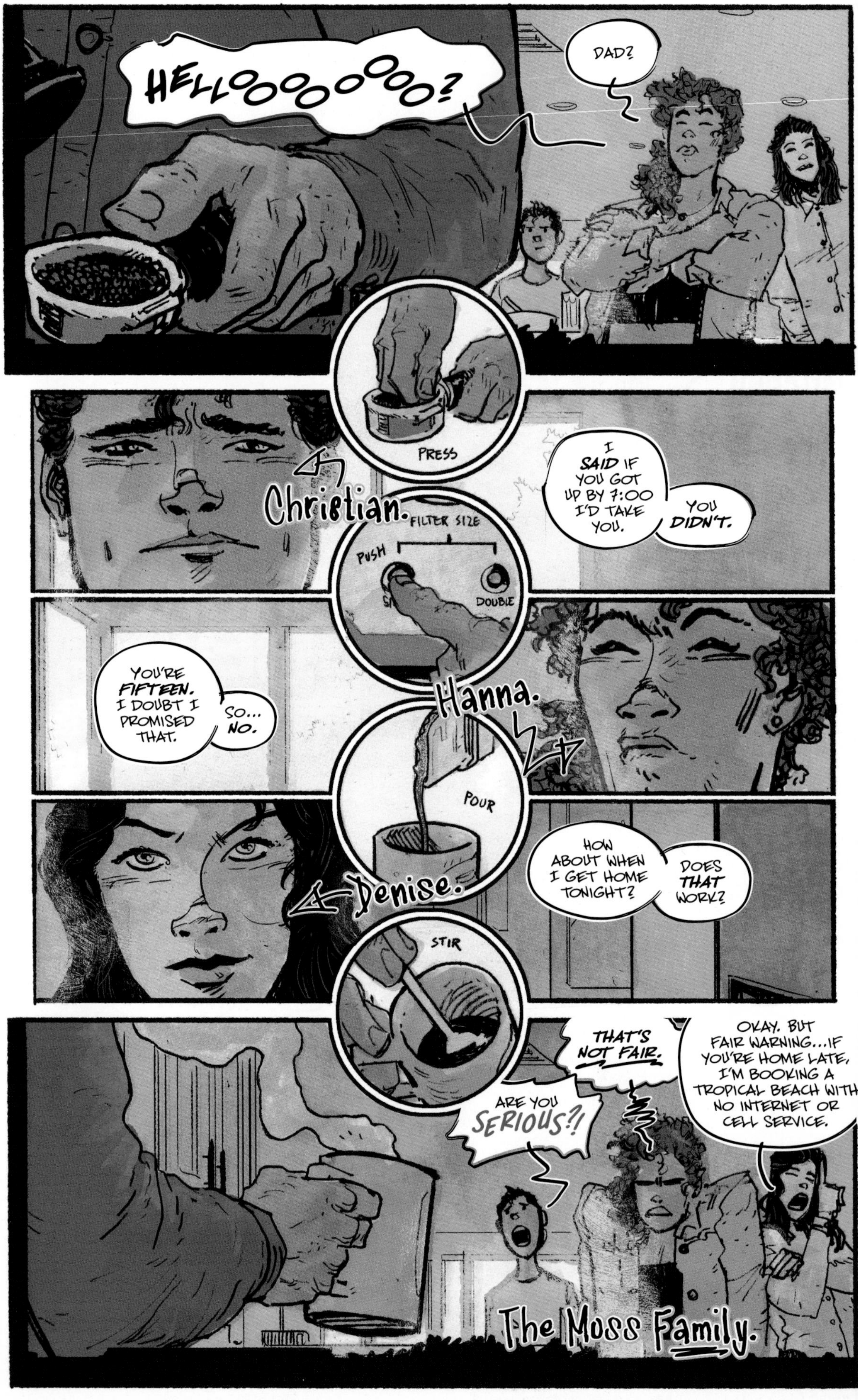
HELLOOOOOOO?
DAD?
PRESS
Christian.
I SAID IF YOU GOT UP BY 7:00 I'D TAKE YOU.
YOU DIDN'T.
FILTER SIZE
PUSH
DOUBLE
YOU'RE FIFTEEN. I DOUBT I PROMISED THAT.
SO... NO.
Hanna.
POUR
HOW ABOUT WHEN I GET HOME TONIGHT?
DOES THAT WORK?
Denise.
STIR
THAT'S NOT FAIR.
OKAY. BUT FAIR WARNING...IF YOU'RE HOME LATE, I'M BOOKING A TROPICAL BEACH WITH NO INTERNET OR CELL SERVICE.
ARE YOU SERIOUS?!
The Moss Family.

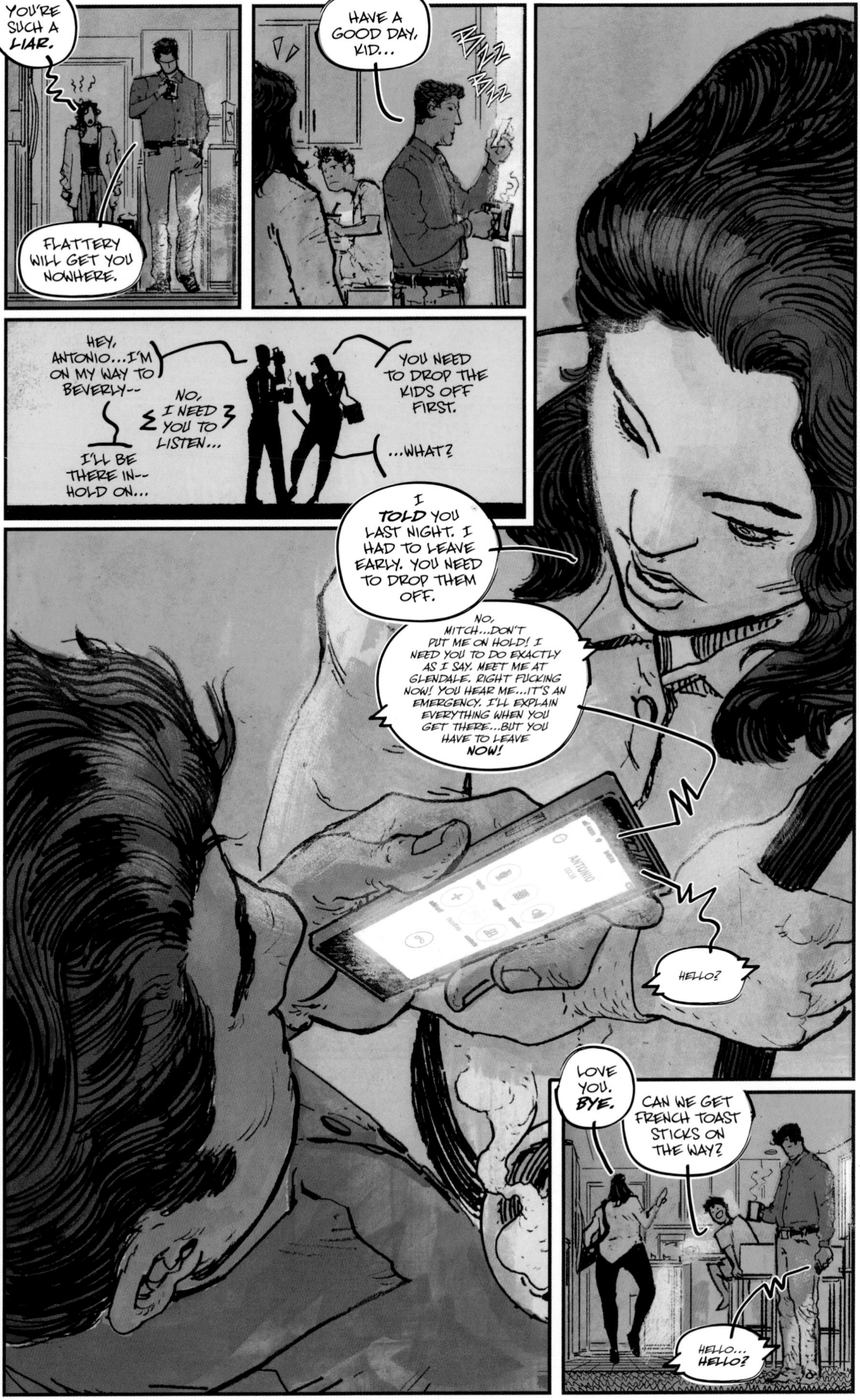
YOU'RE SUCH A LIAR.
FLATTERY WILL GET YOU NOWHERE.
HAVE A GOOD DAY, KID...
BZZ BZZ
HEY, ANTONIO...I'M ON MY WAY TO BEVERLY--
YOU NEED TO DROP THE KIDS OFF FIRST.
NO, I NEED YOU TO LISTEN...
I'LL BE THERE IN-- HOLD ON...
...WHAT?
I TOLD YOU LAST NIGHT. I HAD TO LEAVE EARLY. YOU NEED TO DROP THEM OFF.
NO, MITCH...DON'T PUT ME ON HOLD! I NEED YOU TO DO EXACTLY AS I SAY. MEET ME AT GLENDALE. RIGHT FUCKING NOW! YOU HEAR ME...IT'S AN EMERGENCY. I'LL EXPLAIN EVERYTHING WHEN YOU GET THERE...BUT YOU HAVE TO LEAVE NOW!
ANTONIO
HELLO?
LOVE YOU. BYE.
CAN WE GET FRENCH TOAST STICKS ON THE WAY?
HELLO... HELLO?

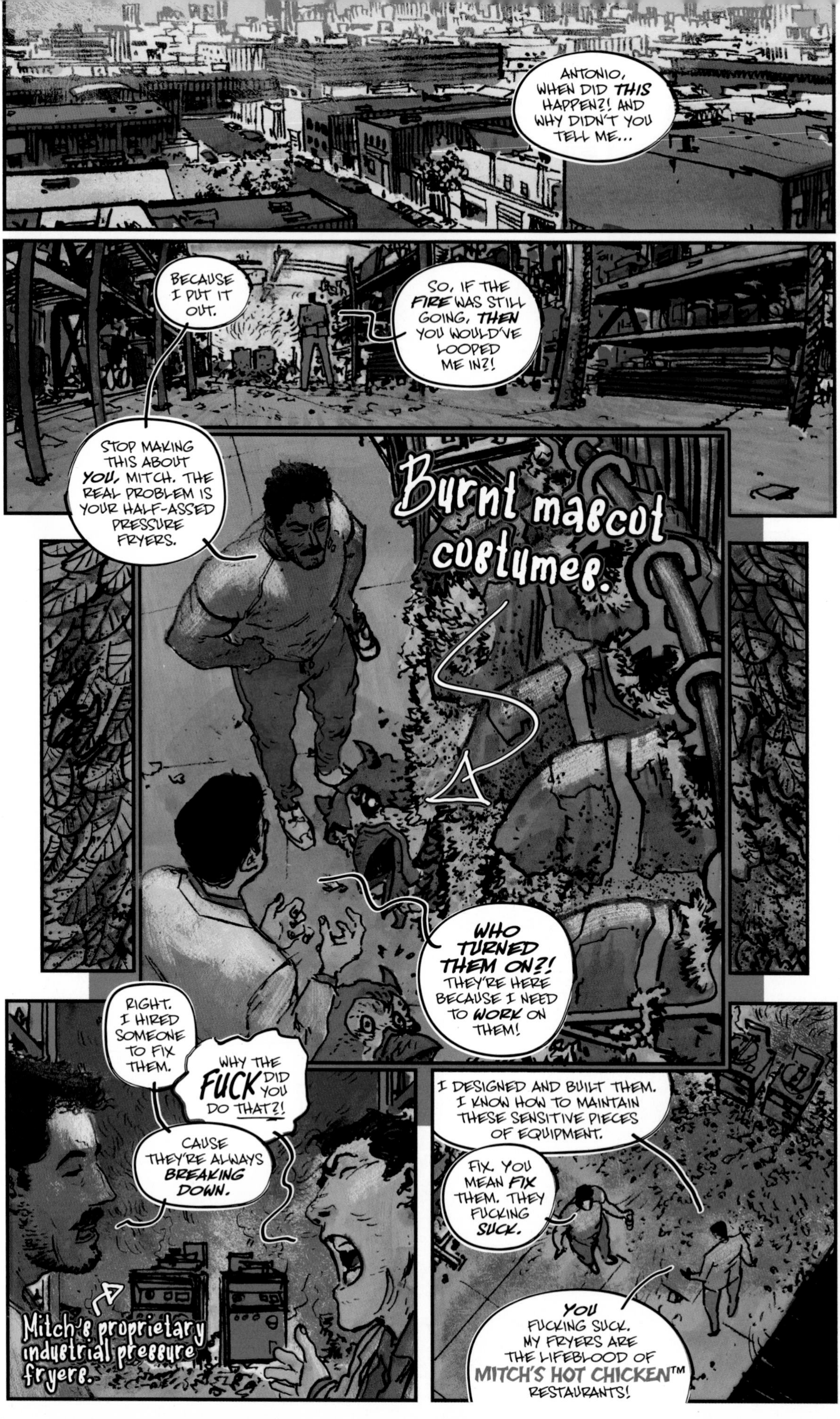

ANTONIO, WHEN DID THIS HAPPEN?! AND WHY DIDN'T YOU TELL ME...
BECAUSE I PUT IT OUT.
SO, IF THE FIRE WAS STILL GOING, THEN YOU WOULD'VE LOOPED ME IN?!
STOP MAKING THIS ABOUT YOU, MITCH. THE REAL PROBLEM IS YOUR HALF-ASSED PRESSURE FRYERS.
Burnt mascot costumes.
WHO TURNED THEM ON?! THEY'RE HERE BECAUSE I NEED TO WORK ON THEM!
RIGHT. I HIRED SOMEONE TO FIX THEM.
WHY THE FUCK DID YOU DO THAT?!
CAUSE THEY'RE ALWAYS BREAKING DOWN.
Mitch's proprietary industrial pressure fryers.
I DESIGNED AND BUILT THEM. I KNOW HOW TO MAINTAIN THESE SENSITIVE PIECES OF EQUIPMENT.
FIX. YOU MEAN FIX THEM. THEY FUCKING SUCK.
YOU FUCKING SUCK. MY FRYERS ARE THE LIFEBLOOD OF MITCH'S HOT CHICKEN™ RESTAURANTS!

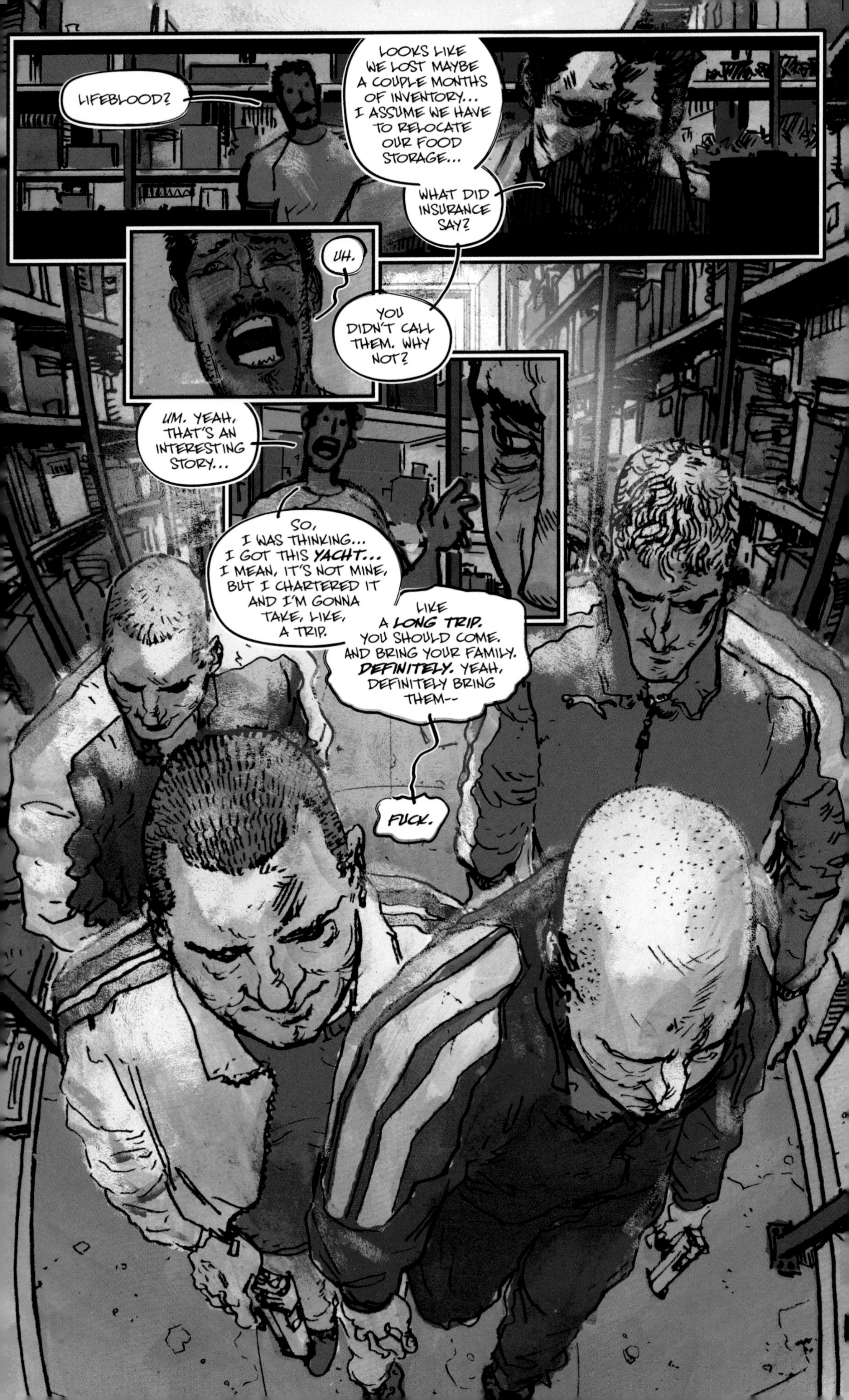
LIFEBLOOD?
LOOKS LIKE WE LOST MAYBE A COUPLE MONTHS OF INVENTORY... I ASSUME WE HAVE TO RELOCATE OUR FOOD STORAGE...
WHAT DID INSURANCE SAY?
UH.
YOU DIDN'T CALL THEM. WHY NOT?
UM. YEAH, THAT'S AN INTERESTING STORY...
SO, I WAS THINKING... I GOT THIS YACHT... I MEAN, IT'S NOT MINE, BUT I CHARTERED IT AND I'M GONNA TAKE, LIKE, A TRIP.
LIKE A LONG TRIP. YOU SHOULD COME. AND BRING YOUR FAMILY. DEFINITELY. YEAH, DEFINITELY BRING THEM--
FUCK.

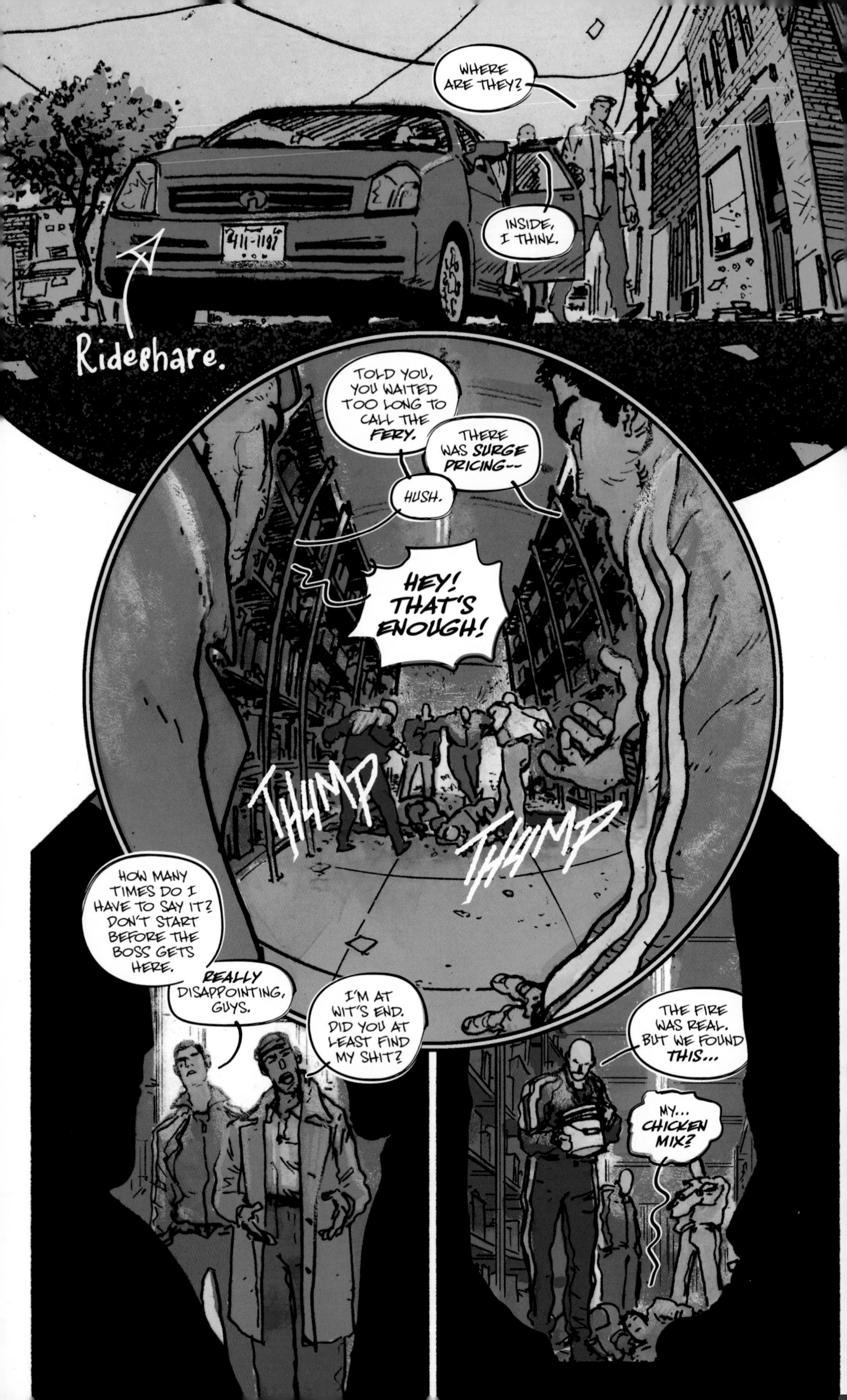
WHERE ARE THEY?
INSIDE, I THINK.
411-1192
Rideshare.
TOLD YOU, YOU WAITED TOO LONG TO CALL THE FERY.
THERE WAS SURGE PRICING--
HUSH.
HEY! THAT'S ENOUGH!
THUMP
THUMP
HOW MANY TIMES DO I HAVE TO SAY IT? DON'T START BEFORE THE BOSS GETS HERE.
REALLY DISAPPOINTING, GUYS.
I'M AT WIT'S END. DID YOU AT LEAST FIND MY SHIT?
THE FIRE WAS REAL. BUT WE FOUND THIS...
MY... CHICKEN MIX?

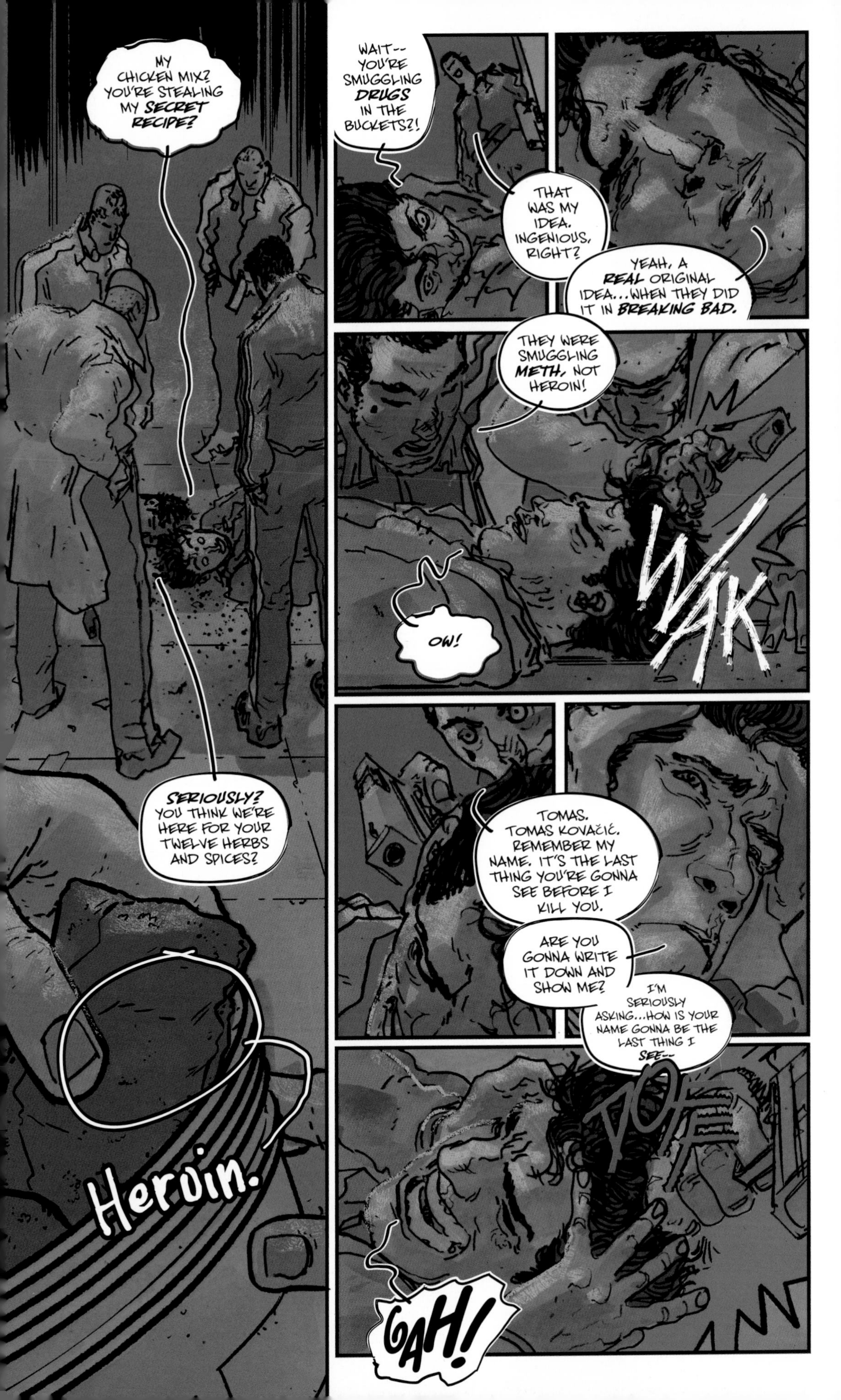

MY CHICKEN MIX? YOU'RE STEALING MY SECRET RECIPE?
SERIOUSLY? YOU THINK WE'RE HERE FOR YOUR TWELVE HERBS AND SPICES?
Heroin.
WAIT-- YOU'RE SMUGGLING DRUGS IN THE BUCKETS?!
THAT WAS MY IDEA. INGENIOUS, RIGHT?
YEAH, A REAL ORIGINAL IDEA...WHEN THEY DID IT IN BREAKING BAD.
THEY WERE SMUGGLING METH, NOT HEROIN!
WAK
OW!
TOMAS. TOMAS KOVAČIĆ. REMEMBER MY NAME. IT'S THE LAST THING YOU'RE GONNA SEE BEFORE I KILL YOU.
ARE YOU GONNA WRITE IT DOWN AND SHOW ME?
I'M SERIOUSLY ASKING...HOW IS YOUR NAME GONNA BE THE LAST THING I SEE--
POF
GAH!

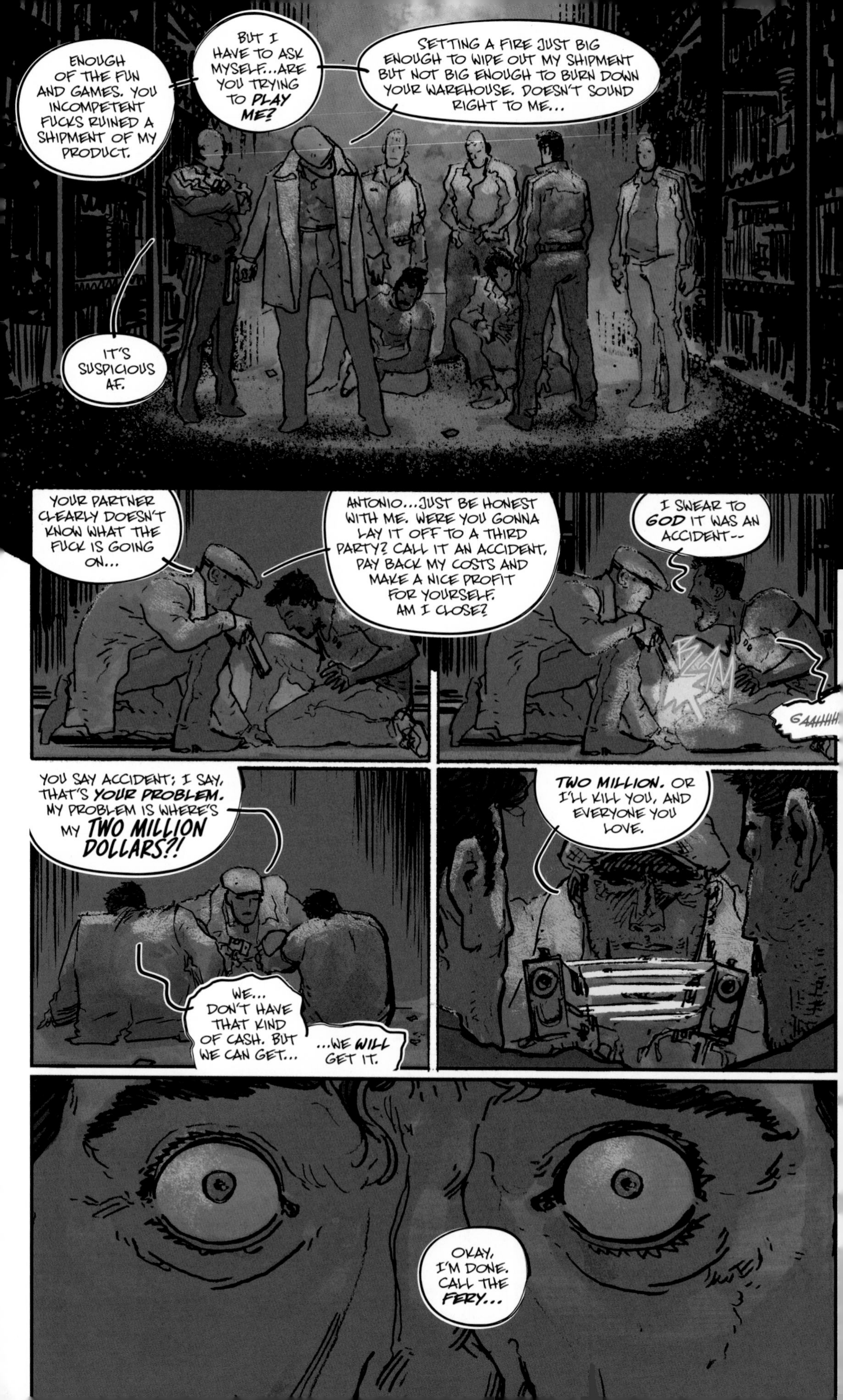

ENOUGH OF THE FUN AND GAMES. YOU INCOMPETENT FUCKS RUINED A SHIPMENT OF MY PRODUCT.
BUT I HAVE TO ASK MYSELF...ARE YOU TRYING TO PLAY ME?
SETTING A FIRE JUST BIG ENOUGH TO WIPE OUT MY SHIPMENT BUT NOT BIG ENOUGH TO BURN DOWN YOUR WAREHOUSE. DOESN'T SOUND RIGHT TO ME...
IT'S SUSPICIOUS AF.
YOUR PARTNER CLEARLY DOESN'T KNOW WHAT THE FUCK IS GOING ON...
ANTONIO...JUST BE HONEST WITH ME. WERE YOU GONNA LAY IT OFF TO A THIRD PARTY? CALL IT AN ACCIDENT, PAY BACK MY COSTS AND MAKE A NICE PROFIT FOR YOURSELF. AM I CLOSE?
I SWEAR TO GOD IT WAS AN ACCIDENT--
BLAM
GAAHHH
YOU SAY ACCIDENT; I SAY, THAT'S YOUR PROBLEM. MY PROBLEM IS WHERE'S MY TWO MILLION DOLLARS?!
WE... DON'T HAVE THAT KIND OF CASH. BUT WE CAN GET...
...WE WILL GET IT.
TWO MILLION. OR I'LL KILL YOU, AND EVERYONE YOU LOVE.
OKAY, I'M DONE. CALL THE FERY...

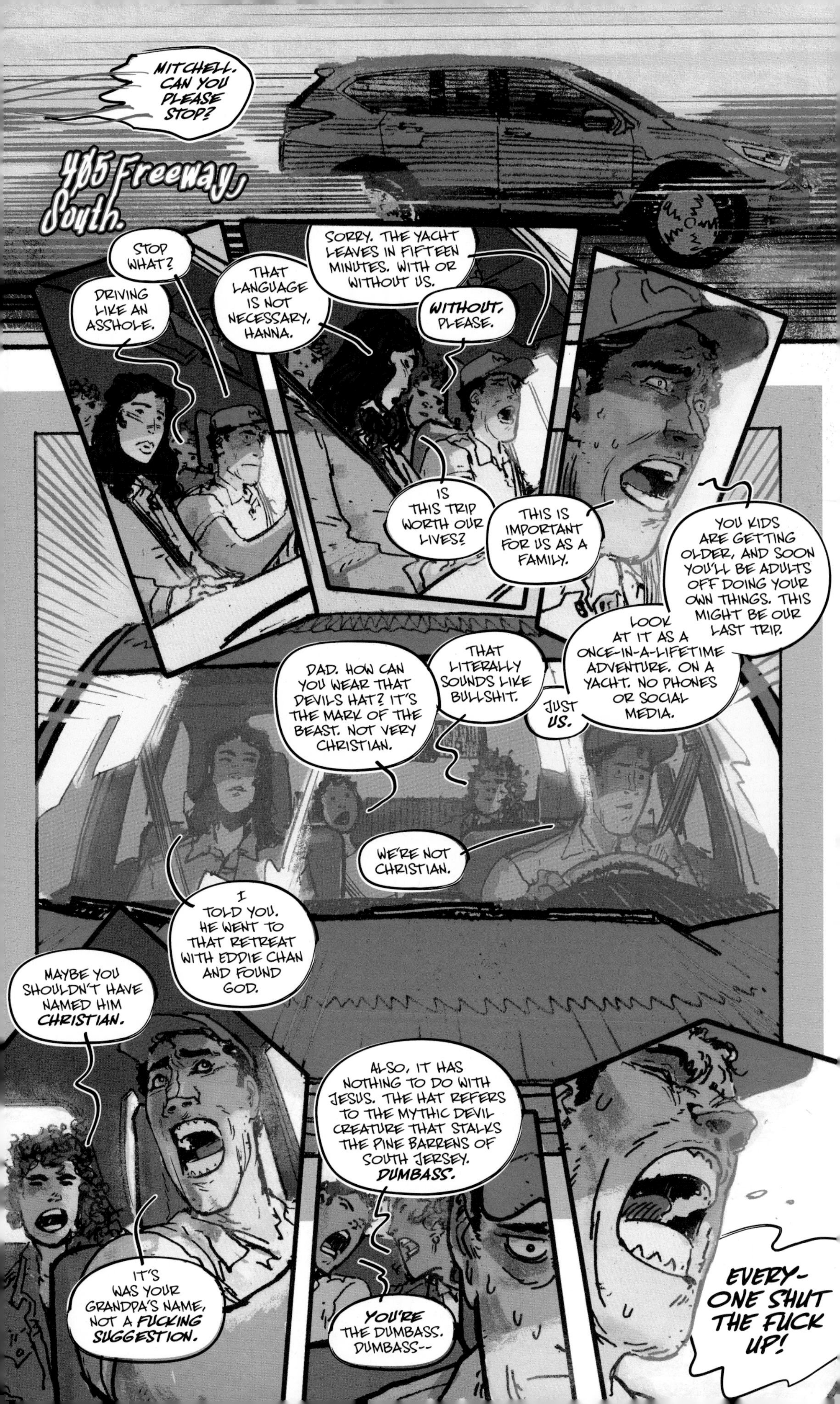
MITCHELL. CAN YOU PLEASE STOP?
405 Freeway, South.
STOP WHAT?
DRIVING LIKE AN ASSHOLE.
THAT LANGUAGE IS NOT NECESSARY, HANNA.
SORRY. THE YACHT LEAVES IN FIFTEEN MINUTES. WITH OR WITHOUT US.
WITHOUT, PLEASE.
IS THIS TRIP WORTH OUR LIVES?
THIS IS IMPORTANT FOR US AS A FAMILY.
YOU KIDS ARE GETTING OLDER, AND SOON YOU'LL BE ADULTS OFF DOING YOUR OWN THINGS. THIS MIGHT BE OUR LAST TRIP.
LOOK AT IT AS A ONCE-IN-A-LIFETIME ADVENTURE. ON A YACHT. NO PHONES OR SOCIAL MEDIA.
JUST US.
THAT LITERALLY SOUNDS LIKE BULLSHIT.
DAD. HOW CAN YOU WEAR THAT DEVILS HAT? IT'S THE MARK OF THE BEAST. NOT VERY CHRISTIAN.
WE'RE NOT CHRISTIAN.
I TOLD YOU. HE WENT TO THAT RETREAT WITH EDDIE CHAN AND FOUND GOD.
MAYBE YOU SHOULDN'T HAVE NAMED HIM CHRISTIAN.
IT'S WAS YOUR GRANDPA'S NAME, NOT A FUCKING SUGGESTION.
ALSO, IT HAS NOTHING TO DO WITH JESUS. THE HAT REFERS TO THE MYTHIC DEVIL CREATURE THAT STALKS THE PINE BARRENS OF SOUTH JERSEY. DUMBASS.
YOU'RE THE DUMBASS. DUMBASS--
EVERY-ONE SHUT THE FUCK UP!

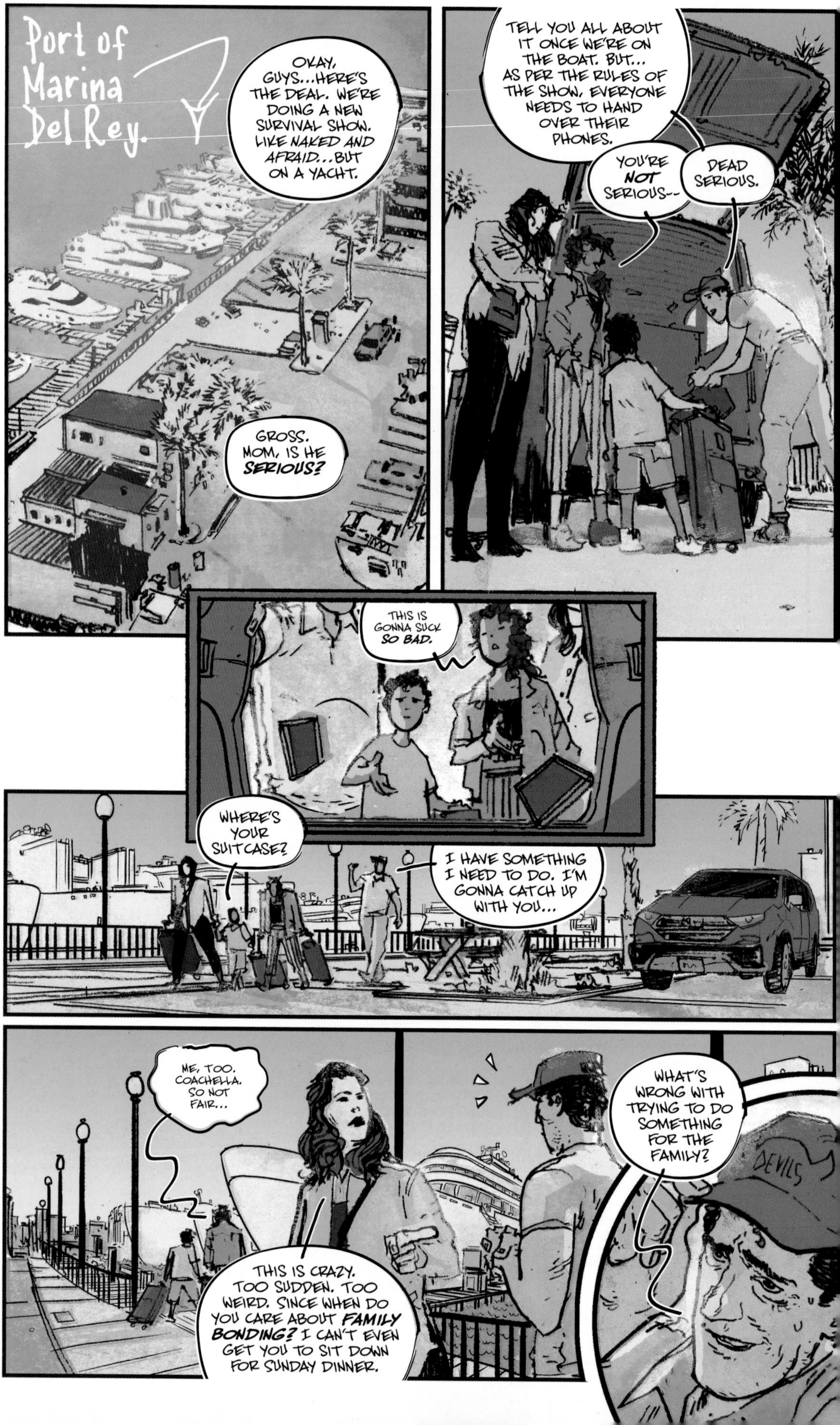
Port of Marina Del Rey.
OKAY, GUYS...HERE'S THE DEAL. WE'RE DOING A NEW SURVIVAL SHOW. LIKE NAKED AND AFRAID...BUT ON A YACHT.
GROSS. MOM, IS HE SERIOUS?
TELL YOU ALL ABOUT IT ONCE WE'RE ON THE BOAT. BUT... AS PER THE RULES OF THE SHOW, EVERYONE NEEDS TO HAND OVER THEIR PHONES.
YOU'RE NOT SERIOUS--
DEAD SERIOUS.
THIS IS GONNA SUCK SO BAD.
WHERE'S YOUR SUITCASE?
I HAVE SOMETHING I NEED TO DO. I'M GONNA CATCH UP WITH YOU...
ME, TOO. COACHELLA. SO NOT FAIR...
THIS IS CRAZY. TOO SUDDEN. TOO WEIRD. SINCE WHEN DO YOU CARE ABOUT FAMILY BONDING? I CAN'T EVEN GET YOU TO SIT DOWN FOR SUNDAY DINNER.
WHAT'S WRONG WITH TRYING TO DO SOMETHING FOR THE FAMILY?
DEVILS

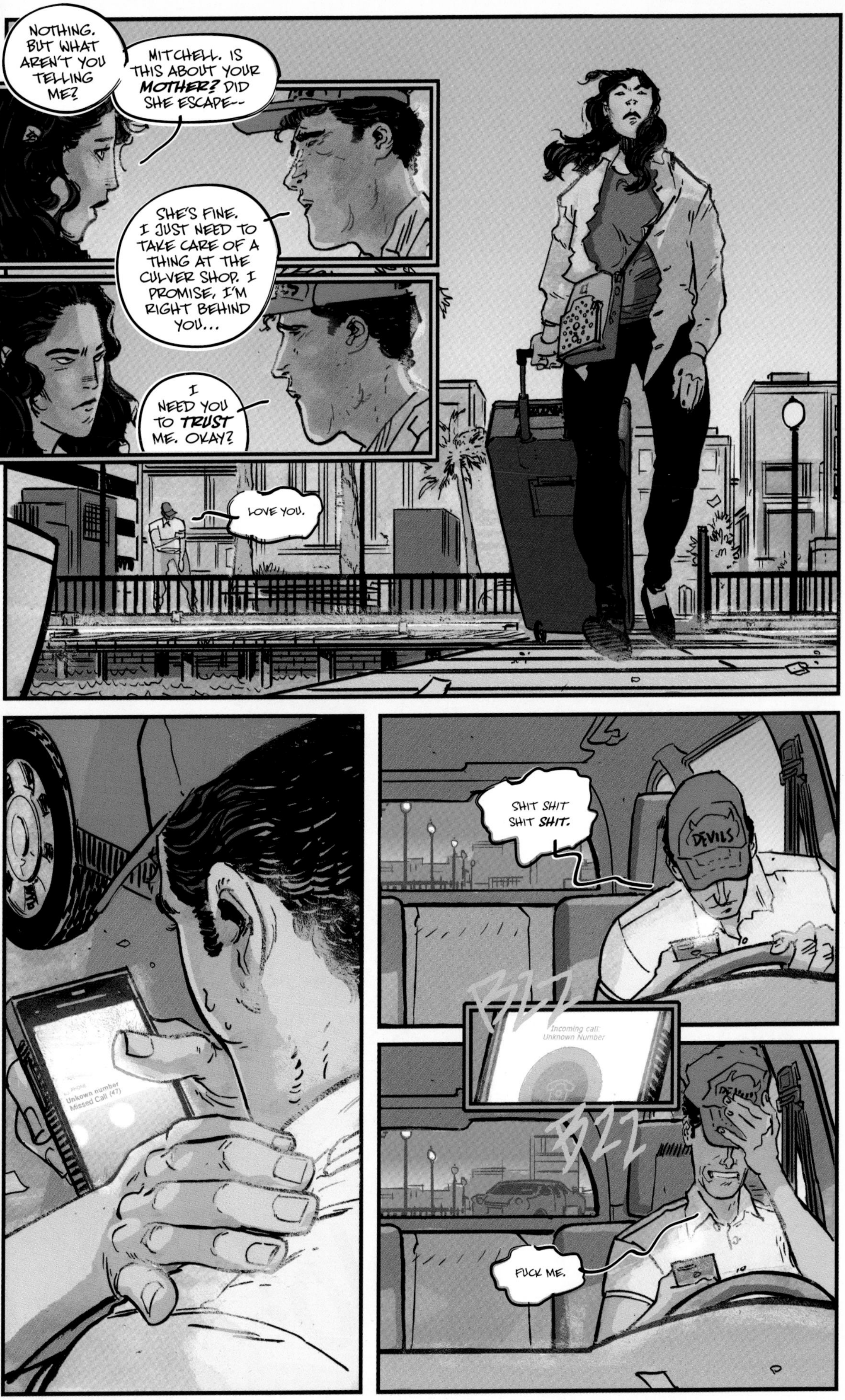

NOTHING. BUT WHAT AREN'T YOU TELLING ME?
MITCHELL. IS THIS ABOUT YOUR MOTHER? DID SHE ESCAPE--
SHE'S FINE. I JUST NEED TO TAKE CARE OF A THING AT THE CULVER SHOP. I PROMISE, I'M RIGHT BEHIND YOU...
I NEED YOU TO TRUST ME. OKAY?
LOVE YOU.
Unkown number
Missed Call (47)
SHIT SHIT SHIT SHIT.
DEVILS
BZZ
Incoming call:
Unknown Number
BZZ
FUCK ME.

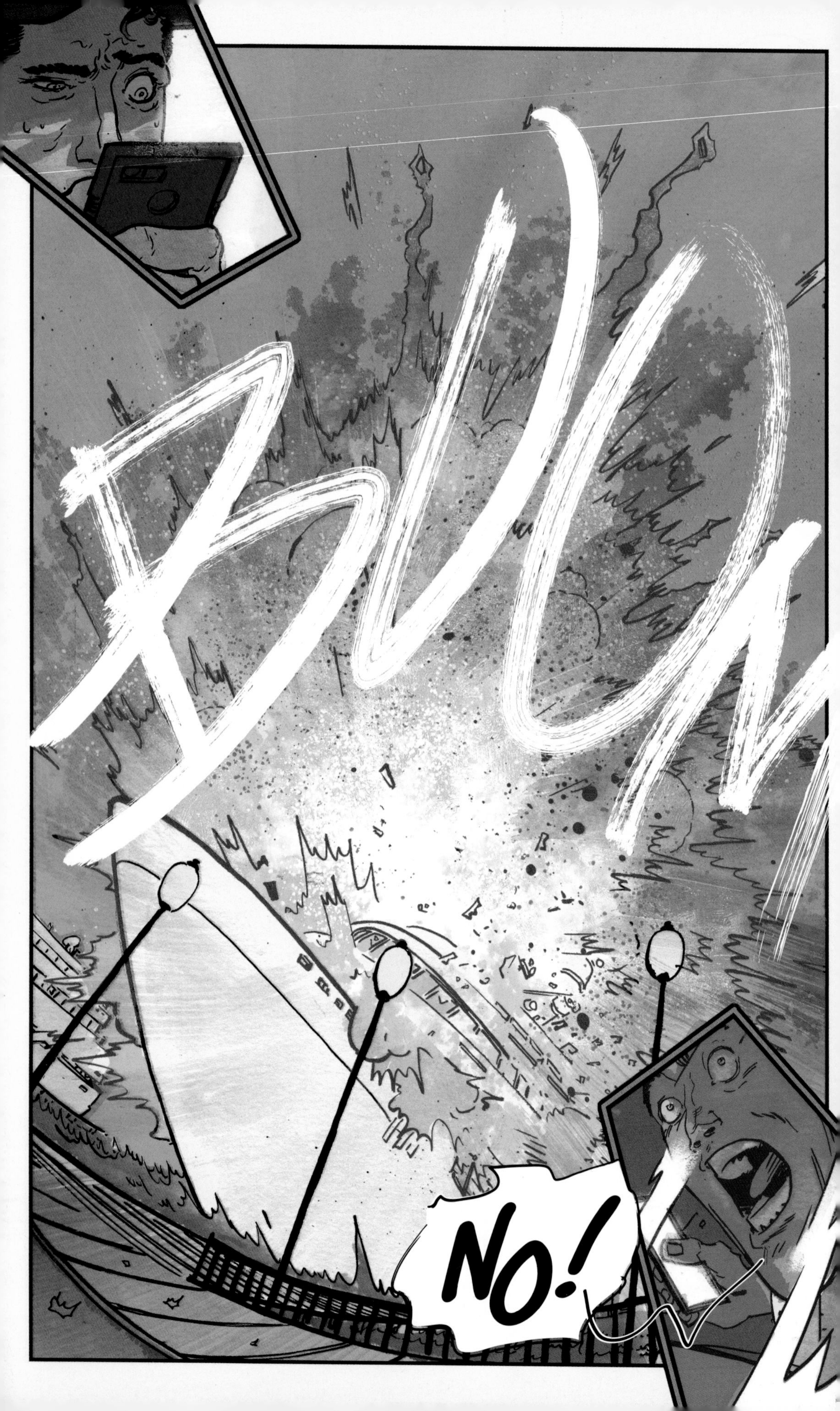
NO!

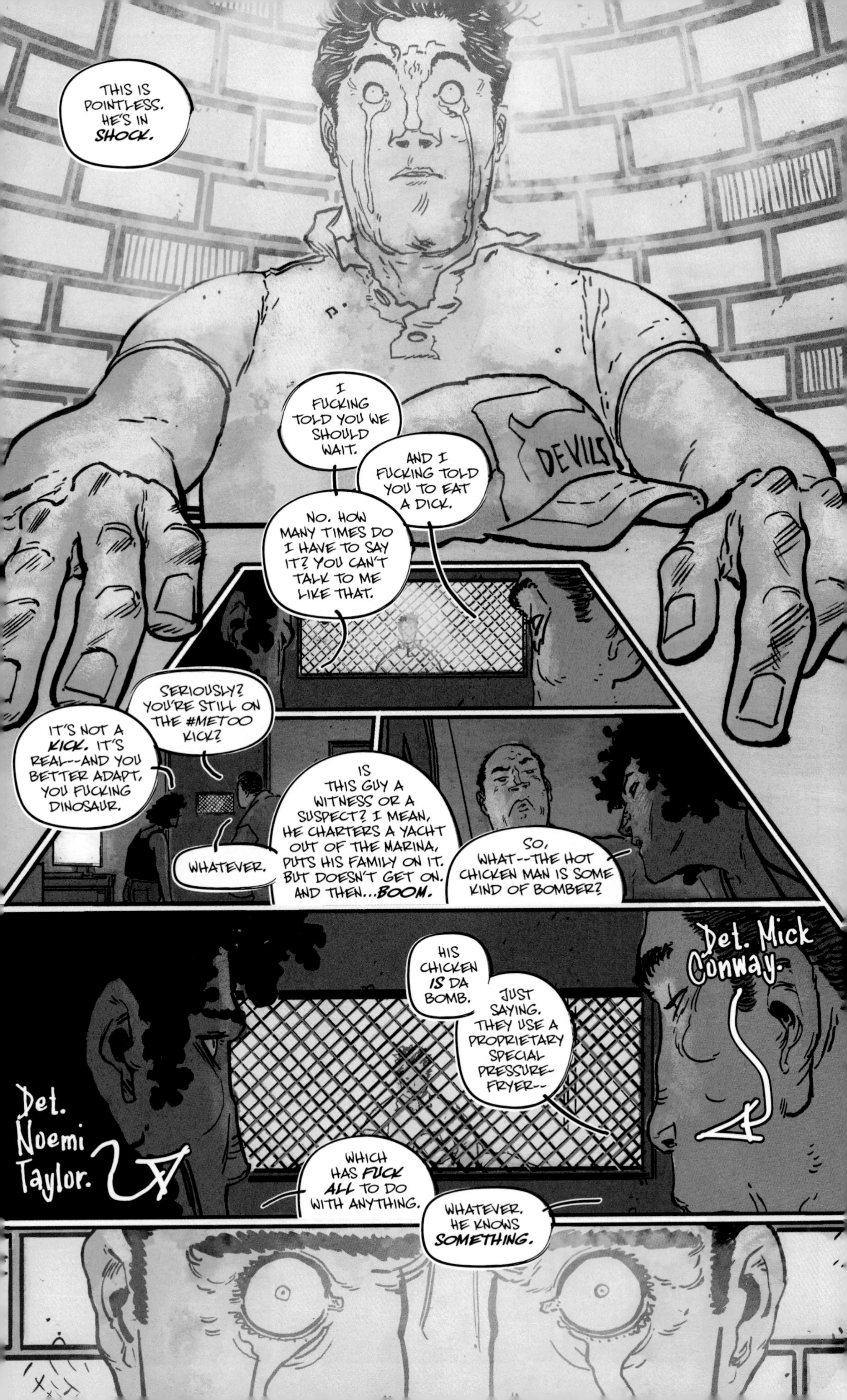

THIS IS POINTLESS. HE'S IN SHOCK.
I FUCKING TOLD YOU WE SHOULD WAIT.
AND I FUCKING TOLD YOU TO EAT A DICK.
NO. HOW MANY TIMES DO I HAVE TO SAY IT? YOU CAN'T TALK TO ME LIKE THAT.
SERIOUSLY? YOU'RE STILL ON THE #METOO KICK?
IT'S NOT A KICK. IT'S REAL--AND YOU BETTER ADAPT, YOU FUCKING DINOSAUR.
WHATEVER.
IS THIS GUY A WITNESS OR A SUSPECT? I MEAN, HE CHARTERS A YACHT OUT OF THE MARINA, PUTS HIS FAMILY ON IT. BUT DOESN'T GET ON. AND THEN...BOOM.
SO, WHAT--THE HOT CHICKEN MAN IS SOME KIND OF BOMBER?
Det. Mick Conway.
HIS CHICKEN IS DA BOMB.
JUST SAYING. THEY USE A PROPRIETARY SPECIAL PRESSURE-FRYER--
Det. Noemi Taylor.
WHICH HAS FUCK ALL TO DO WITH ANYTHING.
WHATEVER. HE KNOWS SOMETHING.

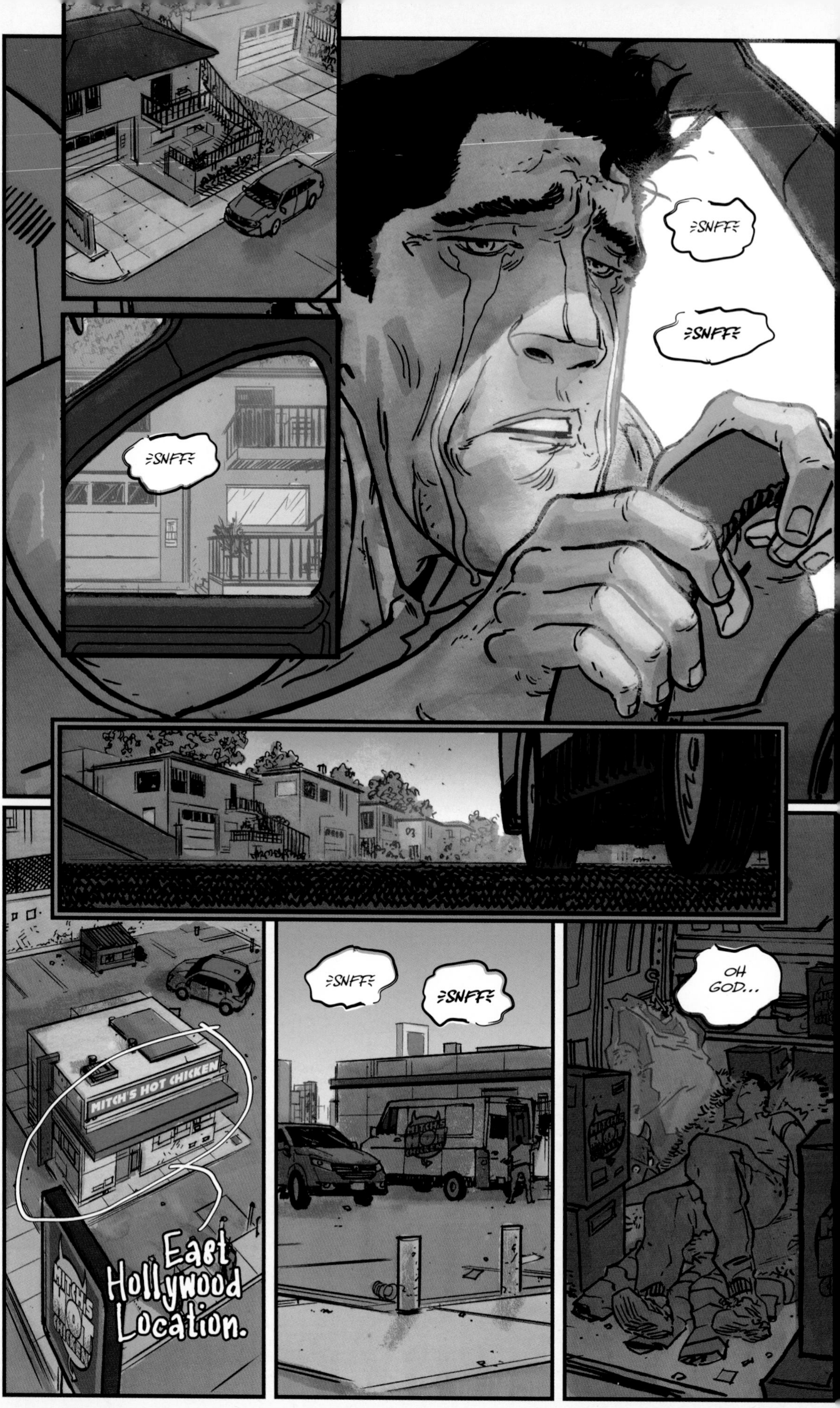
SNFF
SNFF
SNFF
MITCH'S HOT CHICKEN
East Hollywood Location.
SNFF
SNFF
OH GOD...

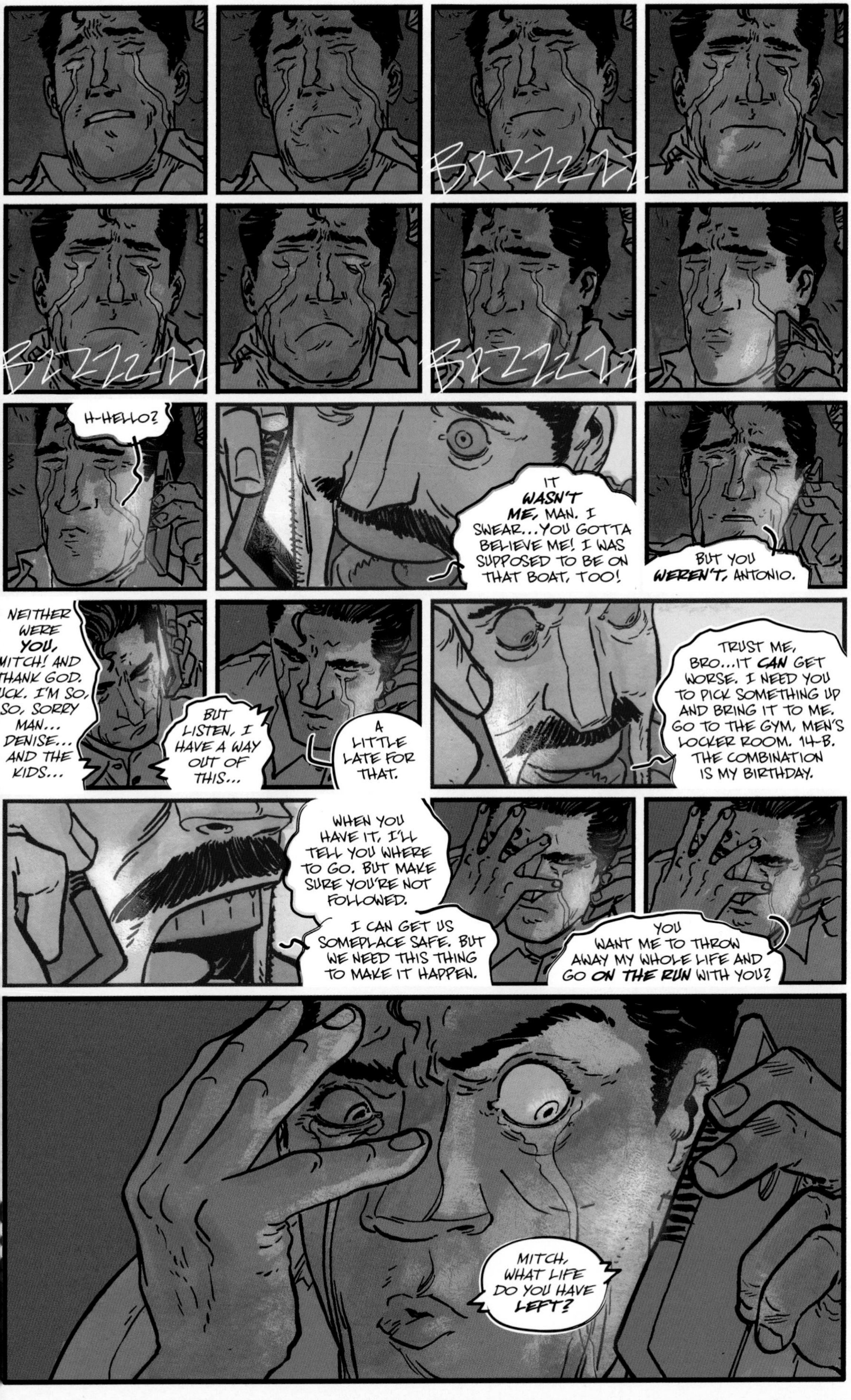
BZZZZZZ
BZZZZZZ
BZZZZZZ
H-HELLO?
IT WASN'T ME, MAN. I SWEAR...YOU GOTTA BELIEVE ME! I WAS SUPPOSED TO BE ON THAT BOAT, TOO!
BUT YOU WEREN'T, ANTONIO.
NEITHER WERE YOU, MITCH! AND THANK GOD. UCK. I'M SO, SO, SORRY MAN... DENISE... AND THE KIDS...
BUT LISTEN, I HAVE A WAY OUT OF THIS...
A LITTLE LATE FOR THAT.
TRUST ME, BRO...IT CAN GET WORSE. I NEED YOU TO PICK SOMETHING UP AND BRING IT TO ME. GO TO THE GYM, MEN'S LOCKER ROOM. 14-B. THE COMBINATION IS MY BIRTHDAY.
WHEN YOU HAVE IT, I'LL TELL YOU WHERE TO GO. BUT MAKE SURE YOU'RE NOT FOLLOWED.
I CAN GET US SOMEPLACE SAFE. BUT WE NEED THIS THING TO MAKE IT HAPPEN.
YOU WANT ME TO THROW AWAY MY WHOLE LIFE AND GO ON THE RUN WITH YOU?
MITCH, WHAT LIFE DO YOU HAVE LEFT?

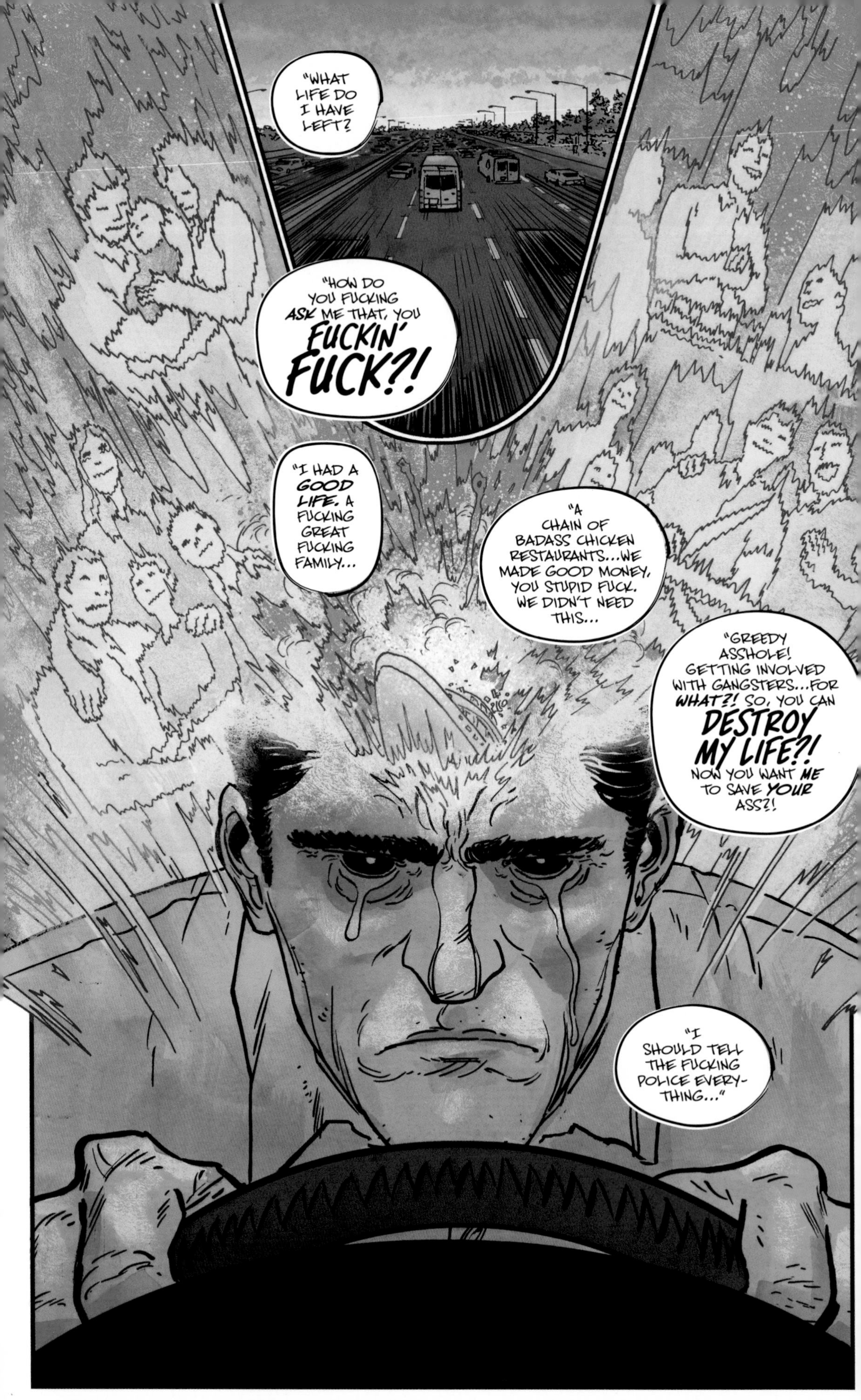
"WHAT LIFE DO I HAVE LEFT?
"HOW DO YOU FUCKING ASK ME THAT, YOU FUCKIN' FUCK?!
"I HAD A GOOD LIFE. A FUCKING GREAT FUCKING FAMILY...
"A CHAIN OF BADASS CHICKEN RESTAURANTS...WE MADE GOOD MONEY, YOU STUPID FUCK. WE DIDN'T NEED THIS...
"GREEDY ASSHOLE! GETTING INVOLVED WITH GANGSTERS...FOR WHAT?! SO, YOU CAN DESTROY MY LIFE?! NOW YOU WANT ME TO SAVE YOUR ASS?!
"I SHOULD TELL THE FUCKING POLICE EVERY-THING..."

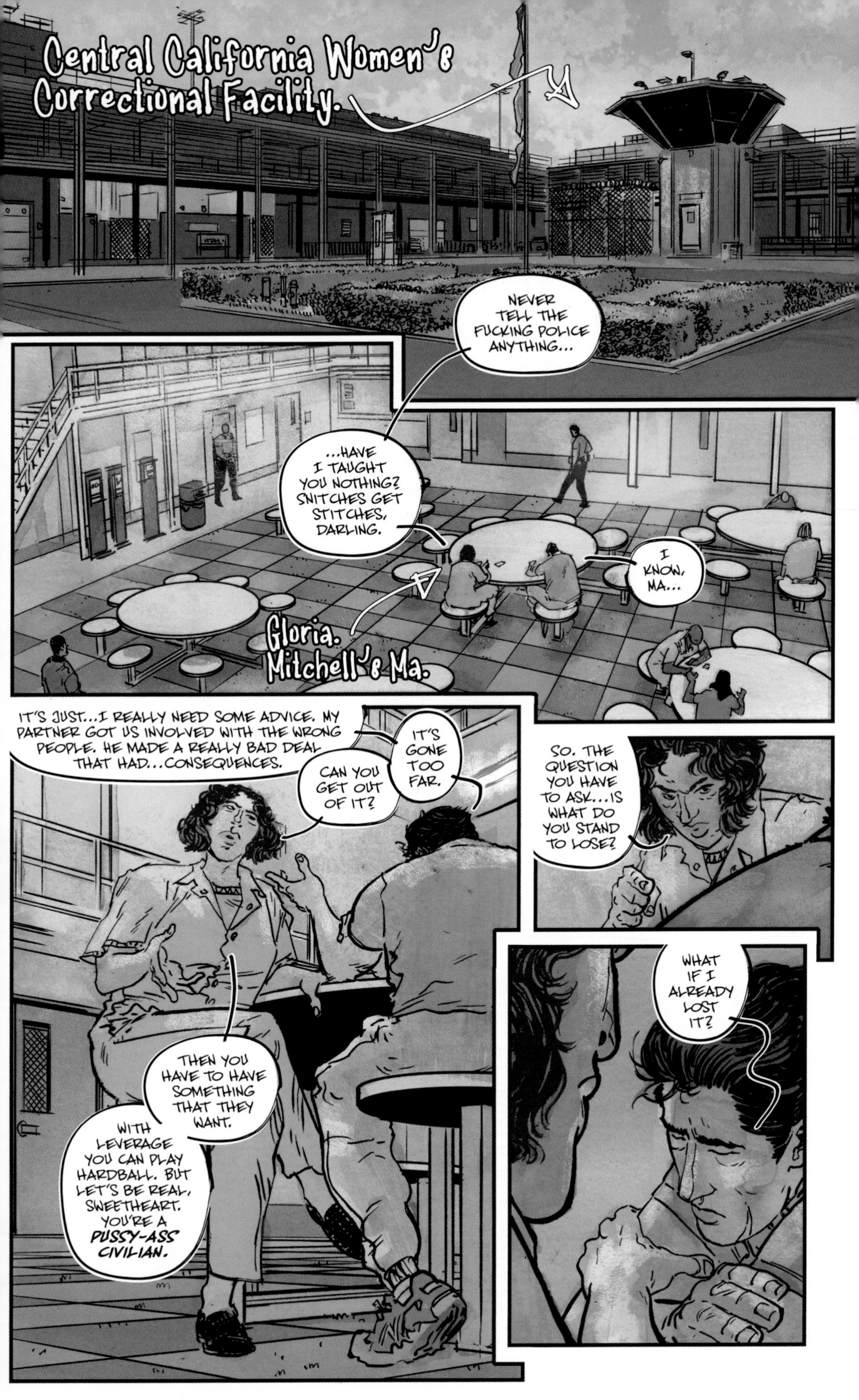
Central California Women's Correctional Facility.
NEVER TELL THE FUCKING POLICE ANYTHING...
...HAVE I TAUGHT YOU NOTHING? SNITCHES GET STITCHES, DARLING.
I KNOW, MA...
Gloria. Mitchell's Ma.
IT'S JUST...I REALLY NEED SOME ADVICE. MY PARTNER GOT US INVOLVED WITH THE WRONG PEOPLE. HE MADE A REALLY BAD DEAL THAT HAD...CONSEQUENCES.
IT'S GONE TOO FAR.
CAN YOU GET OUT OF IT?
THEN YOU HAVE TO HAVE SOMETHING THAT THEY WANT.
WITH LEVERAGE YOU CAN PLAY HARDBALL. BUT LET'S BE REAL, SWEETHEART. YOU'RE A PUSSY-ASS CIVILIAN.
SO. THE QUESTION YOU HAVE TO ASK...IS WHAT DO YOU STAND TO LOSE?
WHAT IF I ALREADY LOST IT?

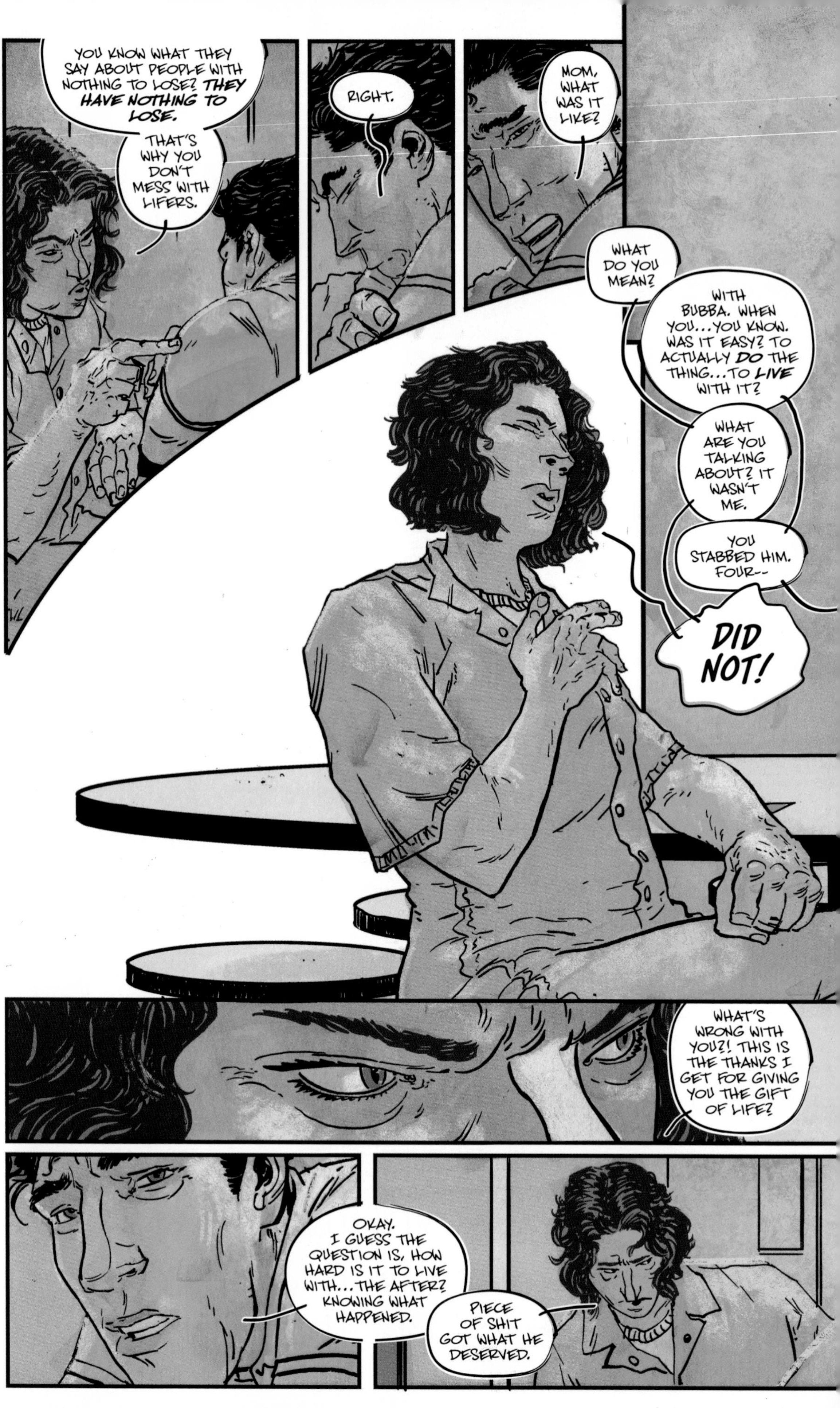
YOU KNOW WHAT THEY SAY ABOUT PEOPLE WITH NOTHING TO LOSE? **THEY HAVE NOTHING TO LOSE.**
THAT'S WHY YOU DON'T MESS WITH LIFERS.
RIGHT.
MOM, WHAT WAS IT LIKE?
WHAT DO YOU MEAN?
WITH BUBBA. WHEN YOU...YOU KNOW. WAS IT EASY? TO ACTUALLY **DO** THE THING...TO **LIVE** WITH IT?
WHAT ARE YOU TALKING ABOUT? IT WASN'T ME.
YOU STABBED HIM. FOUR--
DID NOT!
WHAT'S WRONG WITH YOU?! THIS IS THE THANKS I GET FOR GIVING YOU THE GIFT OF LIFE?
OKAY. I GUESS THE QUESTION IS, HOW HARD IS IT TO LIVE WITH...THE AFTER? KNOWING WHAT HAPPENED.
PIECE OF SHIT GOT WHAT HE DESERVED.

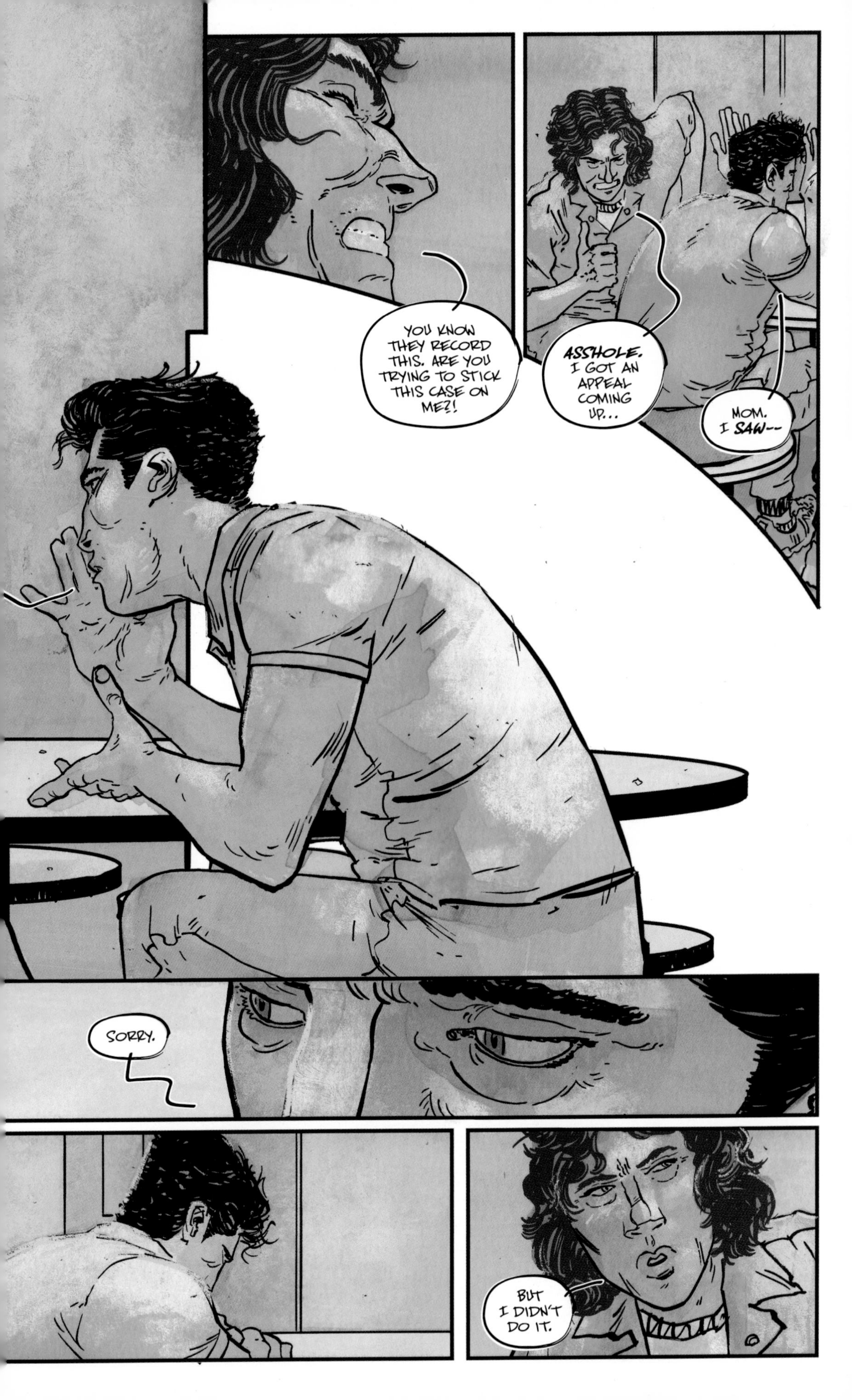
YOU KNOW THEY RECORD THIS. ARE YOU TRYING TO STICK THIS CASE ON ME?!
ASSHOLE. I GOT AN APPEAL COMING UP...
MOM. I SAW--
SORRY.
BUT I DIDN'T DO IT.

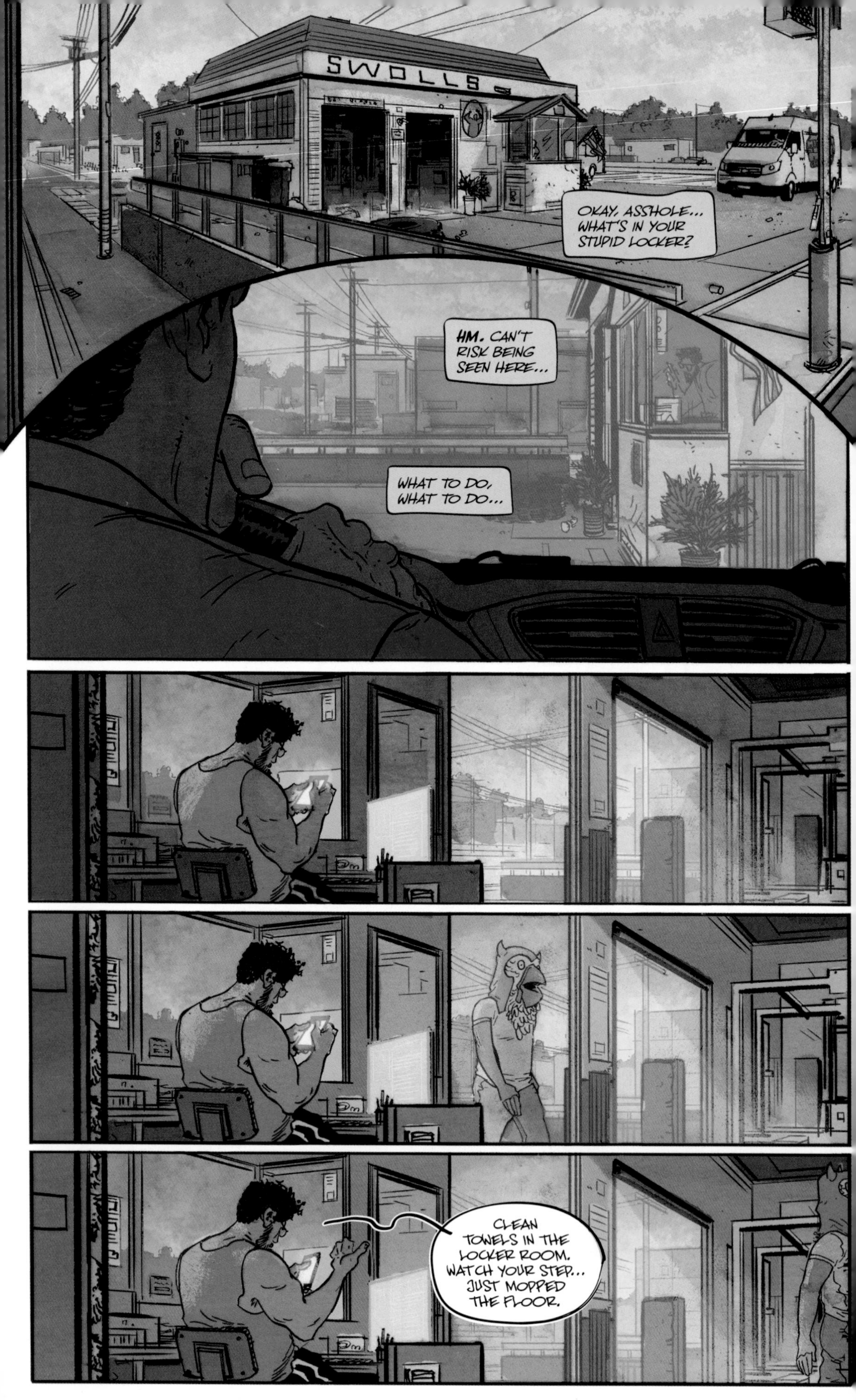
SWOLLS
OKAY, ASSHOLE... WHAT'S IN YOUR STUPID LOCKER?
HM. CAN'T RISK BEING SEEN HERE...
WHAT TO DO, WHAT TO DO...
CLEAN TOWELS IN THE LOCKER ROOM. WATCH YOUR STEP... JUST MOPPED THE FLOOR.

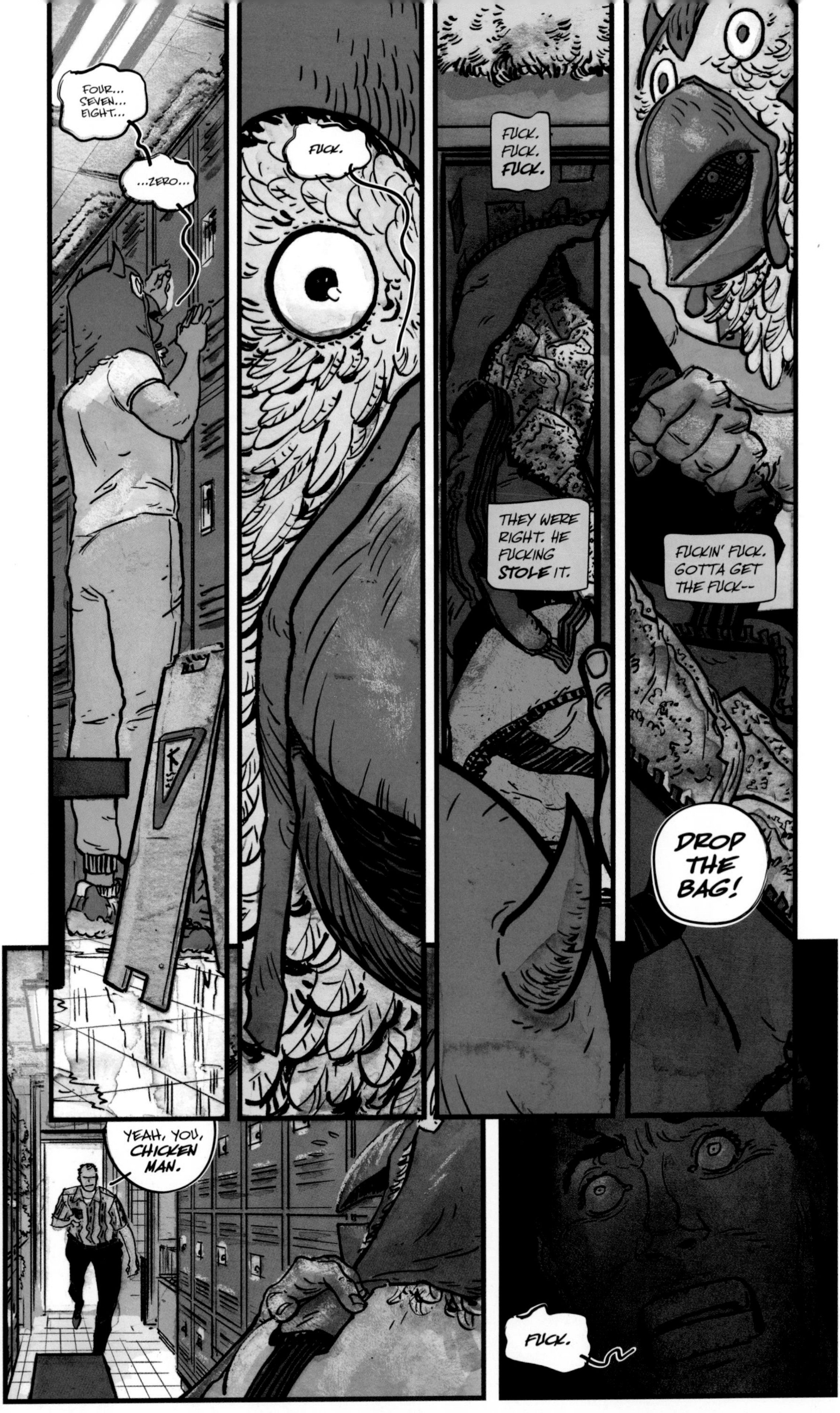
FOUR... SEVEN... EIGHT...
...ZERO...
FUCK.
FUCK. FUCK. FUCK.
THEY WERE RIGHT. HE FUCKING STOLE IT.
FUCKIN' FUCK. GOTTA GET THE FUCK--
DROP THE BAG!
YEAH, YOU, CHICKEN MAN.
FUCK.

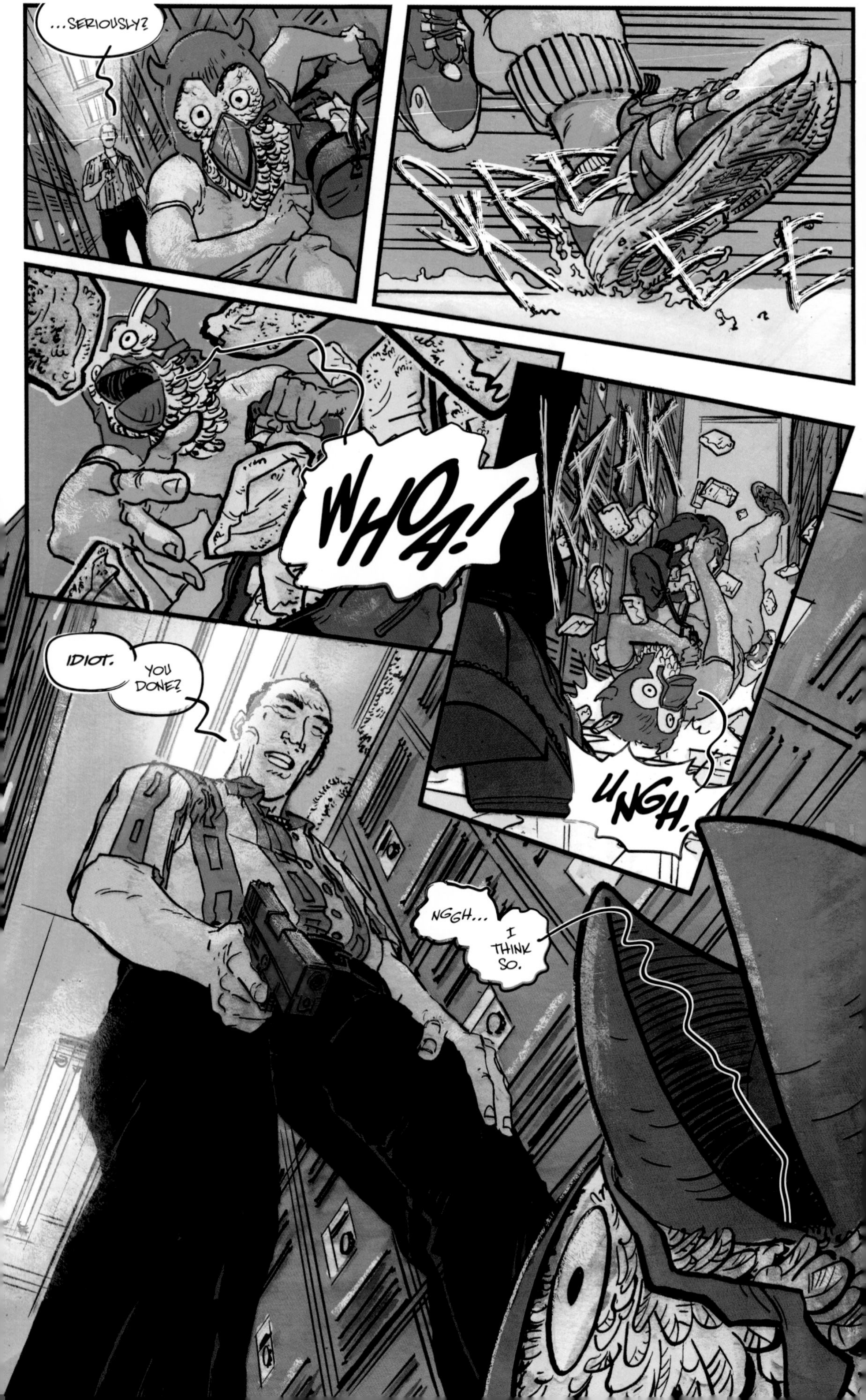
...SERIOUSLY?
SKREEEEE
WHOA!
KRAK
UNGH.
IDIOT.
YOU DONE?
NGGH...
I THINK SO.

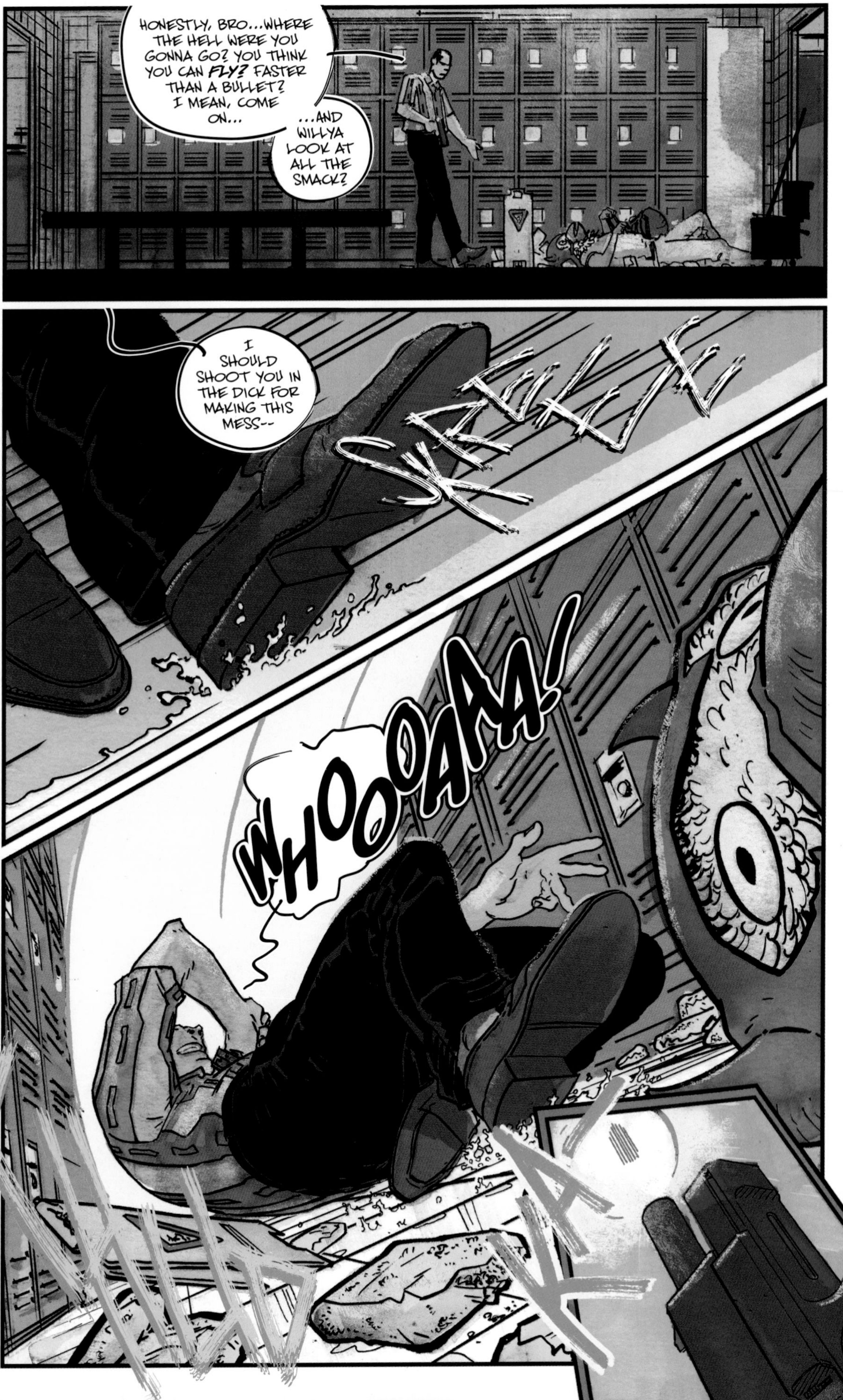
HONESTLY, BRO...WHERE THE HELL WERE YOU GONNA GO? YOU THINK YOU CAN *FLY?* FASTER THAN A BULLET? I MEAN, COME ON...
...AND WILLYA LOOK AT ALL THE SMACK?
I SHOULD SHOOT YOU IN THE DICK FOR MAKING THIS MESS--
WHOOOAAA!

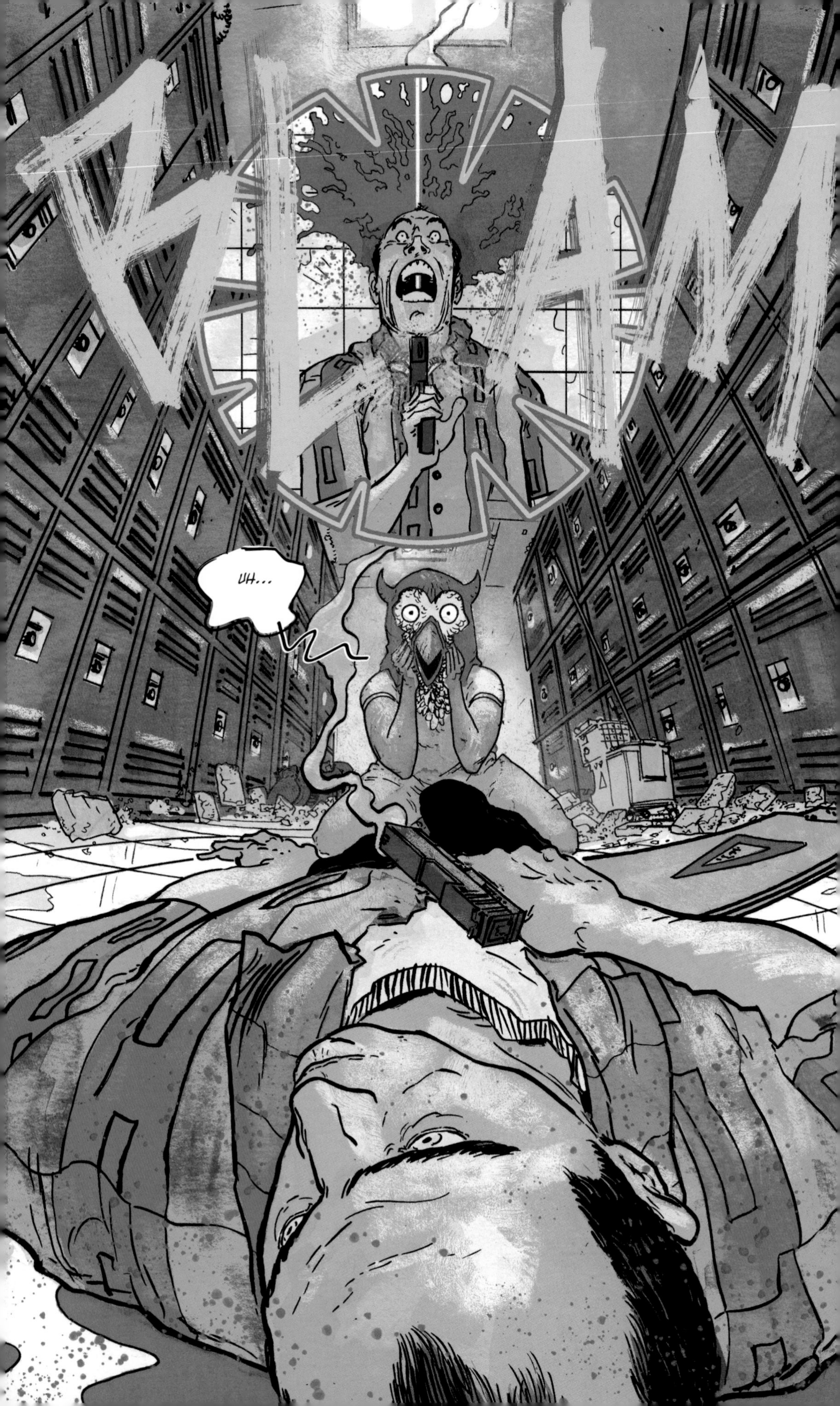
BLAM
UH...

2

LIKE A DEVIL WITH HIS HEAD CUT OFF

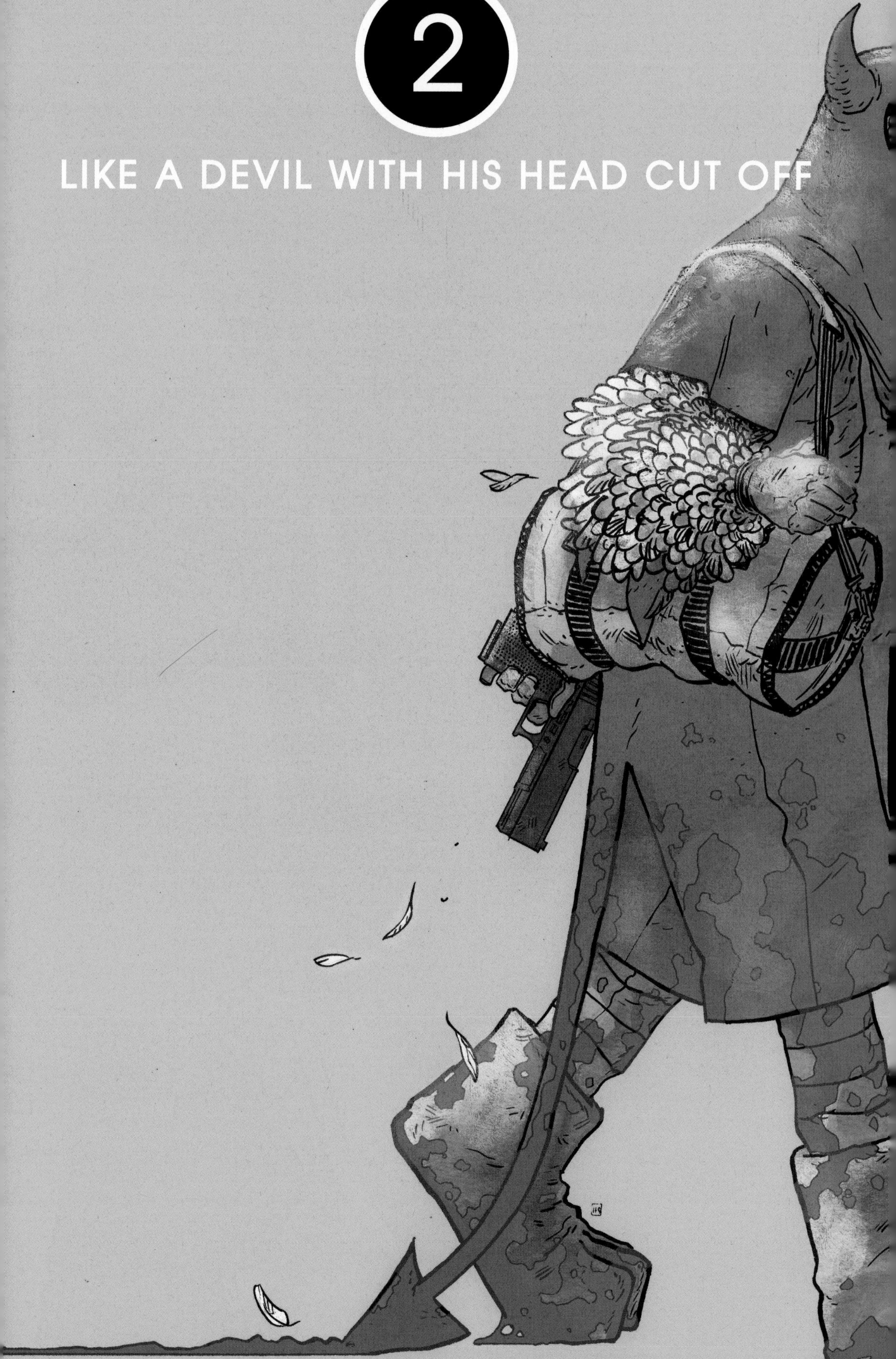

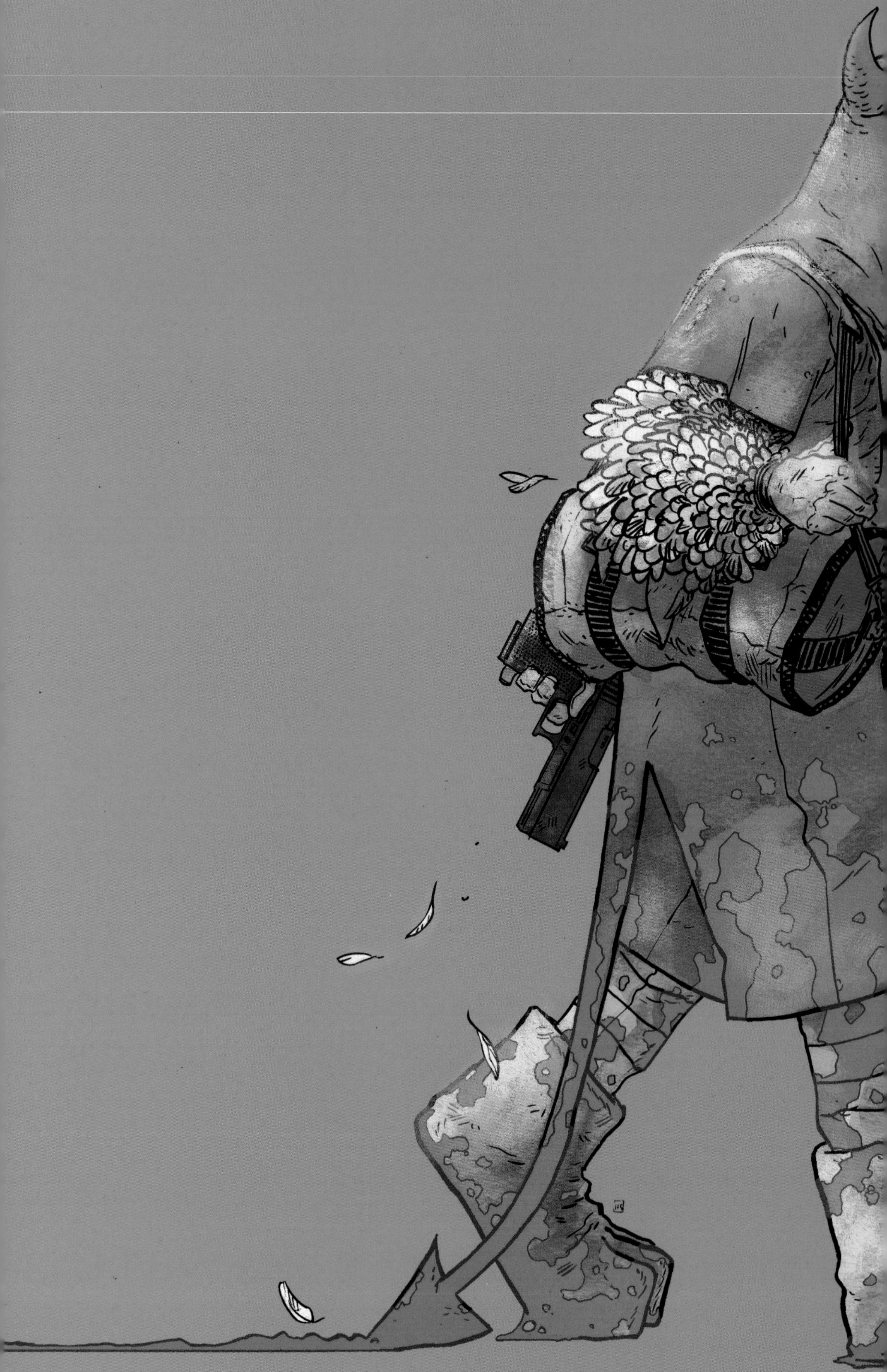

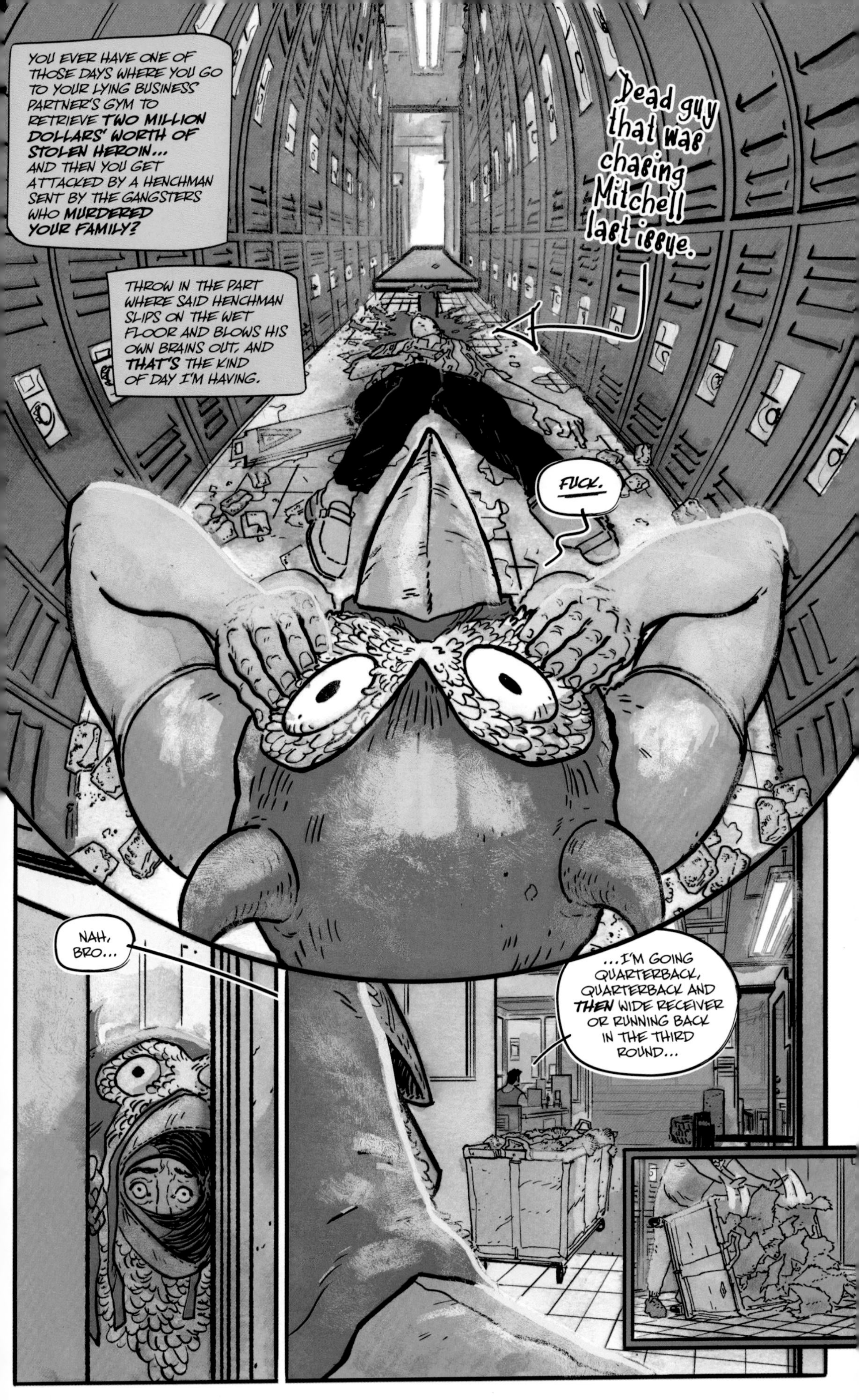
YOU EVER HAVE ONE OF THOSE DAYS WHERE YOU GO TO YOUR LYING BUSINESS PARTNER'S GYM TO RETRIEVE TWO MILLION DOLLARS' WORTH OF STOLEN HEROIN... AND THEN YOU GET ATTACKED BY A HENCHMAN SENT BY THE GANGSTERS WHO MURDERED YOUR FAMILY?
Dead guy that was chasing Mitchell last issue.
THROW IN THE PART WHERE SAID HENCHMAN SLIPS ON THE WET FLOOR AND BLOWS HIS OWN BRAINS OUT, AND THAT'S THE KIND OF DAY I'M HAVING.
FUCK.
NAH, BRO...
...I'M GOING QUARTERBACK, QUARTERBACK AND THEN WIDE RECEIVER OR RUNNING BACK IN THE THIRD ROUND...

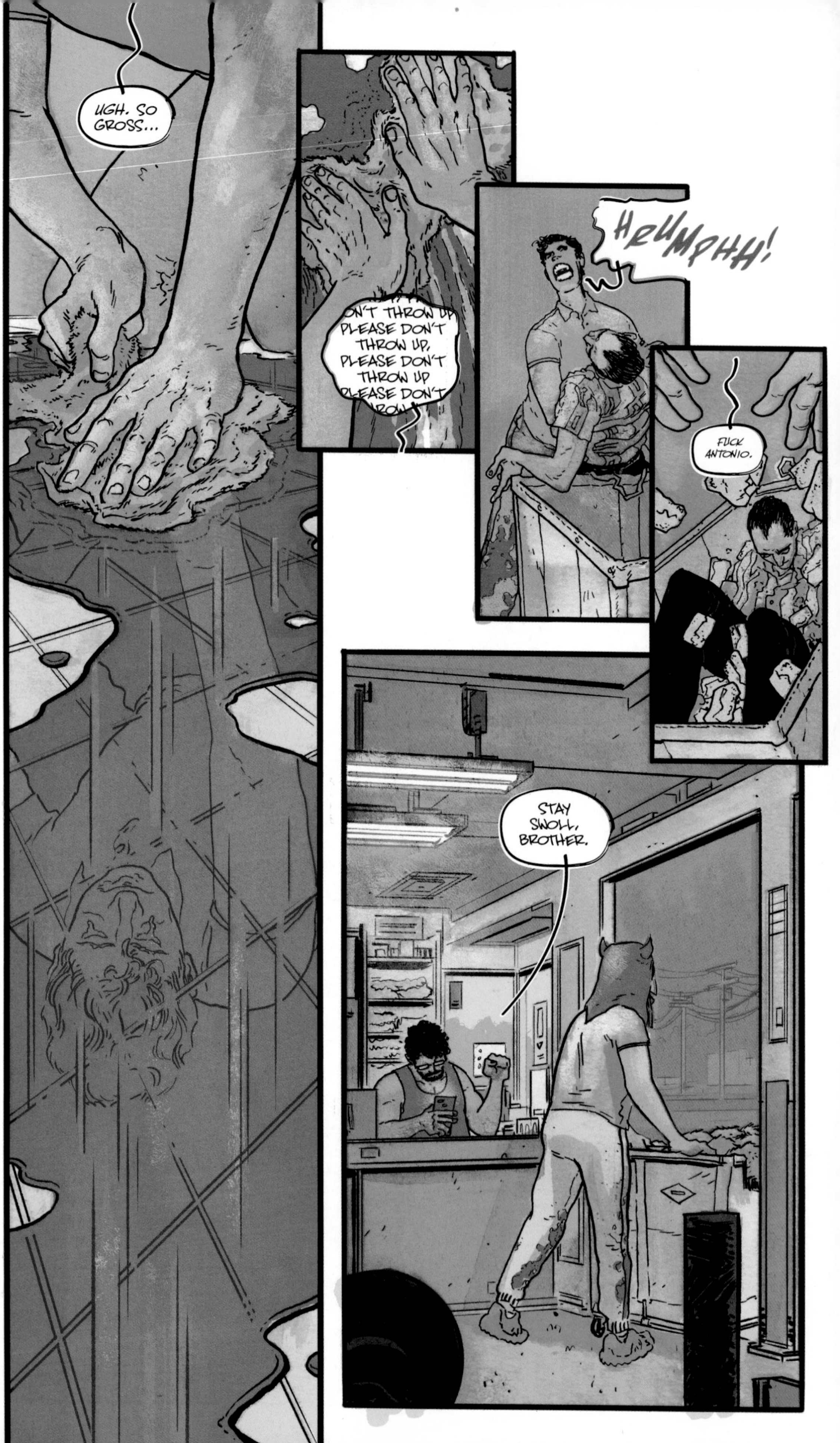
UGH. SO GROSS...
PLEASE DON'T THROW UP, PLEASE DON'T THROW UP PLEASE DON'T
HRUMPHH!
FUCK ANTONIO.
STAY SWOLL, BROTHER.

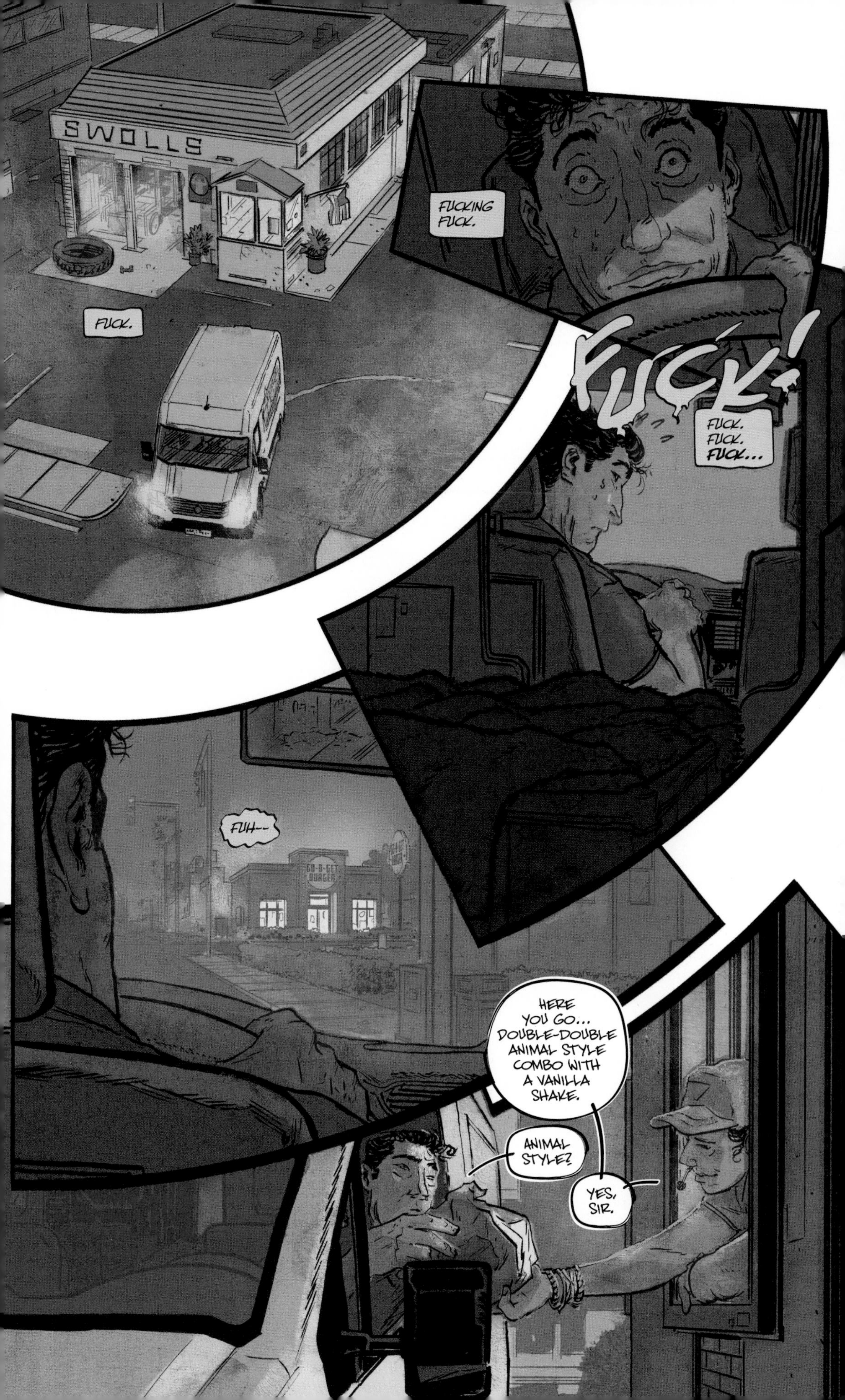
SWOLLS
FUCK.
FUCKING FUCK.
FUCK!
FUCK. FUCK. FUCK...
FUH--
GO-A-GET BURGER
HERE YOU GO... DOUBLE-DOUBLE ANIMAL STYLE COMBO WITH A VANILLA SHAKE.
ANIMAL STYLE?
YES, SIR.

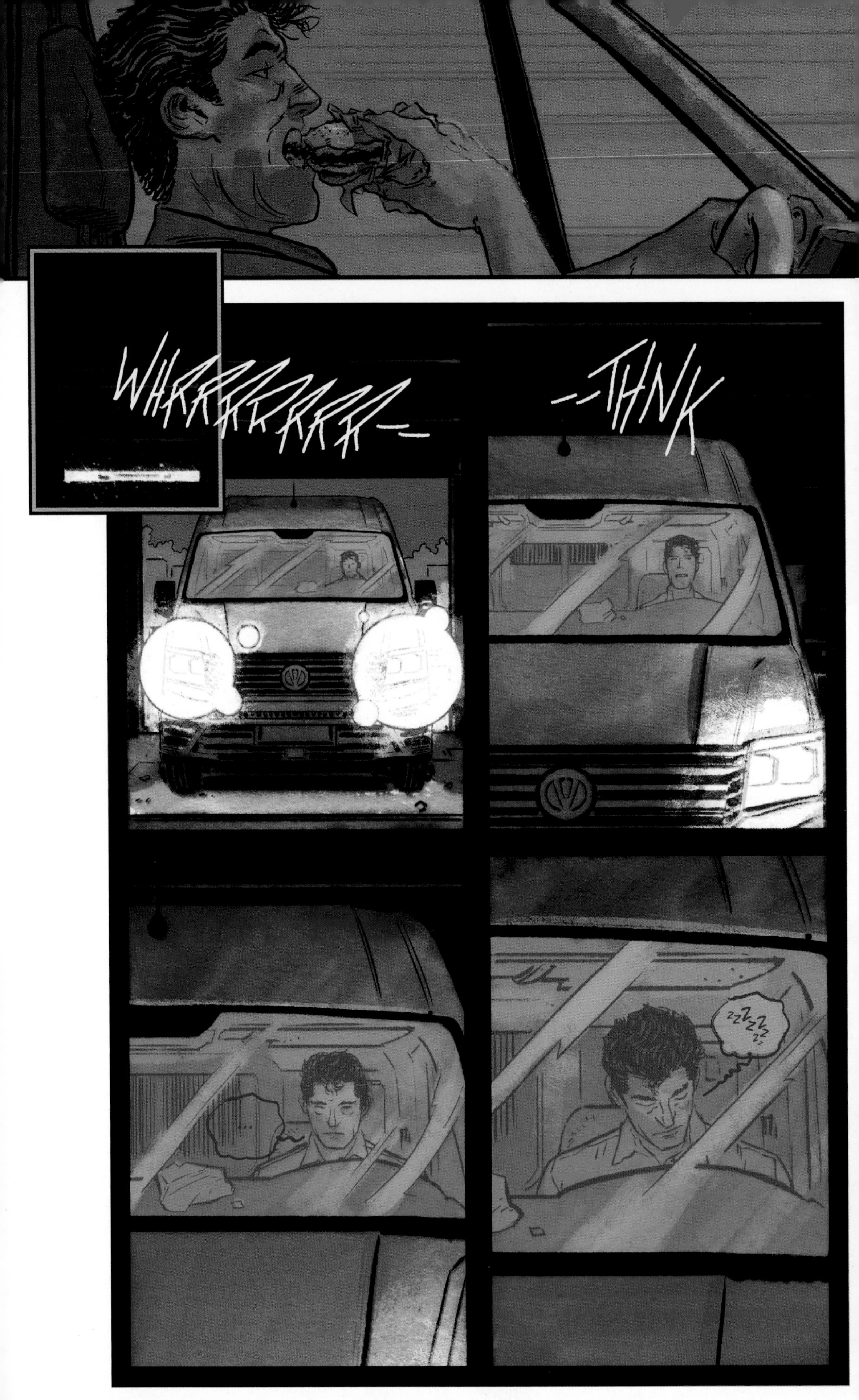

WHRRRRRRRR—
—THNK
ZZZZZZ

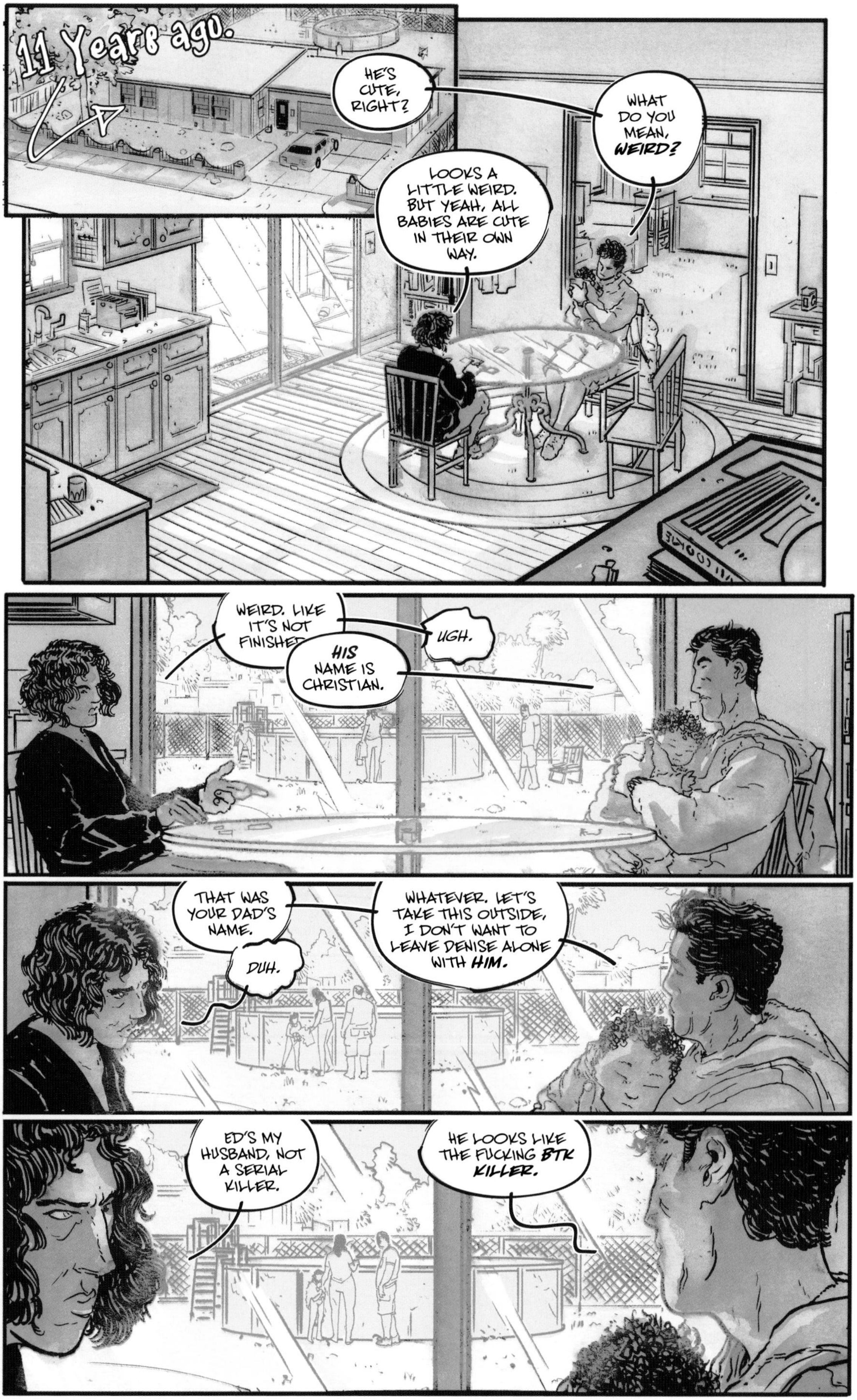
11 Years ago.
HE'S CUTE, RIGHT?
WHAT DO YOU MEAN, WEIRD?
LOOKS A LITTLE WEIRD. BUT YEAH, ALL BABIES ARE CUTE IN THEIR OWN WAY.
WEIRD. LIKE IT'S NOT FINISHED.
UGH.
HIS NAME IS CHRISTIAN.
THAT WAS YOUR DAD'S NAME.
DUH.
WHATEVER. LET'S TAKE THIS OUTSIDE, I DON'T WANT TO LEAVE DENISE ALONE WITH HIM.
ED'S MY HUSBAND, NOT A SERIAL KILLER.
HE LOOKS LIKE THE FUCKING BTK KILLER.

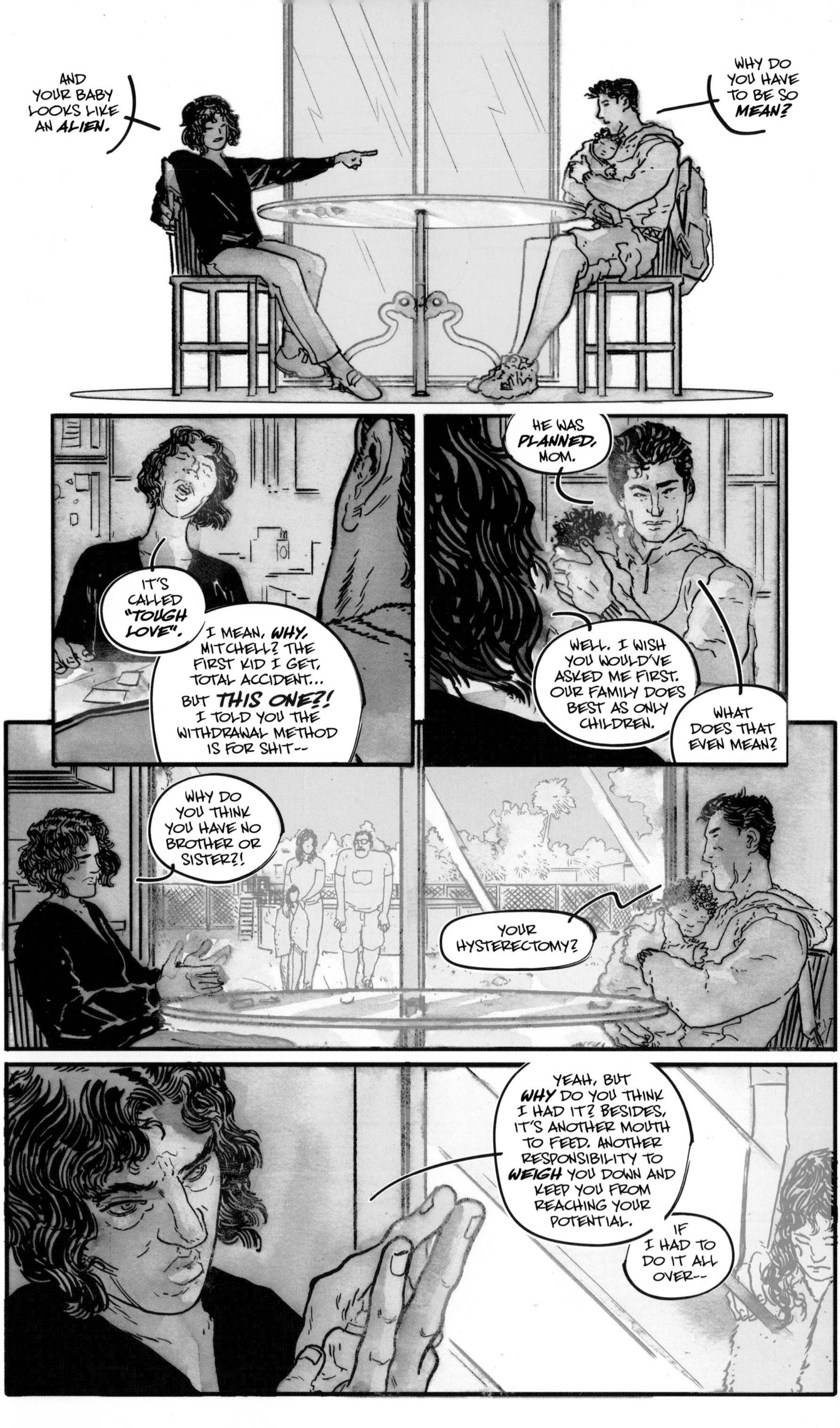
AND YOUR BABY LOOKS LIKE AN ALIEN.
WHY DO YOU HAVE TO BE SO MEAN?
IT'S CALLED "TOUGH LOVE".
I MEAN, WHY, MITCHELL? THE FIRST KID I GET, TOTAL ACCIDENT... BUT THIS ONE?! I TOLD YOU THE WITHDRAWAL METHOD IS FOR SHIT--
HE WAS PLANNED, MOM.
WELL. I WISH YOU WOULD'VE ASKED ME FIRST. OUR FAMILY DOES BEST AS ONLY CHILDREN.
WHAT DOES THAT EVEN MEAN?
WHY DO YOU THINK YOU HAVE NO BROTHER OR SISTER?!
YOUR HYSTERECTOMY?
YEAH, BUT WHY DO YOU THINK I HAD IT? BESIDES, IT'S ANOTHER MOUTH TO FEED. ANOTHER RESPONSIBILITY TO WEIGH YOU DOWN AND KEEP YOU FROM REACHING YOUR POTENTIAL.
IF I HAD TO DO IT ALL OVER--

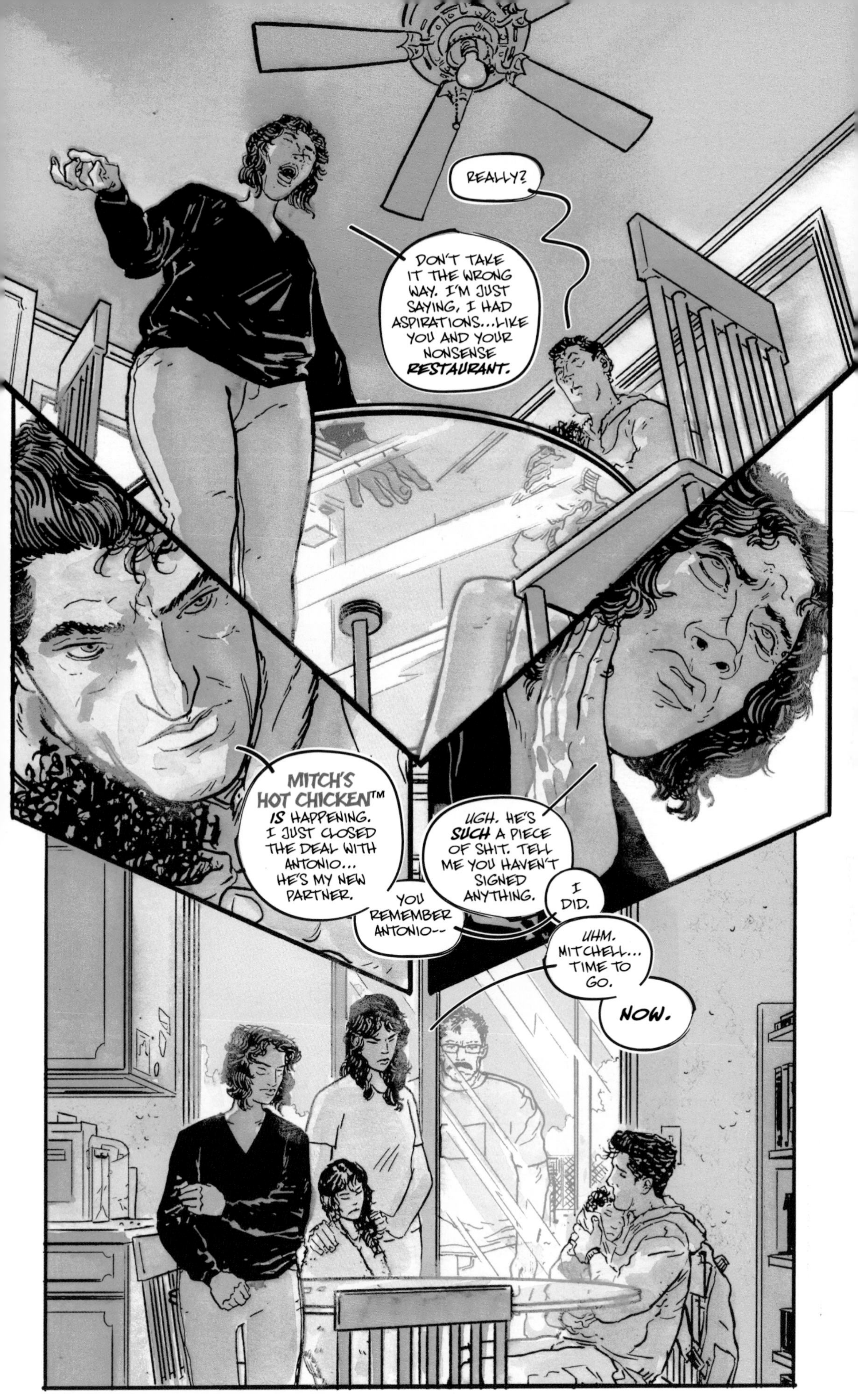
DON'T TAKE IT THE WRONG WAY. I'M JUST SAYING, I HAD ASPIRATIONS...LIKE YOU AND YOUR NONSENSE **RESTAURANT.**
REALLY?
MITCH'S HOT CHICKEN™ ***IS*** HAPPENING. I JUST CLOSED THE DEAL WITH ANTONIO... HE'S MY NEW PARTNER.
YOU REMEMBER ANTONIO--
UGH. HE'S ***SUCH*** A PIECE OF SHIT. TELL ME YOU HAVEN'T SIGNED ANYTHING.
I DID.
UHM. MITCHELL... TIME TO GO.
NOW.

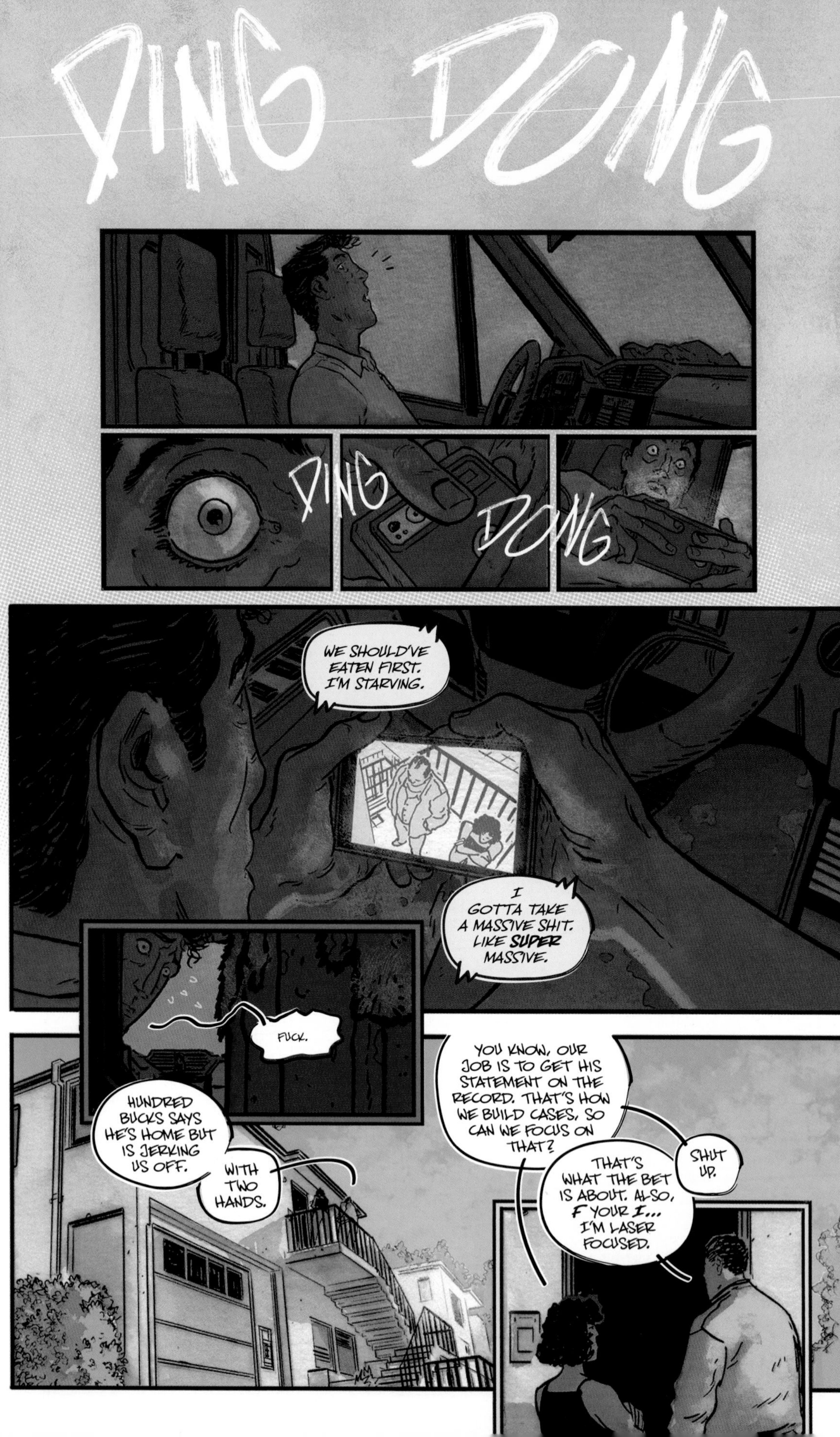
DING DONG
DING
DONG
WE SHOULD'VE EATEN FIRST. I'M STARVING.
I GOTTA TAKE A MASSIVE SHIT. LIKE SUPER MASSIVE.
FUCK.
HUNDRED BUCKS SAYS HE'S HOME BUT IS JERKING US OFF.
WITH TWO HANDS.
YOU KNOW, OUR JOB IS TO GET HIS STATEMENT ON THE RECORD. THAT'S HOW WE BUILD CASES, SO CAN WE FOCUS ON THAT?
SHUT UP.
THAT'S WHAT THE BET IS ABOUT. ALSO, F YOUR I... I'M LASER FOCUSED.

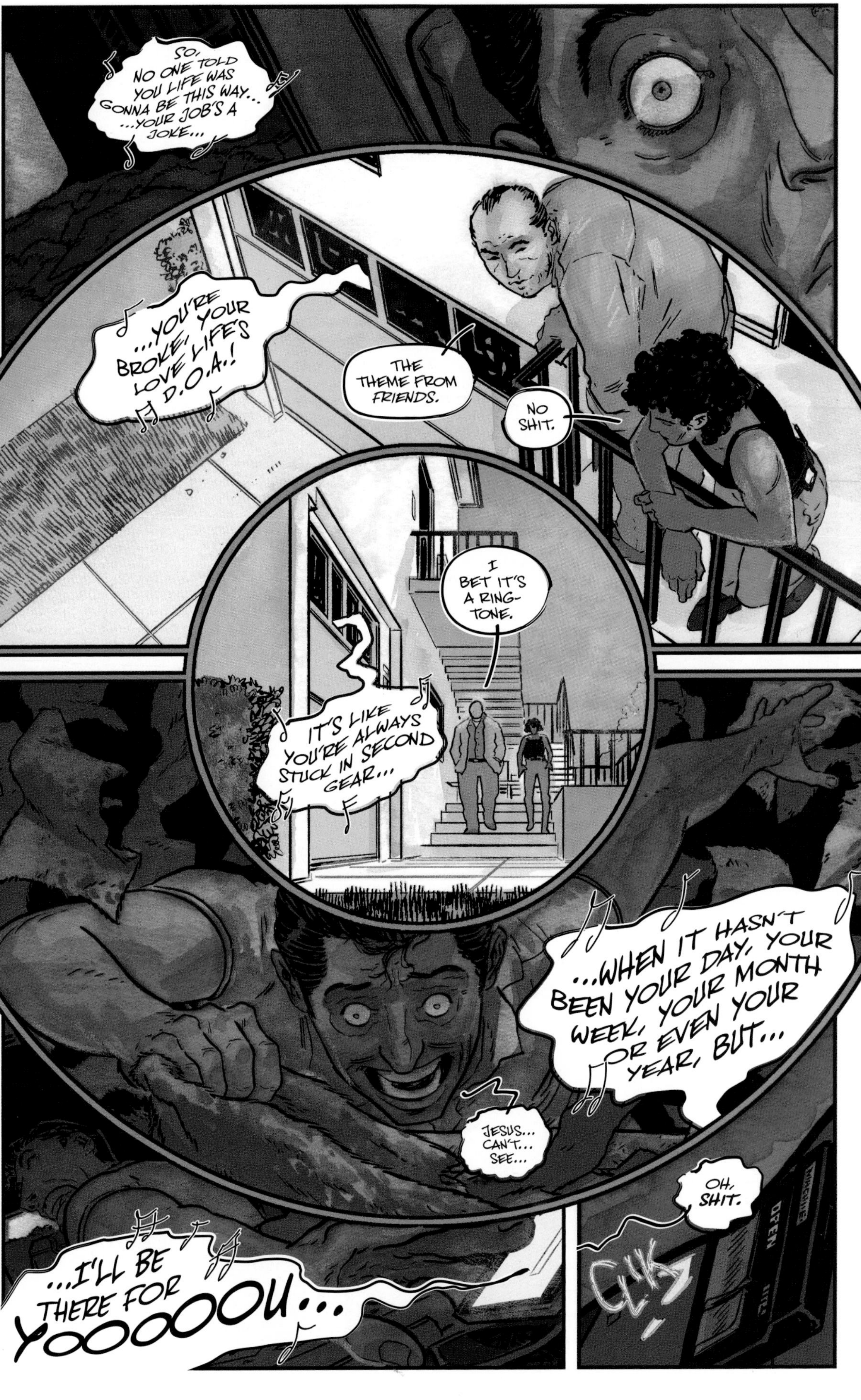
SO, NO ONE TOLD YOU LIFE WAS GONNA BE THIS WAY... ...YOUR JOB'S A JOKE...
...YOU'RE BROKE, YOUR LOVE LIFE'S D.O.A.!
THE THEME FROM FRIENDS.
NO SHIT.
I BET IT'S A RING-TONE.
IT'S LIKE YOU'RE ALWAYS STUCK IN SECOND GEAR...
...WHEN IT HASN'T BEEN YOUR DAY, YOUR WEEK, YOUR MONTH OR EVEN YOUR YEAR, BUT...
JESUS... CAN'T... SEE...
...I'LL BE THERE FOR YOOOOOU...
OH, SHIT.
CLIK
OPEN

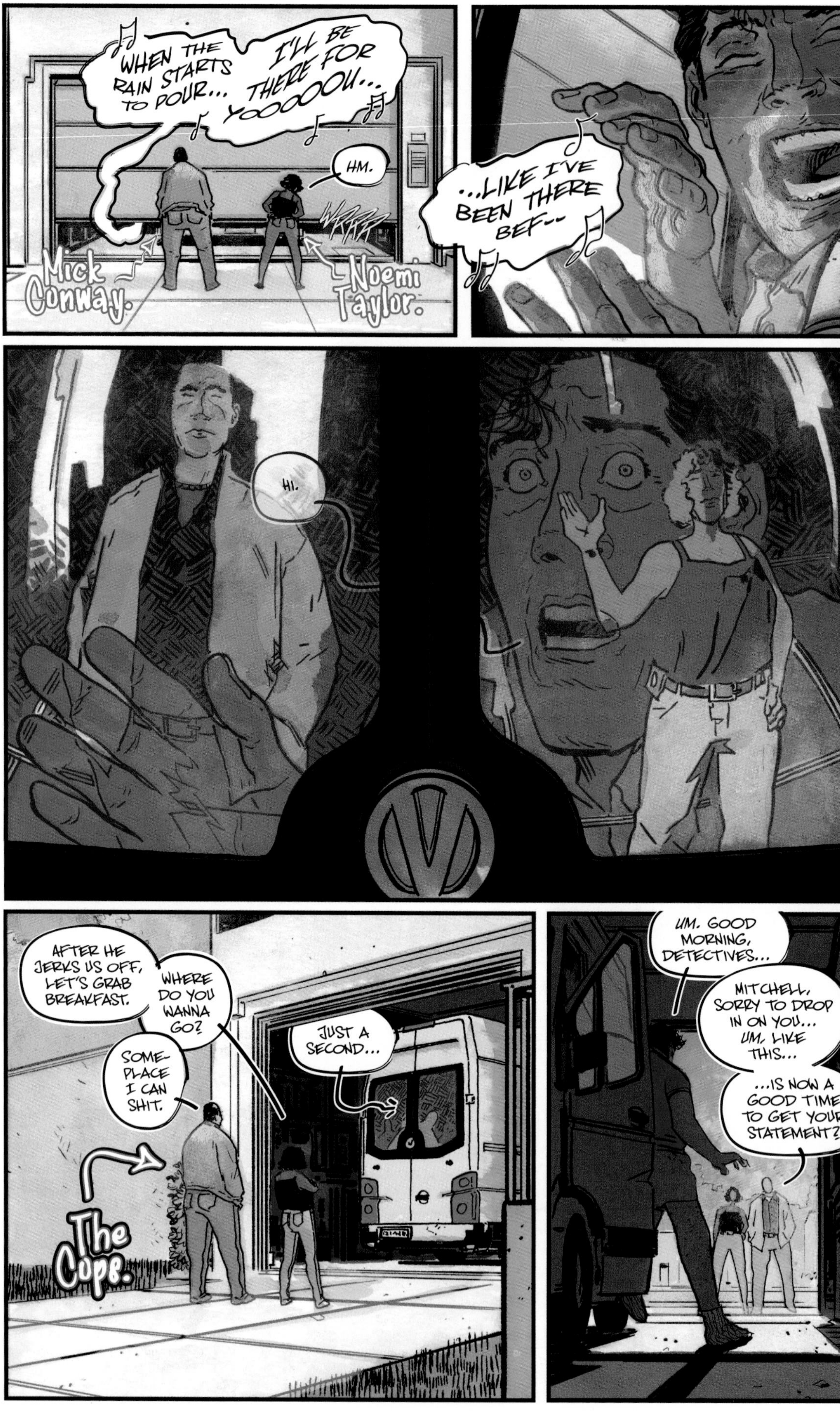
WHEN THE RAIN STARTS TO POUR... I'LL BE THERE FOR YOOOOOOU...
HM.
WRRR
Mick Conway.
Noemi Taylor.
...LIKE I'VE BEEN THERE BEF--
HI.
AFTER HE JERKS US OFF, LET'S GRAB BREAKFAST.
WHERE DO YOU WANNA GO?
SOME-PLACE I CAN SHIT.
JUST A SECOND...
The Cops.
UM. GOOD MORNING, DETECTIVES...
MITCHELL, SORRY TO DROP IN ON YOU... UM, LIKE THIS...
...IS NOW A GOOD TIME TO GET YOUR STATEMENT?

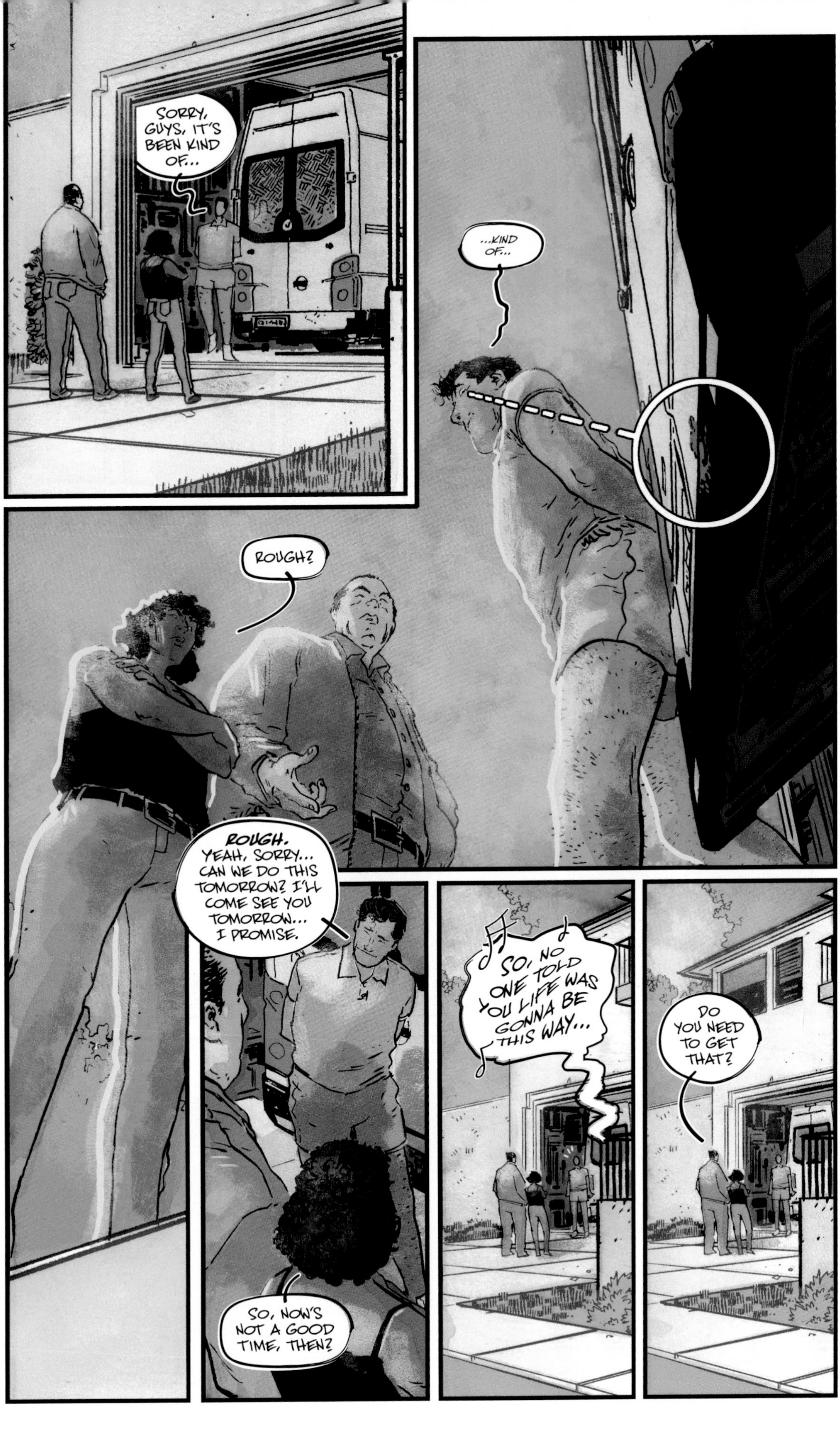
SORRY, GUYS, IT'S BEEN KIND OF...
...KIND OF...
ROUGH?
ROUGH. YEAH, SORRY... CAN WE DO THIS TOMORROW? I'LL COME SEE YOU TOMORROW... I PROMISE.
SO, NOW'S NOT A GOOD TIME, THEN?
SO, NO ONE TOLD YOU LIFE WAS GONNA BE THIS WAY...
DO YOU NEED TO GET THAT?

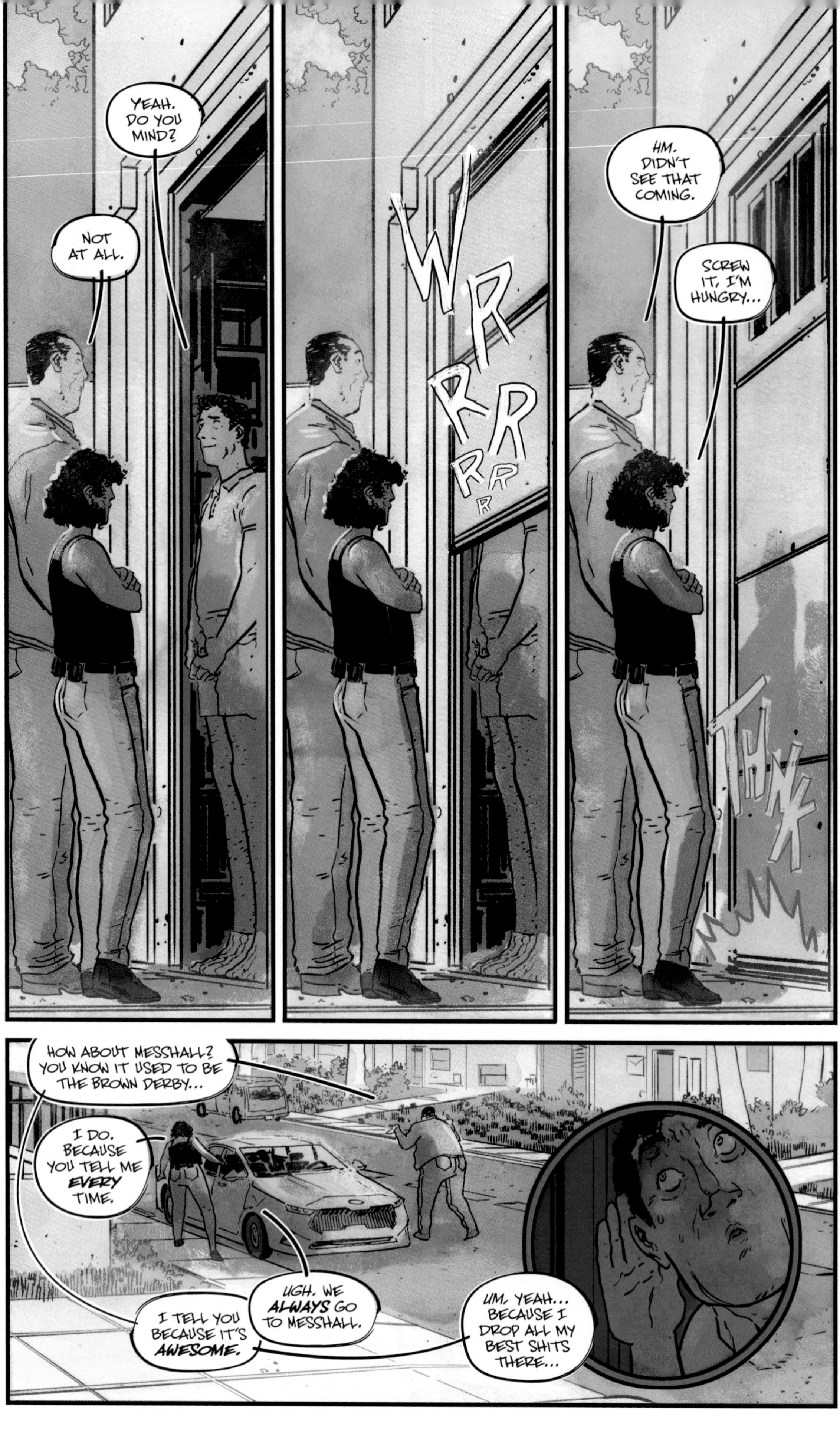
YEAH. DO YOU MIND?
NOT AT ALL.
WRRRRRR
HM. DIDN'T SEE THAT COMING.
SCREW IT, I'M HUNGRY...
THNK
HOW ABOUT MESSHALL? YOU KNOW IT USED TO BE THE BROWN DERBY...
I DO. BECAUSE YOU TELL ME EVERY TIME.
UGH. WE ALWAYS GO TO MESSHALL.
I TELL YOU BECAUSE IT'S AWESOME.
UM, YEAH... BECAUSE I DROP ALL MY BEST SHITS THERE...

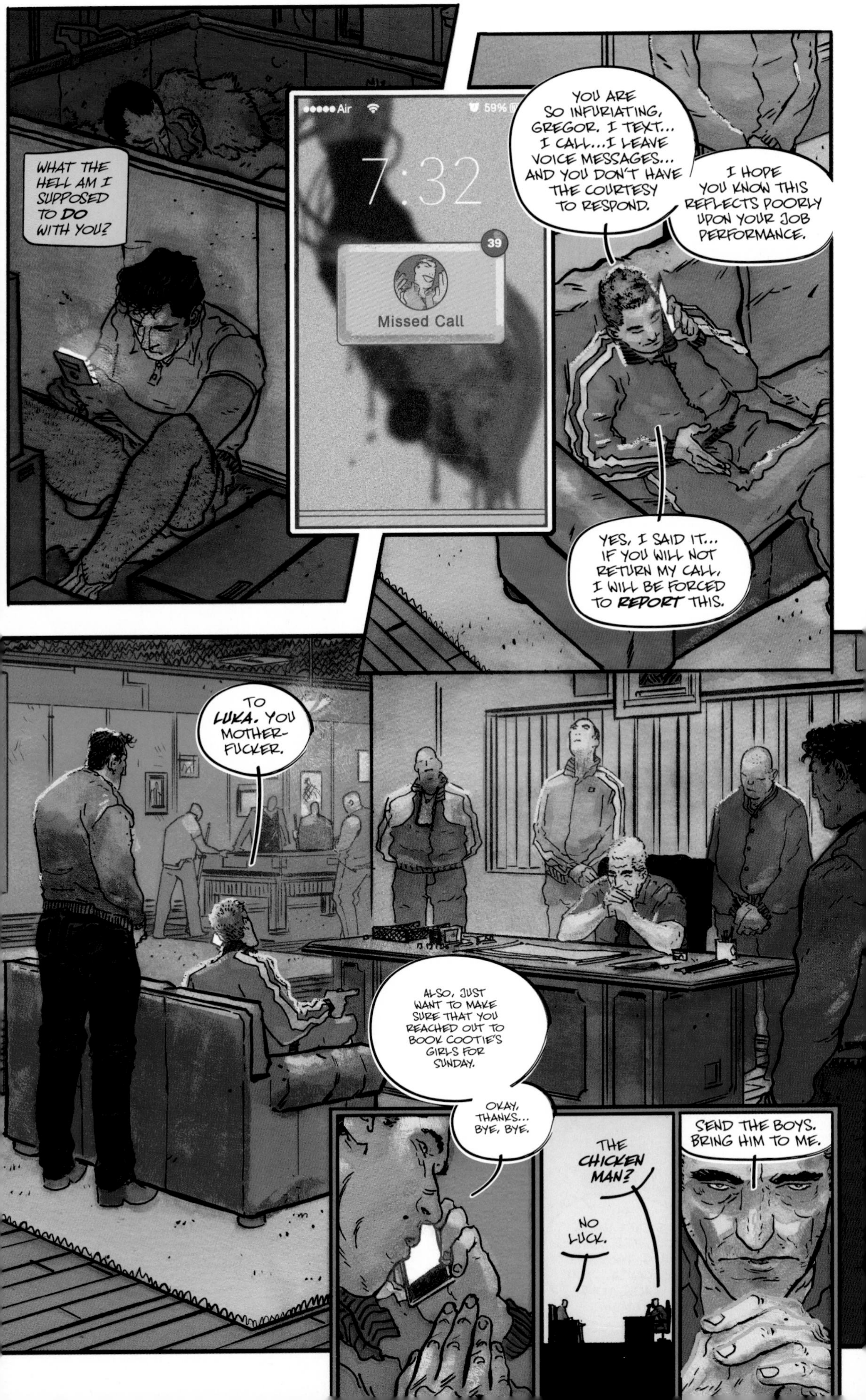
WHAT THE HELL AM I SUPPOSED TO DO WITH YOU?
●●●●● Air 59%
7:32
39
Missed Call
YOU ARE SO INFURIATING, GREGOR. I TEXT... I CALL...I LEAVE VOICE MESSAGES... AND YOU DON'T HAVE THE COURTESY TO RESPOND.
I HOPE YOU KNOW THIS REFLECTS POORLY UPON YOUR JOB PERFORMANCE.
YES, I SAID IT... IF YOU WILL NOT RETURN MY CALL, I WILL BE FORCED TO REPORT THIS.
TO LUKA. YOU MOTHER-FUCKER.
ALSO, JUST WANT TO MAKE SURE THAT YOU REACHED OUT TO BOOK COOTIE'S GIRLS FOR SUNDAY.
OKAY, THANKS... BYE, BYE.
THE CHICKEN MAN?
NO LUCK.
SEND THE BOYS. BRING HIM TO ME.

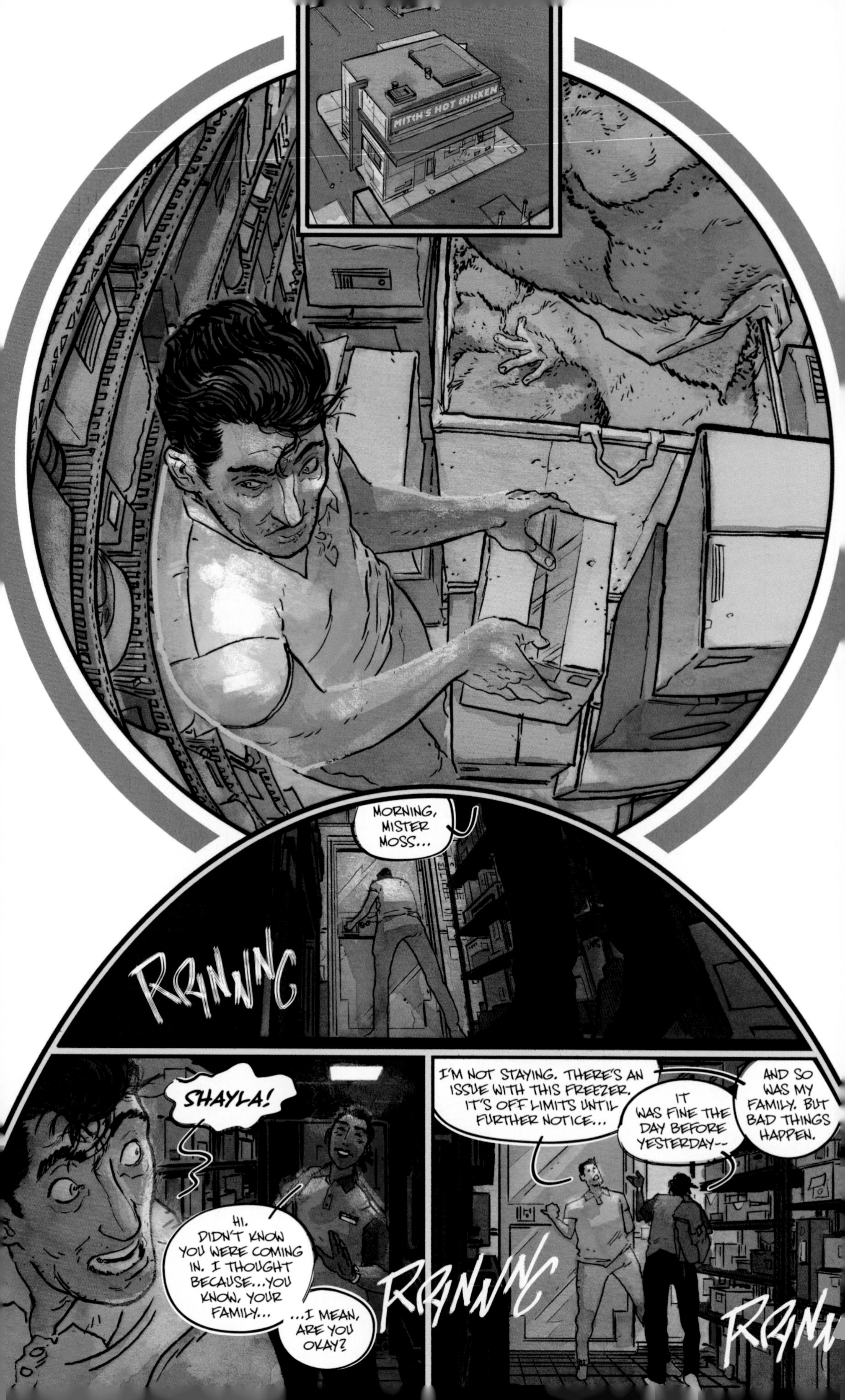
MITCH'S HOT CHICKEN
MORNING, MISTER MOSS...
RRINNNG
SHAYLA!
HI. DIDN'T KNOW YOU WERE COMING IN. I THOUGHT BECAUSE...YOU KNOW, YOUR FAMILY...
...I MEAN, ARE YOU OKAY?
RRINNNG
I'M NOT STAYING. THERE'S AN ISSUE WITH THIS FREEZER. IT'S OFF LIMITS UNTIL FURTHER NOTICE...
IT WAS FINE THE DAY BEFORE YESTERDAY--
AND SO WAS MY FAMILY. BUT BAD THINGS HAPPEN.

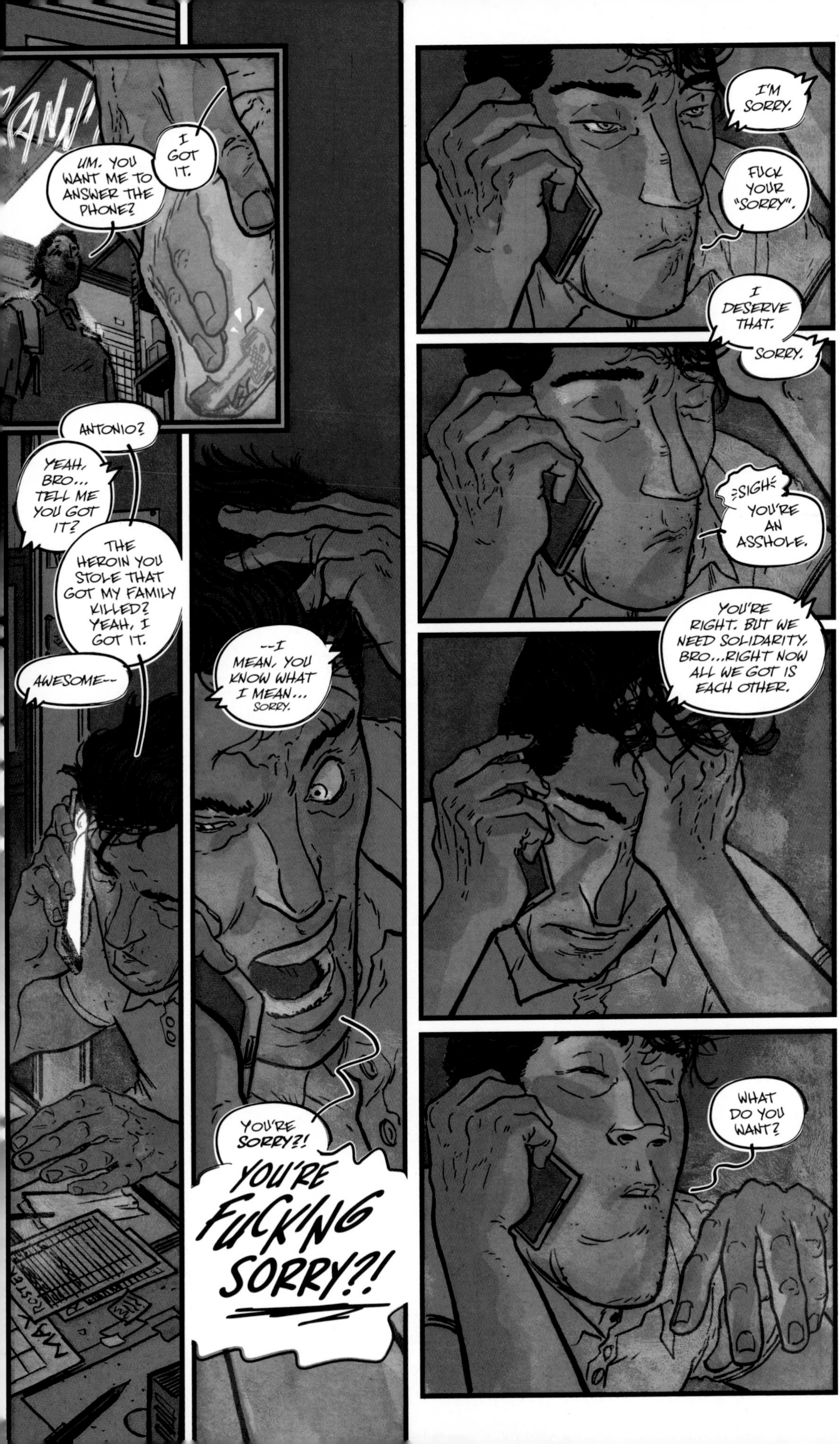
UM. YOU WANT ME TO ANSWER THE PHONE?
I GOT IT.
ANTONIO?
YEAH, BRO... TELL ME YOU GOT IT?
THE HEROIN YOU STOLE THAT GOT MY FAMILY KILLED? YEAH, I GOT IT.
AWESOME--
--I MEAN, YOU KNOW WHAT I MEAN... SORRY.
YOU'RE SORRY?!
YOU'RE FUCKING SORRY?!
I'M SORRY.
FUCK YOUR "SORRY".
I DESERVE THAT.
SORRY.
SIGH
YOU'RE AN ASSHOLE.
YOU'RE RIGHT. BUT WE NEED SOLIDARITY, BRO...RIGHT NOW ALL WE GOT IS EACH OTHER.
WHAT DO YOU WANT?

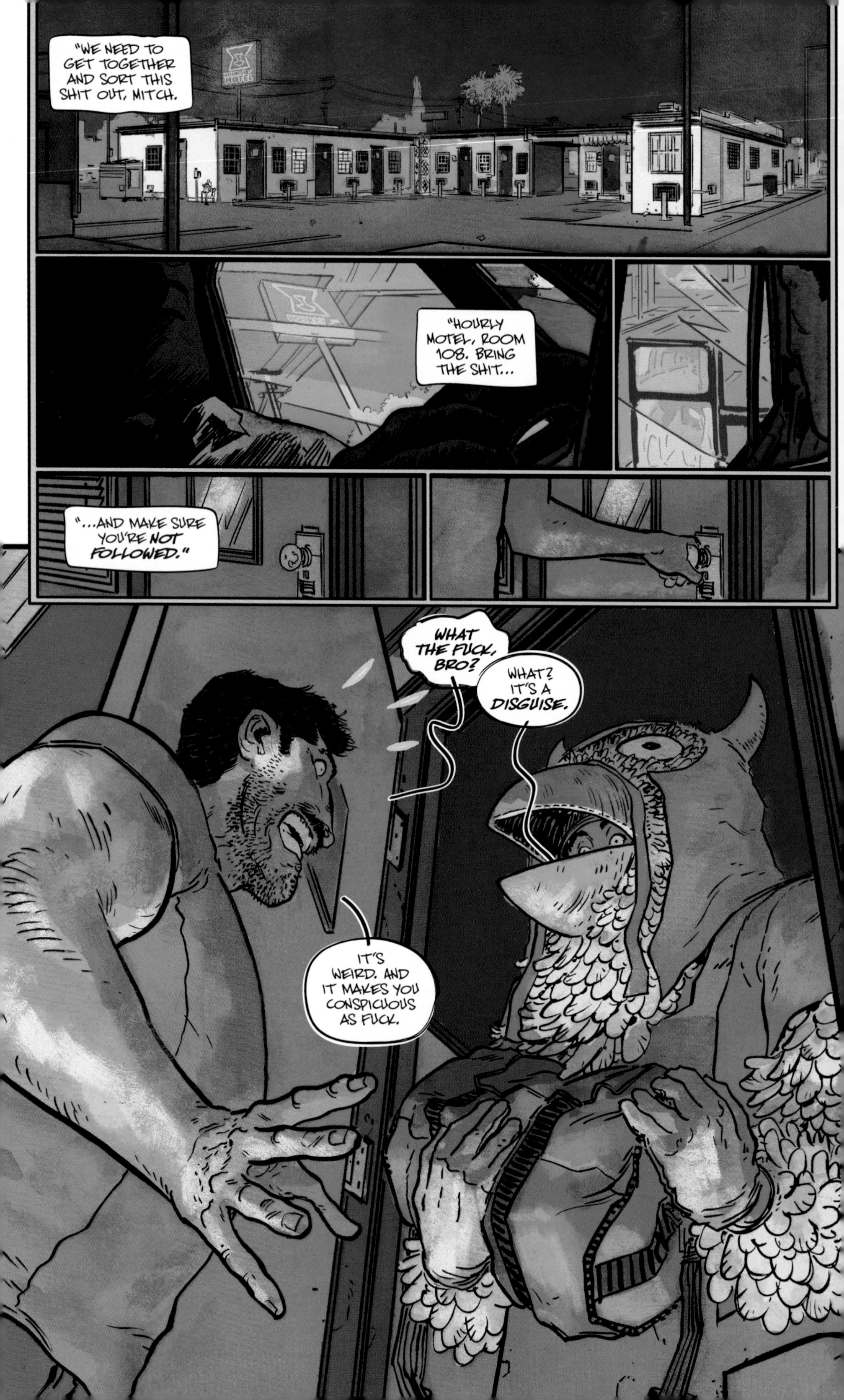
"WE NEED TO GET TOGETHER AND SORT THIS SHIT OUT, MITCH.
"HOURLY MOTEL, ROOM 108. BRING THE SHIT...
"...AND MAKE SURE YOU'RE **NOT FOLLOWED.**"
WHAT THE FUCK, BRO?
WHAT? IT'S A **DISGUISE.**
IT'S WEIRD. AND IT MAKES YOU CONSPICUOUS AS FUCK.

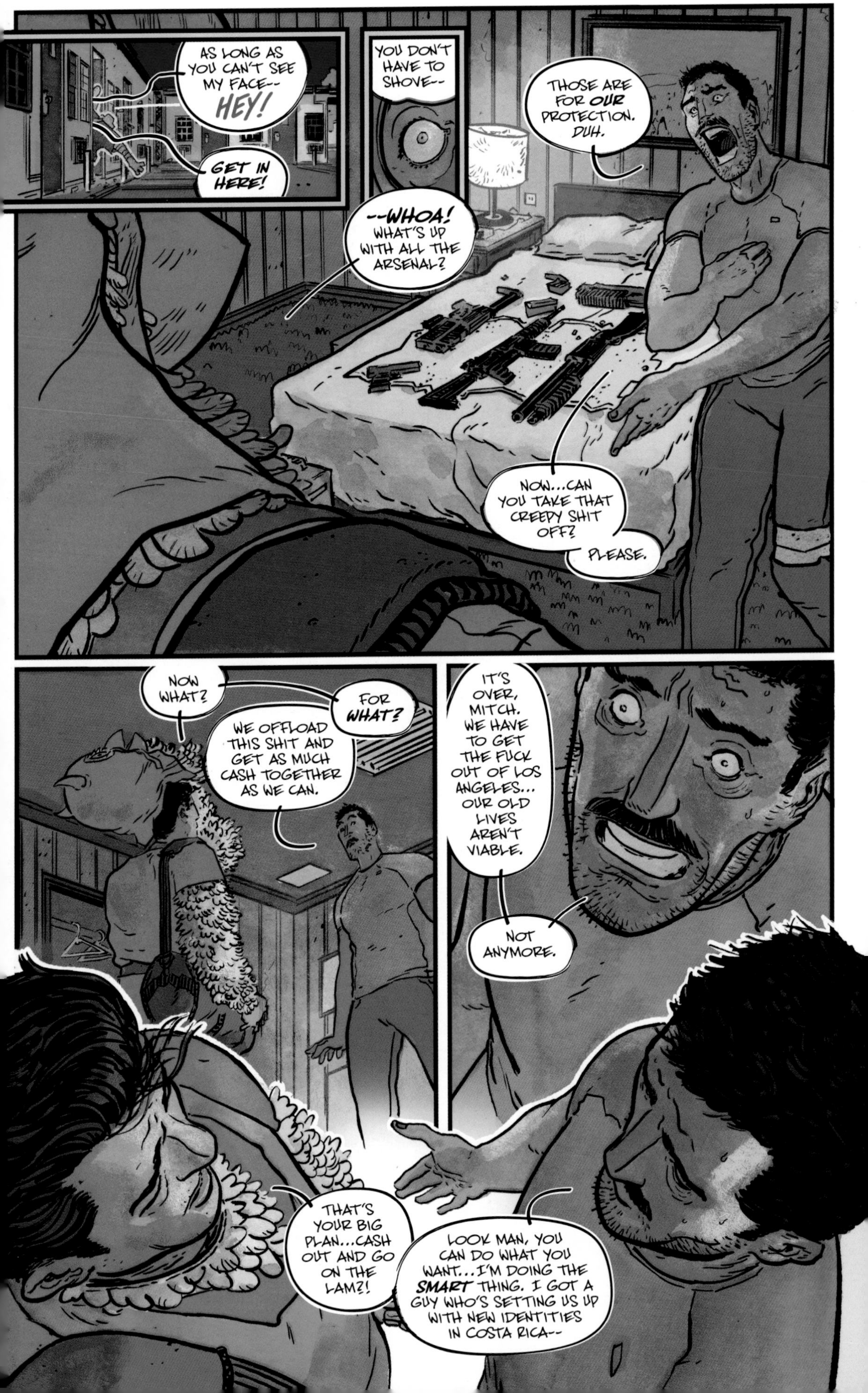
AS LONG AS YOU CAN'T SEE MY FACE-- HEY!
GET IN HERE!
YOU DON'T HAVE TO SHOVE--
--WHOA! WHAT'S UP WITH ALL THE ARSENAL?
THOSE ARE FOR OUR PROTECTION. DUH.
NOW...CAN YOU TAKE THAT CREEPY SHIT OFF?
PLEASE.
NOW WHAT?
FOR WHAT?
WE OFFLOAD THIS SHIT AND GET AS MUCH CASH TOGETHER AS WE CAN.
IT'S OVER, MITCH. WE HAVE TO GET THE FUCK OUT OF LOS ANGELES... OUR OLD LIVES AREN'T VIABLE.
NOT ANYMORE.
THAT'S YOUR BIG PLAN...CASH OUT AND GO ON THE LAM?!
LOOK MAN, YOU CAN DO WHAT YOU WANT...I'M DOING THE SMART THING. I GOT A GUY WHO'S SETTING US UP WITH NEW IDENTITIES IN COSTA RICA--

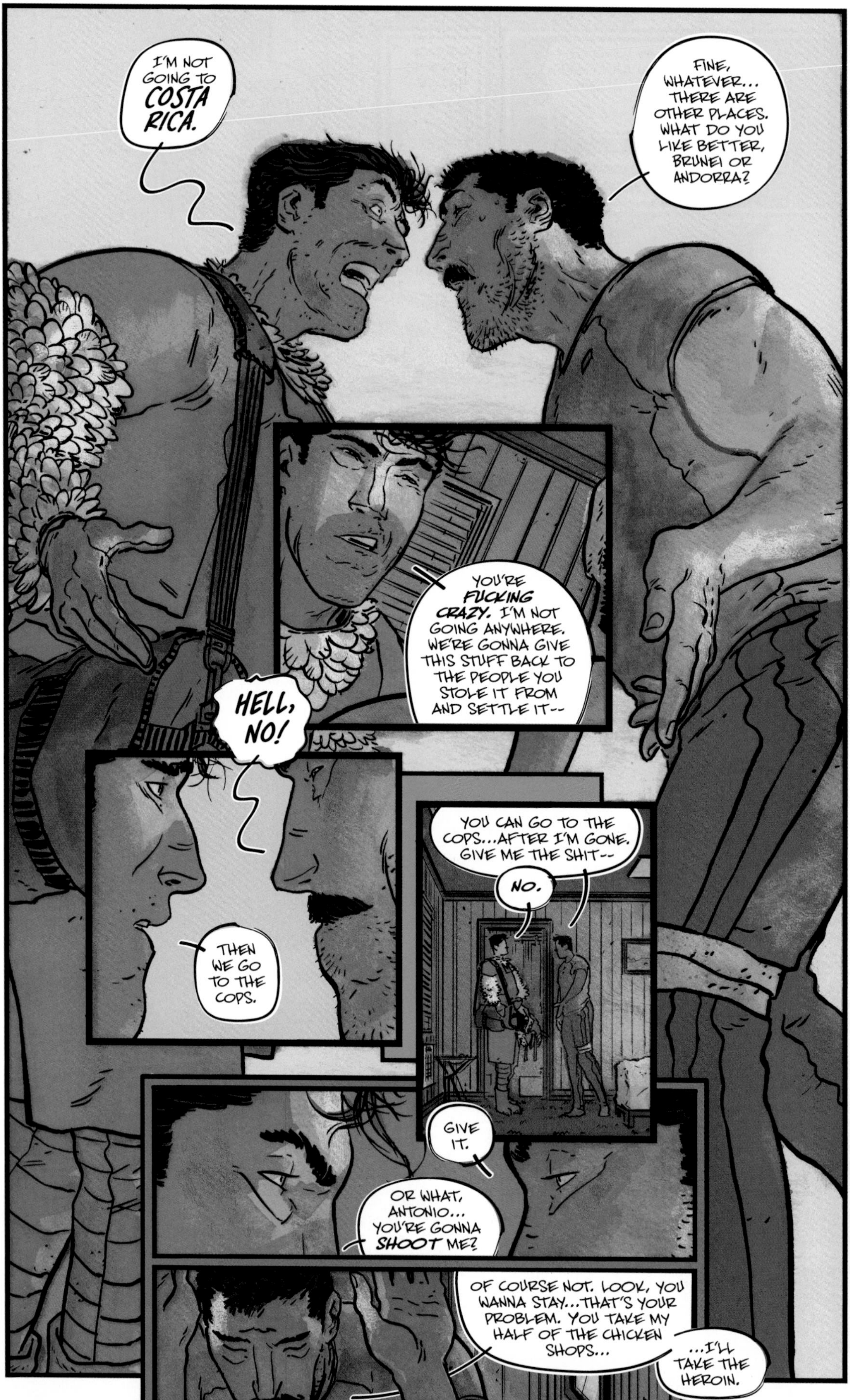
I'M NOT GOING TO COSTA RICA.
FINE, WHATEVER... THERE ARE OTHER PLACES. WHAT DO YOU LIKE BETTER, BRUNEI OR ANDORRA?
YOU'RE FUCKING CRAZY. I'M NOT GOING ANYWHERE. WE'RE GONNA GIVE THIS STUFF BACK TO THE PEOPLE YOU STOLE IT FROM AND SETTLE IT--
HELL, NO!
THEN WE GO TO THE COPS.
YOU CAN GO TO THE COPS...AFTER I'M GONE. GIVE ME THE SHIT--
NO.
GIVE IT.
OR WHAT, ANTONIO... YOU'RE GONNA SHOOT ME?
OF COURSE NOT. LOOK, YOU WANNA STAY...THAT'S YOUR PROBLEM. YOU TAKE MY HALF OF THE CHICKEN SHOPS...
...I'LL TAKE THE HEROIN.

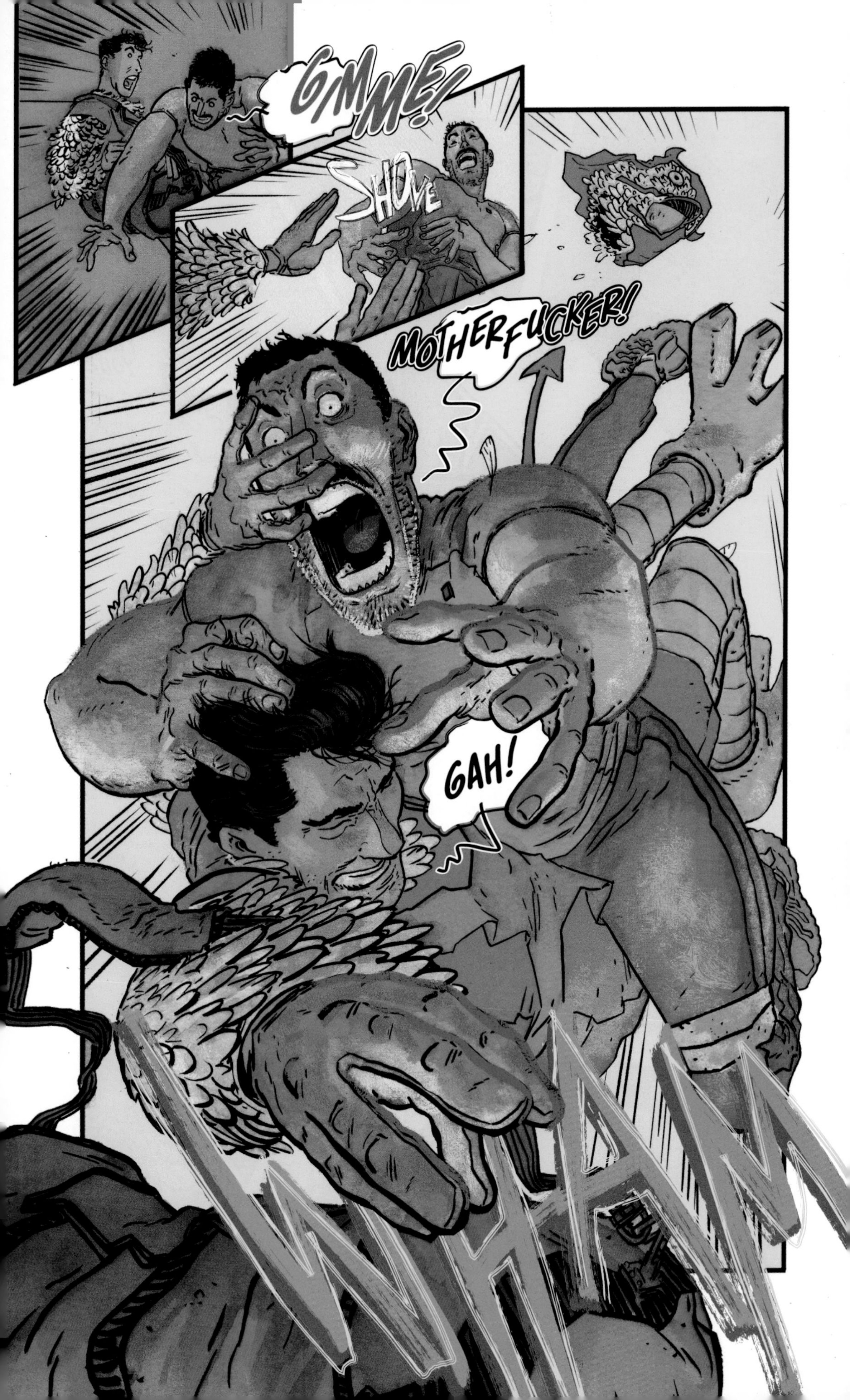
GIMME!
SHOVE
MOTHERFUCKER!
GAH!
WHAM

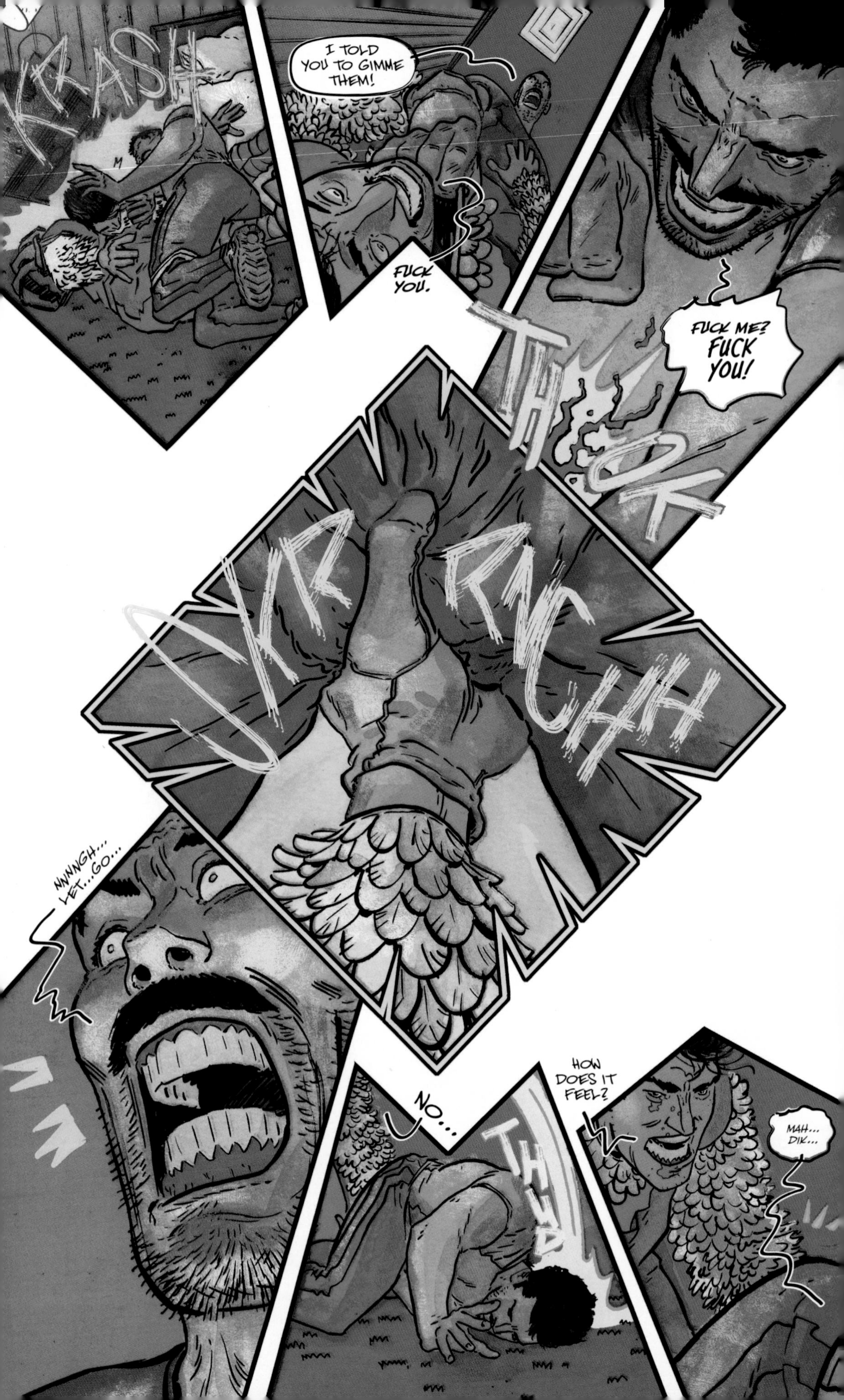

KRASH
M
I TOLD YOU TO GIMME THEM!
FUCK YOU.
FUCK ME? FUCK YOU!
THOOK
KRRUNCHH
NNNNGH... LET...GO...
NO...
THUD
HOW DOES IT FEEL?
MAH... DIK...

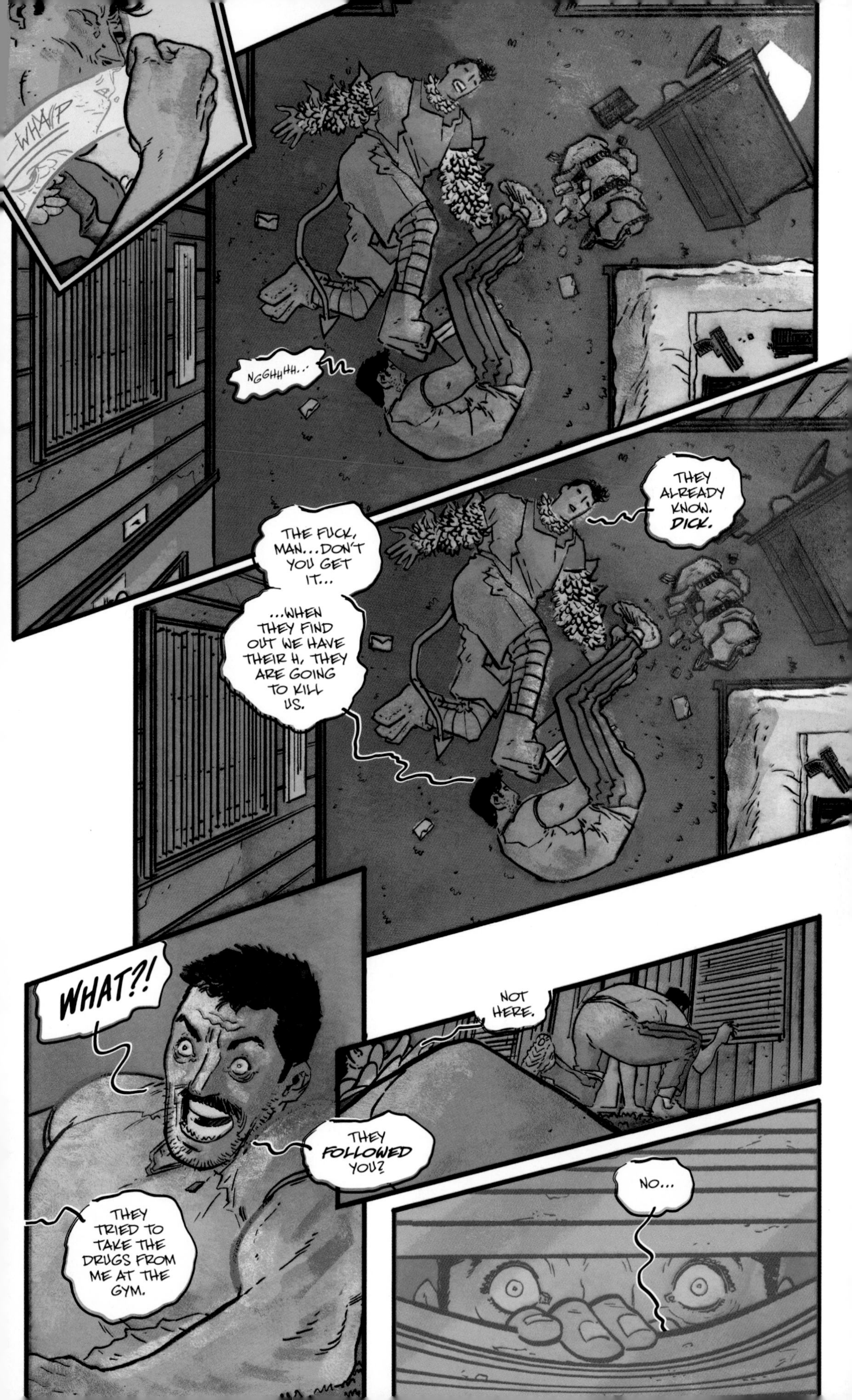
WHAP
NGGHHHH...
THE FUCK, MAN...DON'T YOU GET IT...
...WHEN THEY FIND OUT WE HAVE THEIR H, THEY ARE GOING TO KILL US.
THEY ALREADY KNOW. DICK.
WHAT?!
THEY FOLLOWED YOU?
THEY TRIED TO TAKE THE DRUGS FROM ME AT THE GYM.
NOT HERE.
NO...

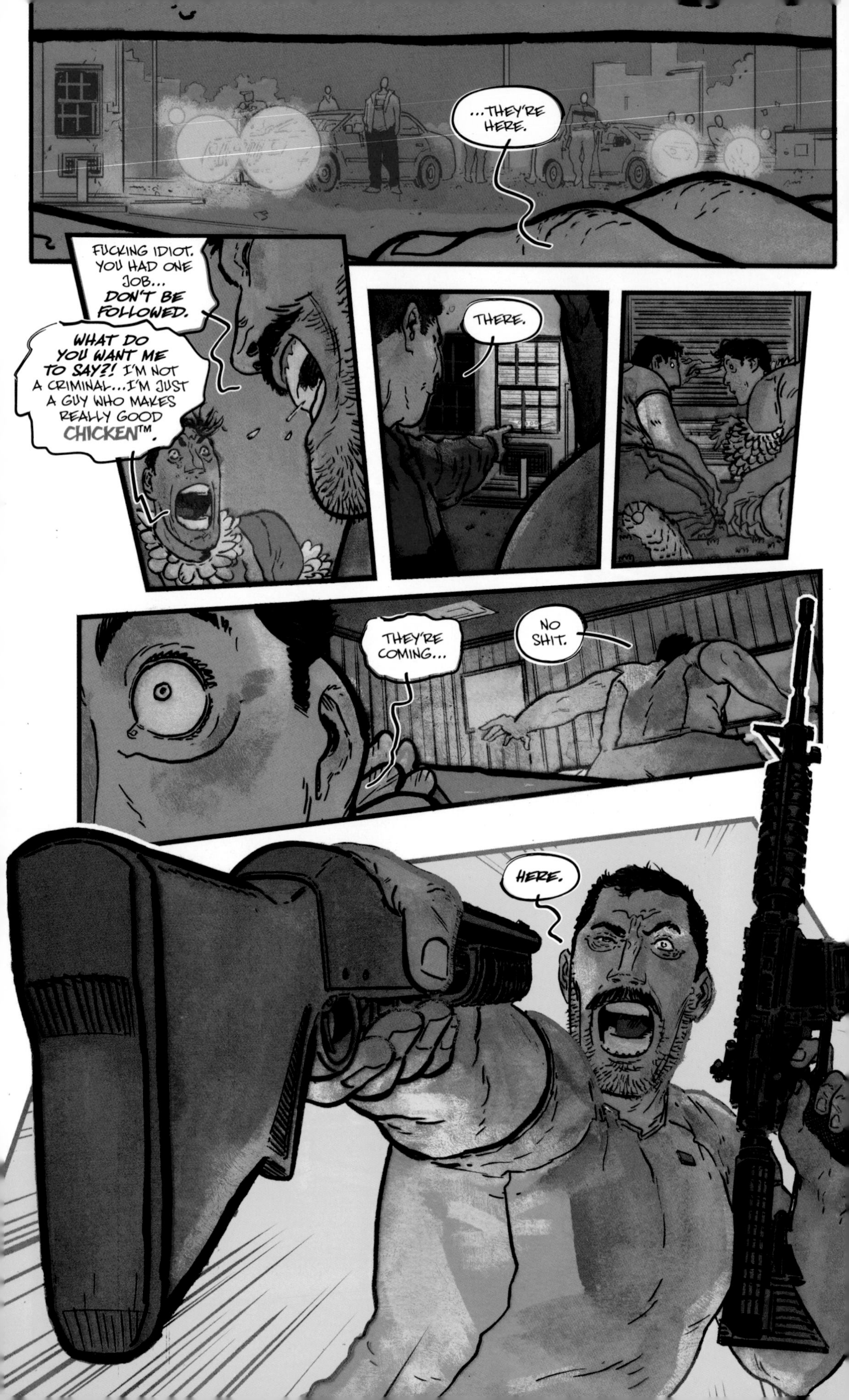
...THEY'RE HERE.
FUCKING IDIOT. YOU HAD ONE JOB... DON'T BE FOLLOWED.
WHAT DO YOU WANT ME TO SAY?! I'M NOT A CRIMINAL...I'M JUST A GUY WHO MAKES REALLY GOOD CHICKEN™.
THERE.
THEY'RE COMING...
NO SHIT.
HERE.

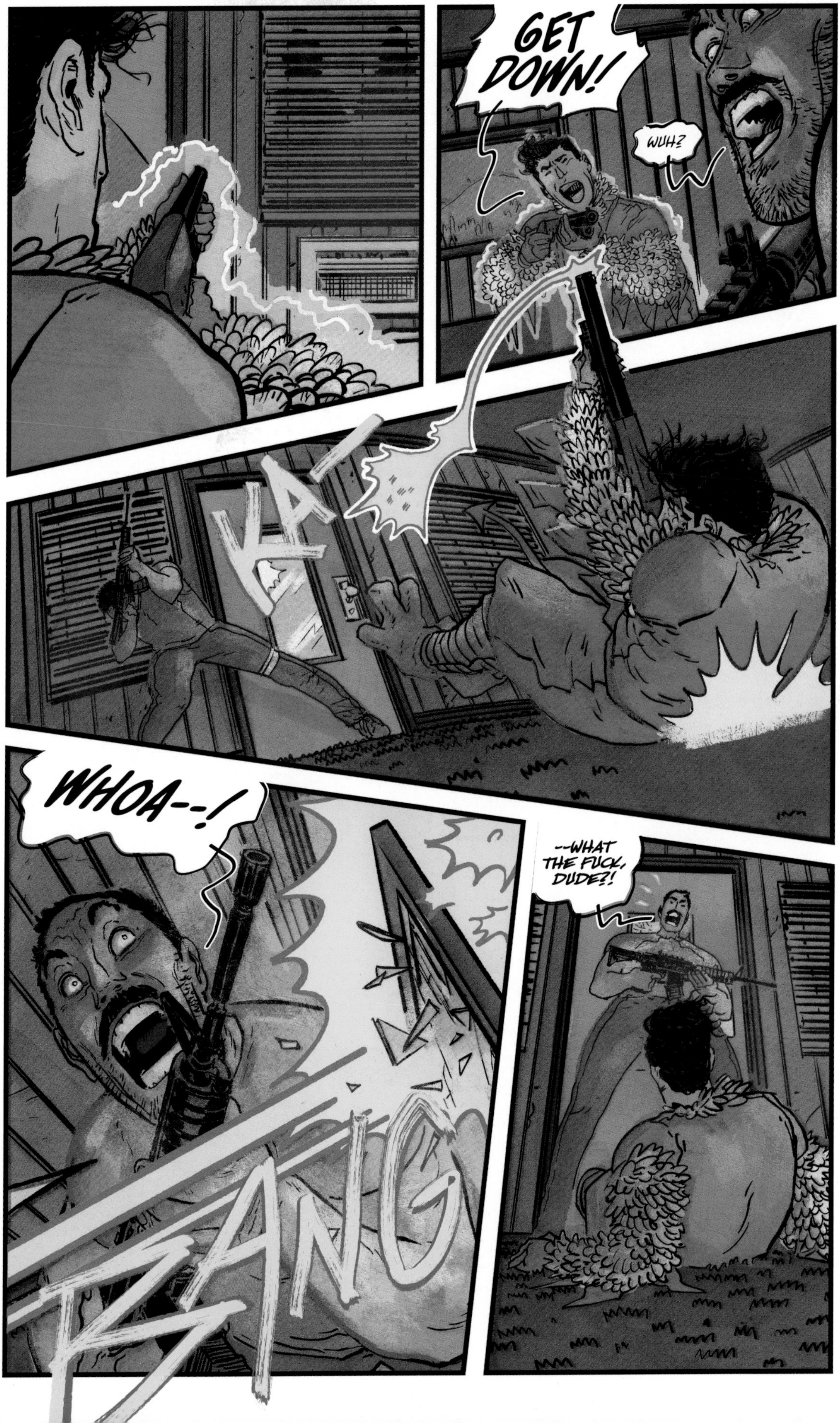
GET DOWN!
WUH?
KA-
WHOA--!
--WHAT THE FUCK, DUDE?!
BANG

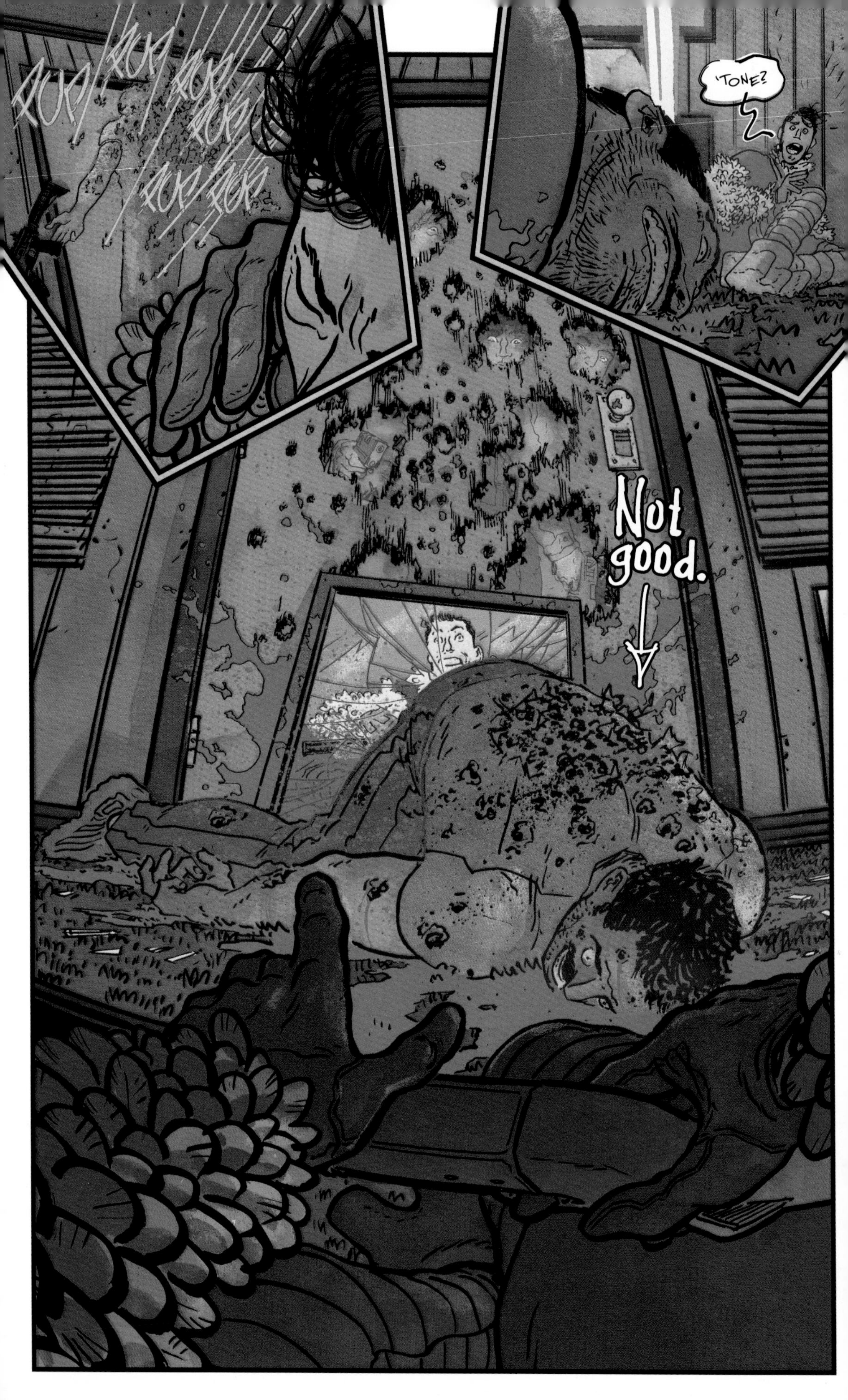
'TONE?
Not good.

3

GIVE THE CHICKEN HIS DUE

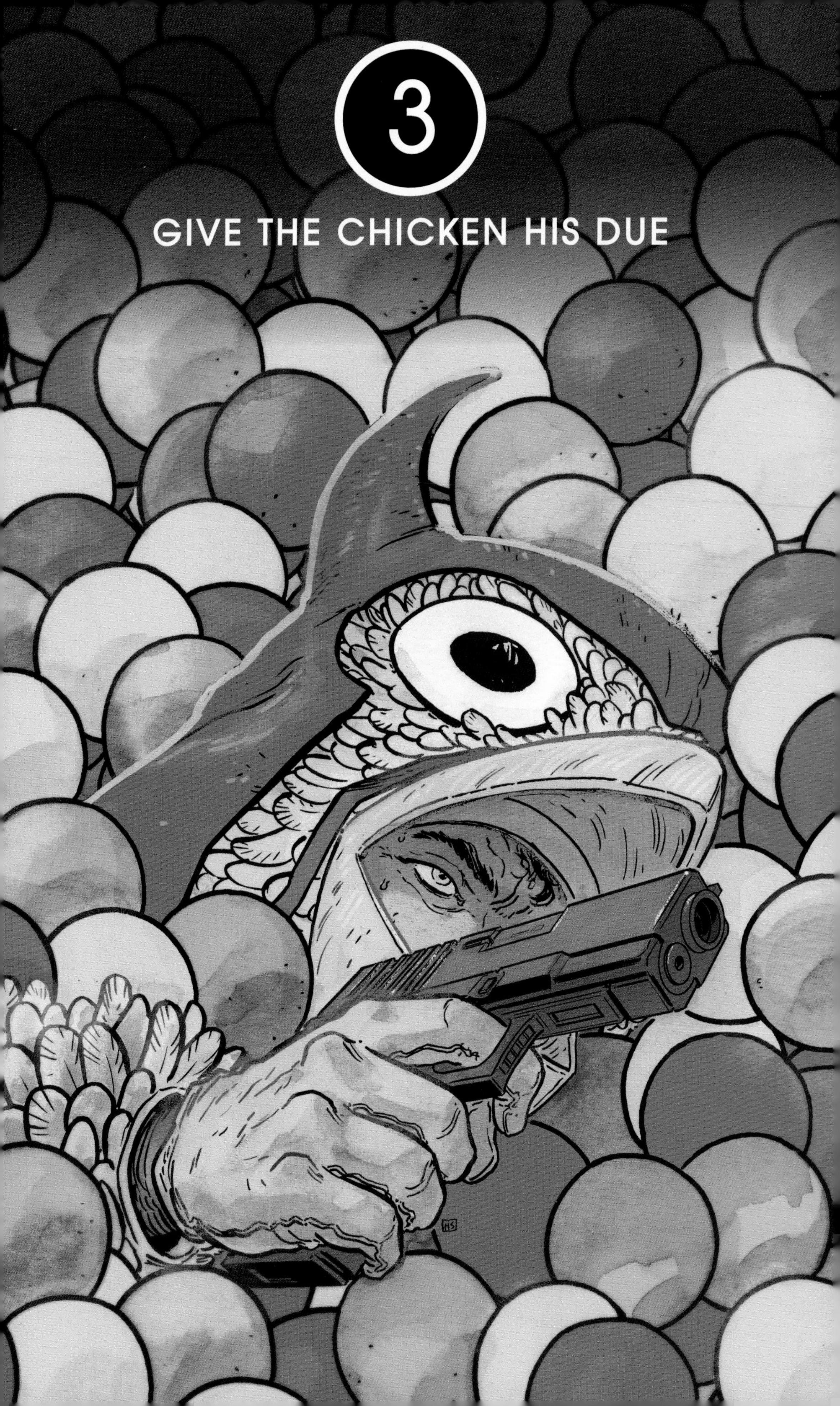

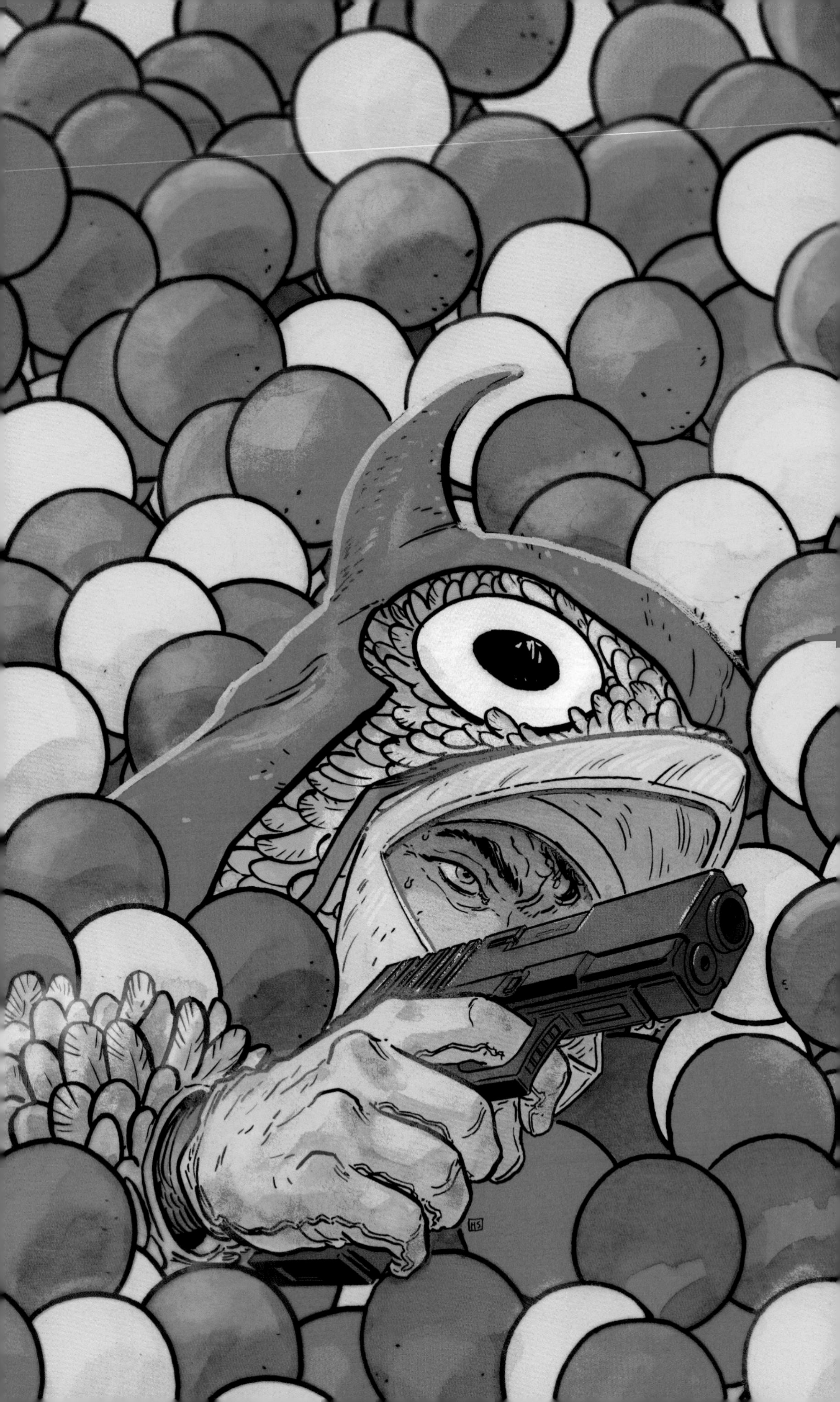

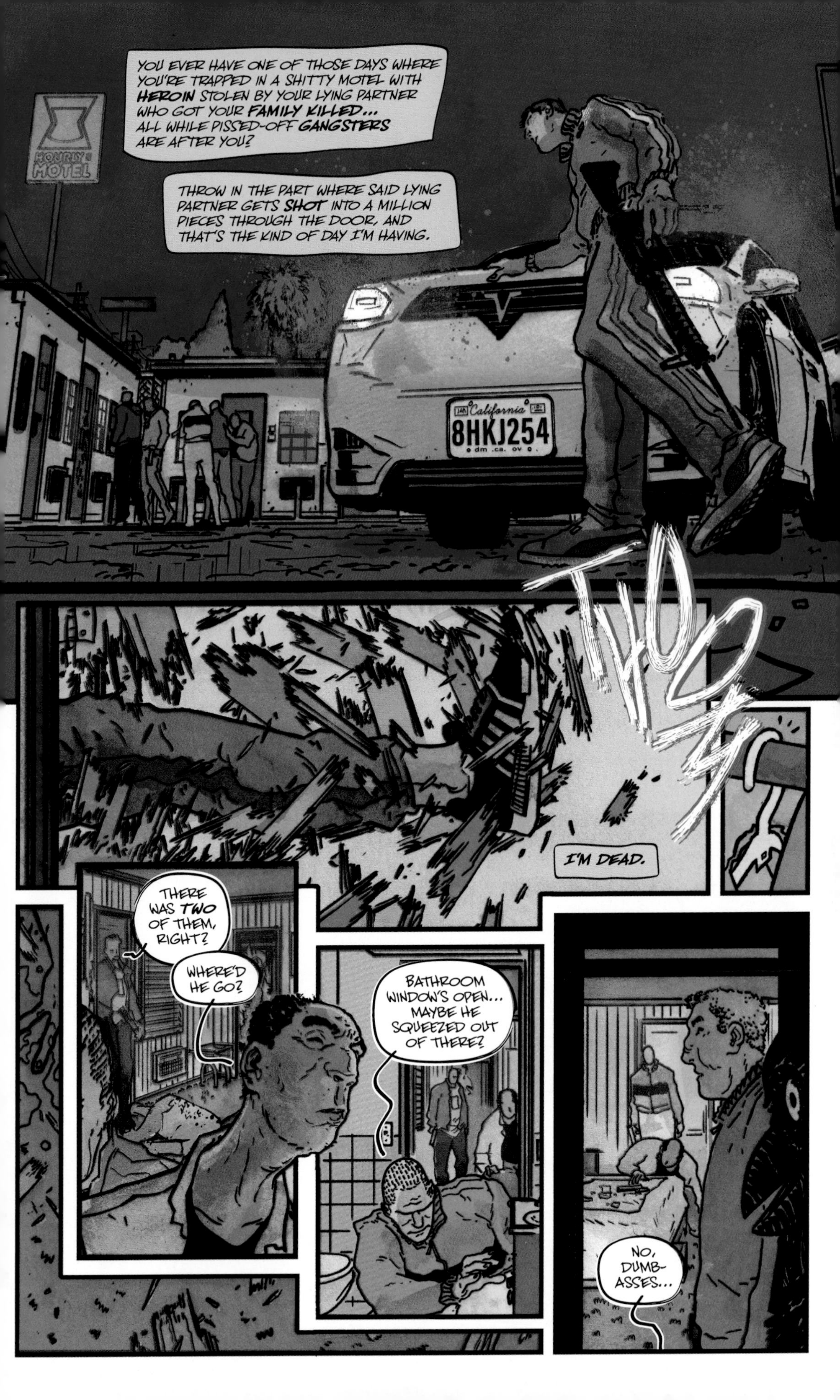

YOU EVER HAVE ONE OF THOSE DAYS WHERE YOU'RE TRAPPED IN A SHITTY MOTEL WITH HEROIN STOLEN BY YOUR LYING PARTNER WHO GOT YOUR FAMILY KILLED... ALL WHILE PISSED-OFF GANGSTERS ARE AFTER YOU?
HOURLY MOTEL
THROW IN THE PART WHERE SAID LYING PARTNER GETS SHOT INTO A MILLION PIECES THROUGH THE DOOR, AND THAT'S THE KIND OF DAY I'M HAVING.
California
8HKJ254
THOOM
I'M DEAD.
THERE WAS TWO OF THEM, RIGHT?
WHERE'D HE GO?
BATHROOM WINDOW'S OPEN... MAYBE HE SQUEEZED OUT OF THERE?
NO, DUMB-ASSES...

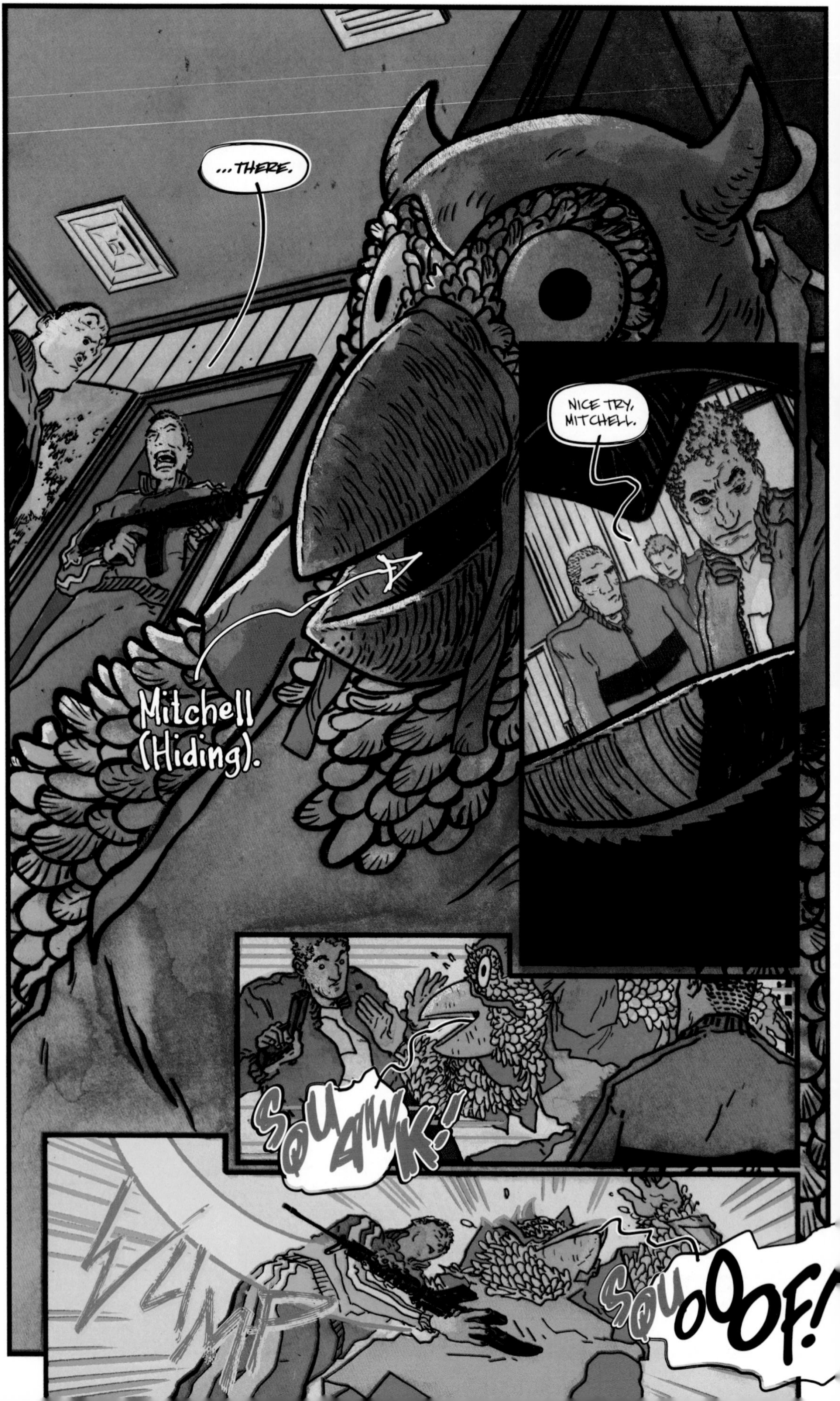

...THERE.
Mitchell (Hiding).
NICE TRY, MITCHELL.
SQUAWK!
THUMP
SQUOOOF!

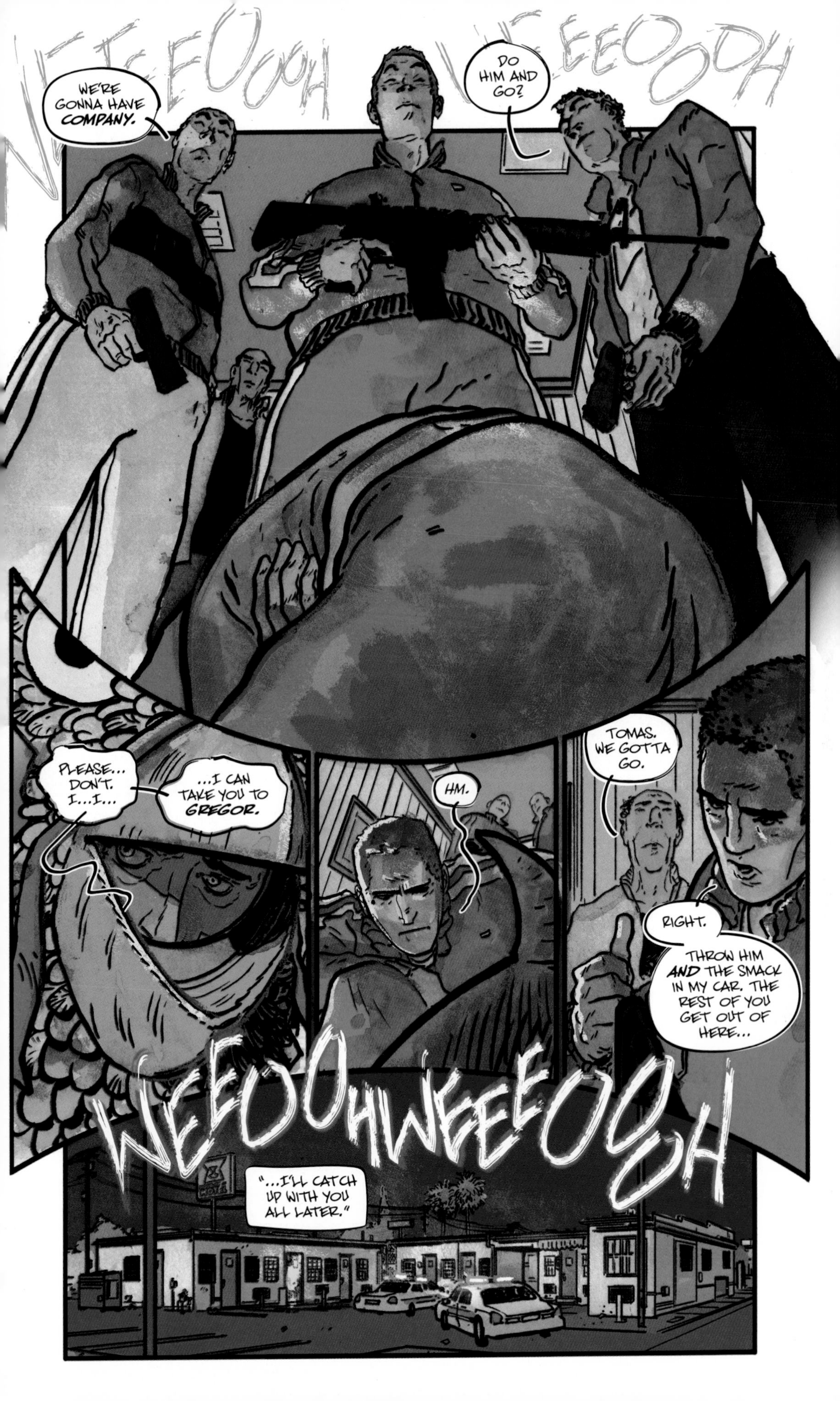
WEEEOOOH WEEEOOOH
WE'RE GONNA HAVE COMPANY.
DO HIM AND GO?
PLEASE... DON'T. I...I...
...I CAN TAKE YOU TO GREGOR.
HM.
TOMAS. WE GOTTA GO.
RIGHT.
THROW HIM AND THE SMACK IN MY CAR. THE REST OF YOU GET OUT OF HERE...
WEEOOHWEEEOOOH
"...I'LL CATCH UP WITH YOU ALL LATER."

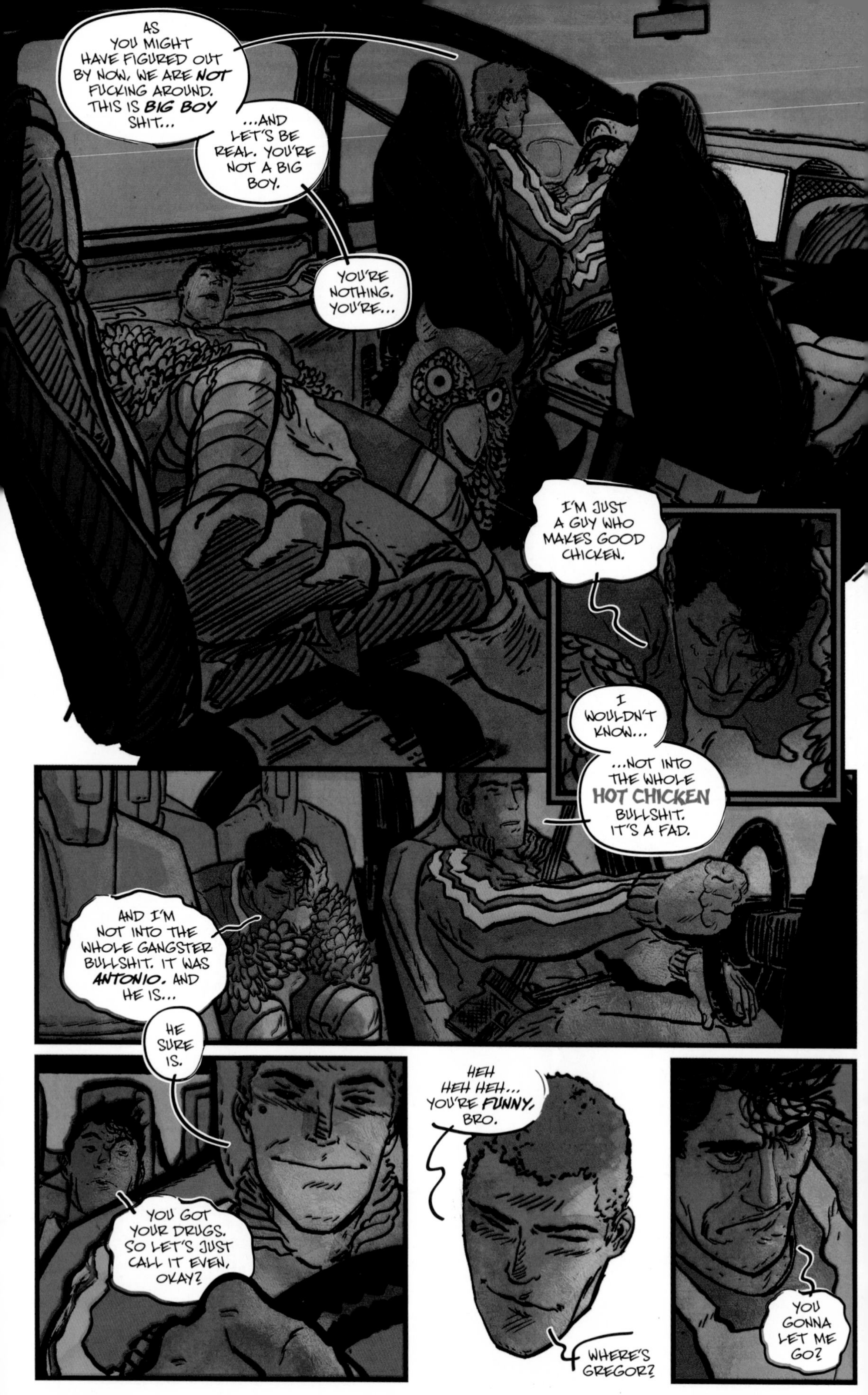
AS YOU MIGHT HAVE FIGURED OUT BY NOW, WE ARE NOT FUCKING AROUND. THIS IS BIG BOY SHIT...
...AND LET'S BE REAL. YOU'RE NOT A BIG BOY.
YOU'RE NOTHING. YOU'RE...
I'M JUST A GUY WHO MAKES GOOD CHICKEN.
I WOULDN'T KNOW...
...NOT INTO THE WHOLE HOT CHICKEN BULLSHIT. IT'S A FAD.
AND I'M NOT INTO THE WHOLE GANGSTER BULLSHIT. IT WAS ANTONIO. AND HE IS...
HE SURE IS.
YOU GOT YOUR DRUGS. SO LET'S JUST CALL IT EVEN, OKAY?
HEH HEH HEH... YOU'RE FUNNY, BRO.
WHERE'S GREGOR?
YOU GONNA LET ME GO?

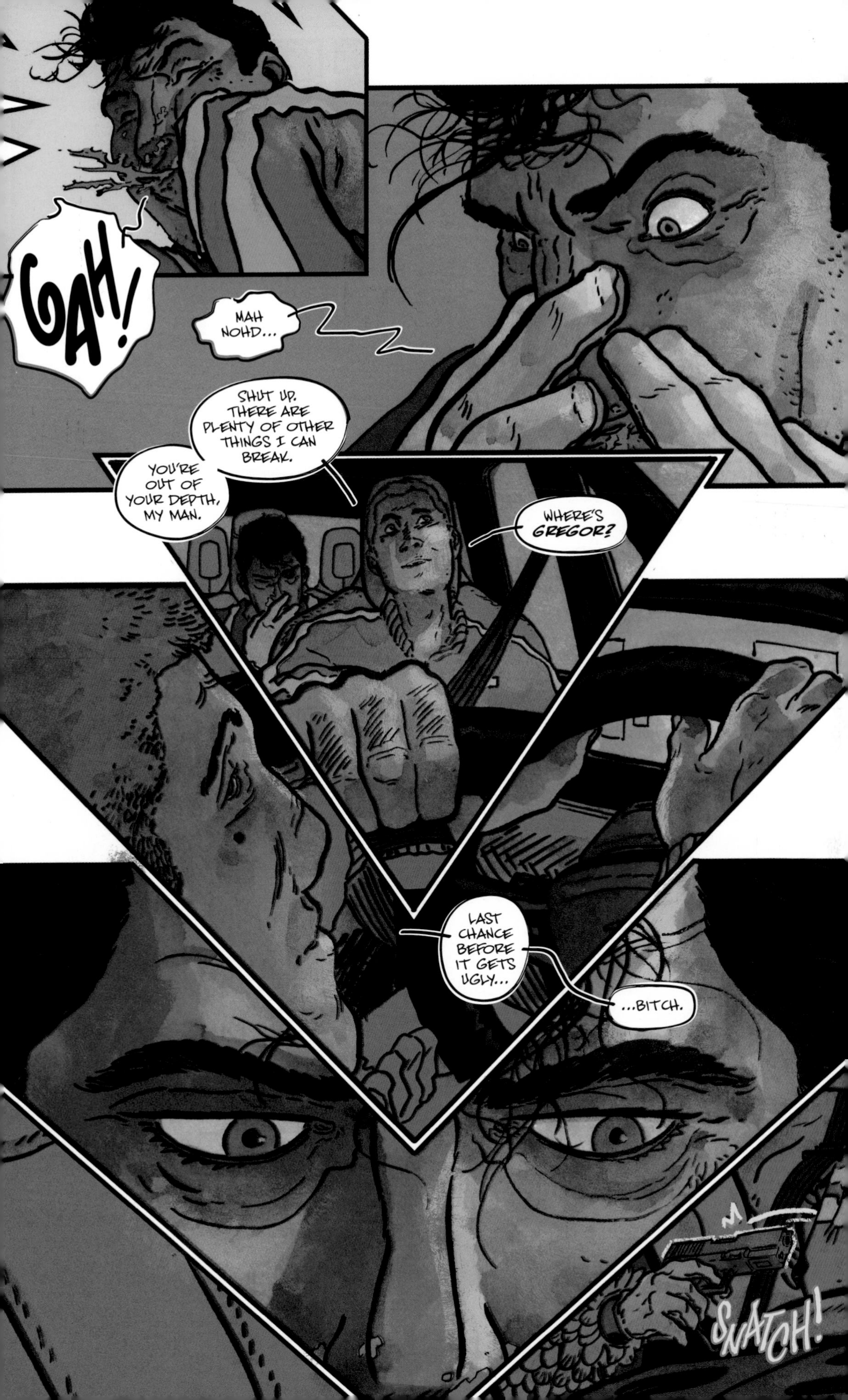
GAH!
MAH NOHD...
SHUT UP. THERE ARE PLENTY OF OTHER THINGS I CAN BREAK.
YOU'RE OUT OF YOUR DEPTH, MY MAN.
WHERE'S GREGOR?
LAST CHANCE BEFORE IT GETS UGLY...
...BITCH.
SNATCH!

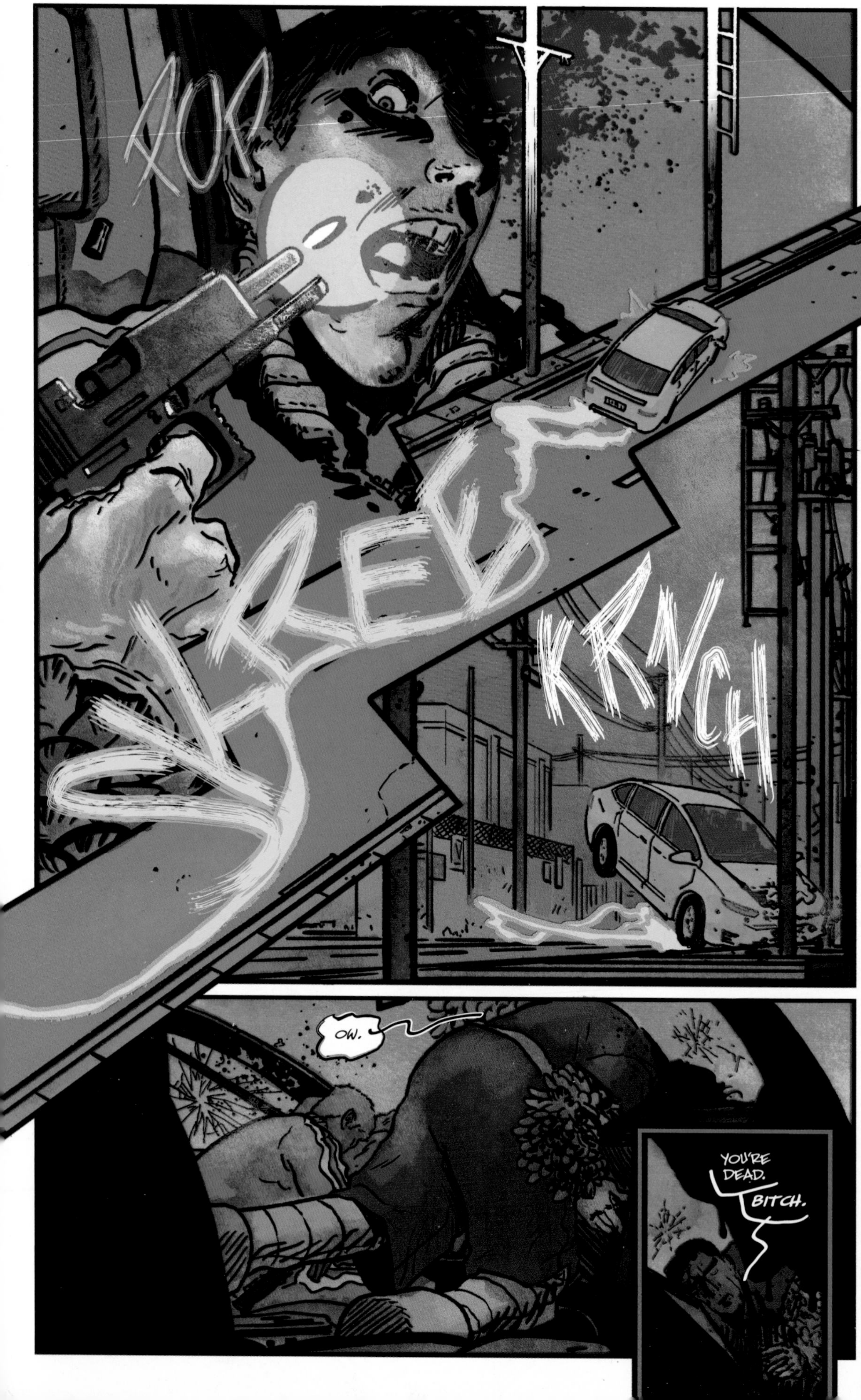
POP
SKREE
KRNCH
OW.
YOU'RE DEAD.
BITCH.

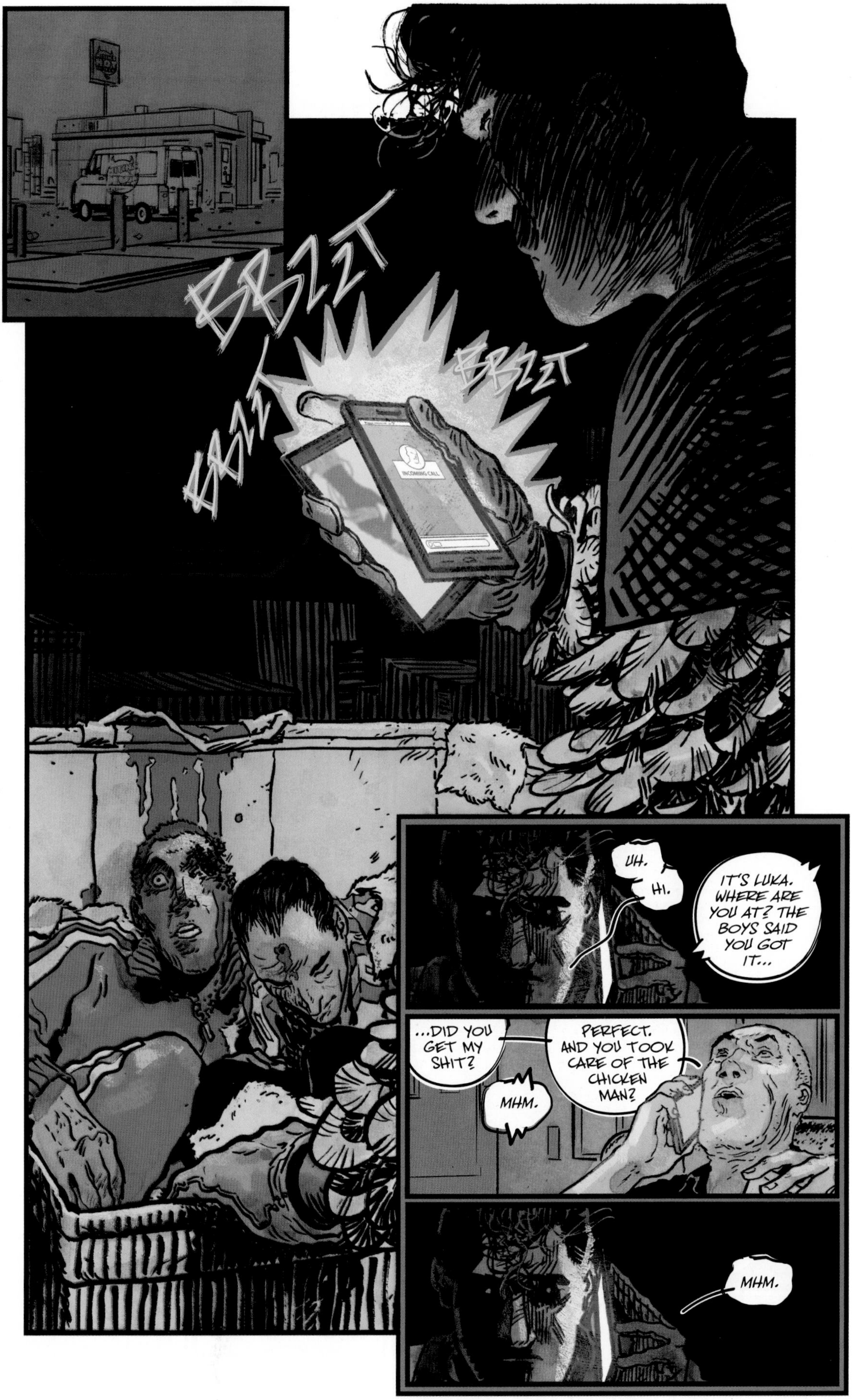

BBZZT
BBZZT
BBZZT
INCOMING CALL
UH.
HI.
IT'S LUKA. WHERE ARE YOU AT? THE BOYS SAID YOU GOT IT...
...DID YOU GET MY SHIT?
MHM.
PERFECT. AND YOU TOOK CARE OF THE CHICKEN MAN?
MHM.

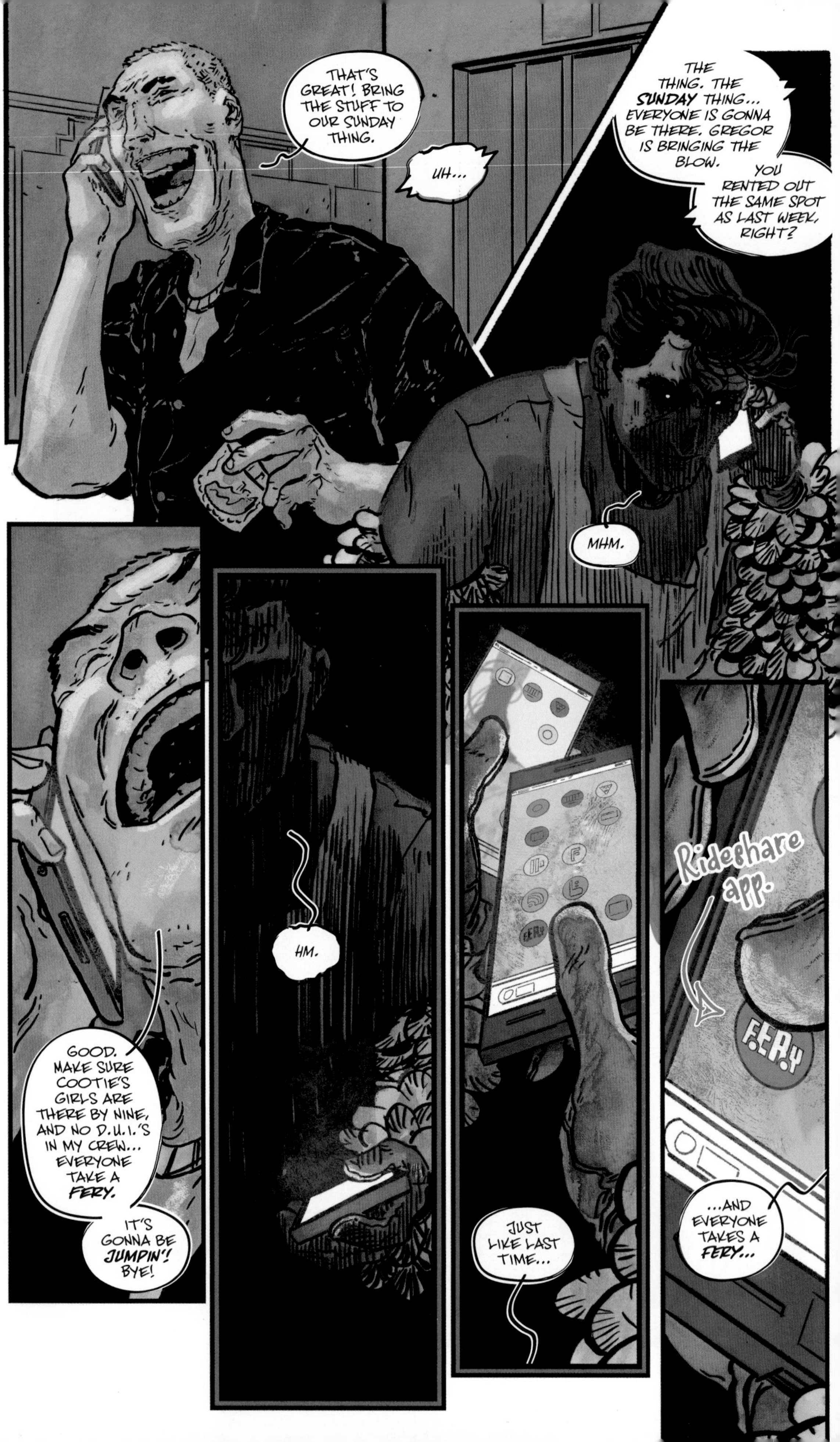

THAT'S GREAT! BRING THE STUFF TO OUR SUNDAY THING.
UH...
THE THING. THE SUNDAY THING... EVERYONE IS GONNA BE THERE. GREGOR IS BRINGING THE BLOW.
YOU RENTED OUT THE SAME SPOT AS LAST WEEK, RIGHT?
MHM.
GOOD. MAKE SURE COOTIE'S GIRLS ARE THERE BY NINE, AND NO D.U.I.'S IN MY CREW... EVERYONE TAKE A FERY.
IT'S GONNA BE JUMPIN'! BYE!
HM.
JUST LIKE LAST TIME...
Rideshare app.
F.E.R.Y
...AND EVERYONE TAKES A FERY...

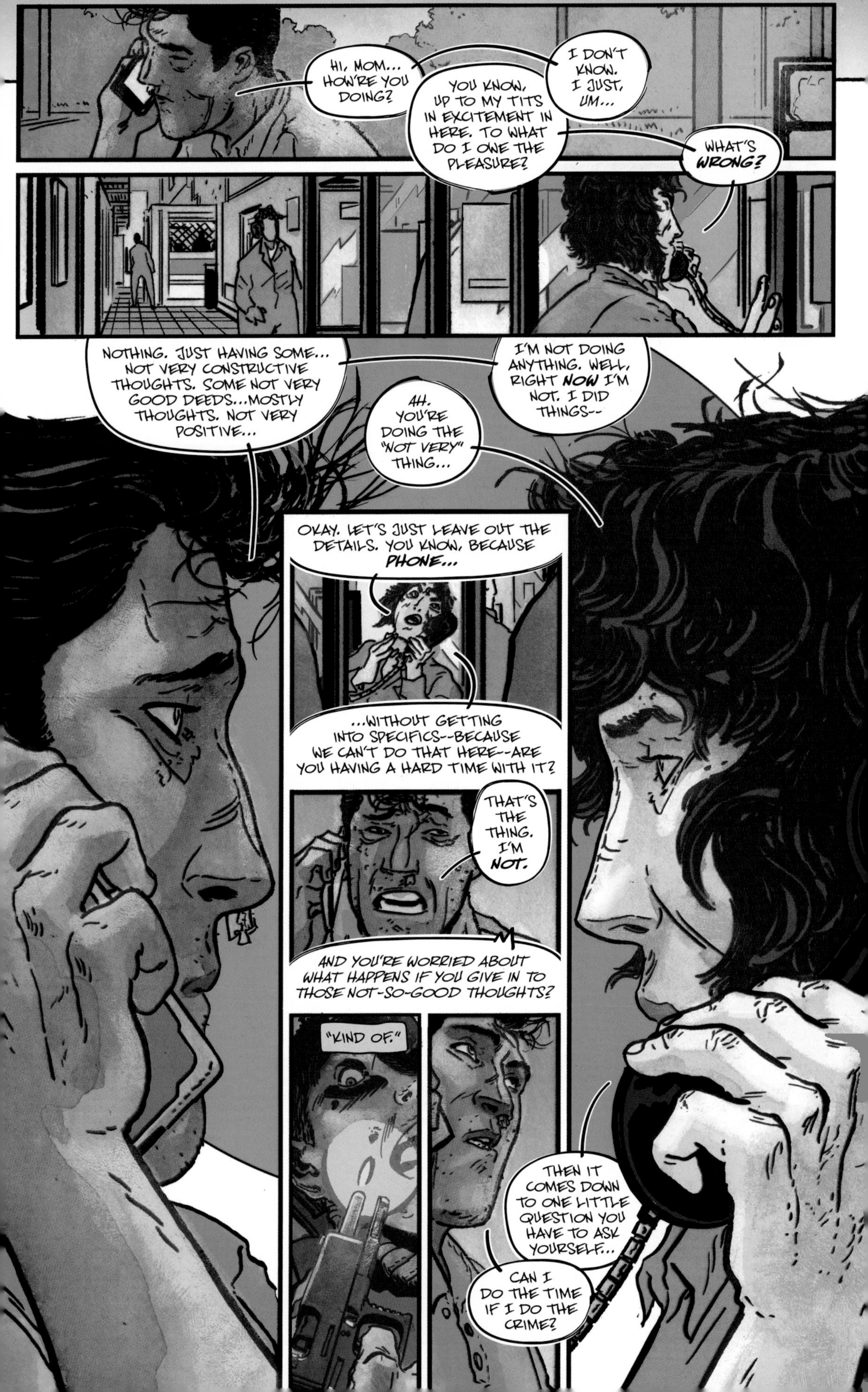
HI, MOM... HOW'RE YOU DOING?
YOU KNOW, UP TO MY TITS IN EXCITEMENT IN HERE. TO WHAT DO I OWE THE PLEASURE?
I DON'T KNOW. I JUST, UM...
WHAT'S **WRONG?**
NOTHING. JUST HAVING SOME... NOT VERY CONSTRUCTIVE THOUGHTS. SOME NOT VERY GOOD DEEDS...MOSTLY THOUGHTS. NOT VERY POSITIVE...
AH. YOU'RE DOING THE "NOT VERY" THING...
I'M NOT DOING ANYTHING. WELL, RIGHT **NOW** I'M NOT. I DID THINGS--
OKAY. LET'S JUST LEAVE OUT THE DETAILS. YOU KNOW, BECAUSE **PHONE...**
...WITHOUT GETTING INTO SPECIFICS--BECAUSE WE CAN'T DO THAT HERE--ARE YOU HAVING A HARD TIME WITH IT?
THAT'S THE THING. I'M **NOT.**
AND YOU'RE WORRIED ABOUT WHAT HAPPENS IF YOU GIVE IN TO THOSE NOT-SO-GOOD THOUGHTS?
"KIND OF."
THEN IT COMES DOWN TO ONE LITTLE QUESTION YOU HAVE TO ASK YOURSELF...
CAN I DO THE TIME IF I DO THE CRIME?

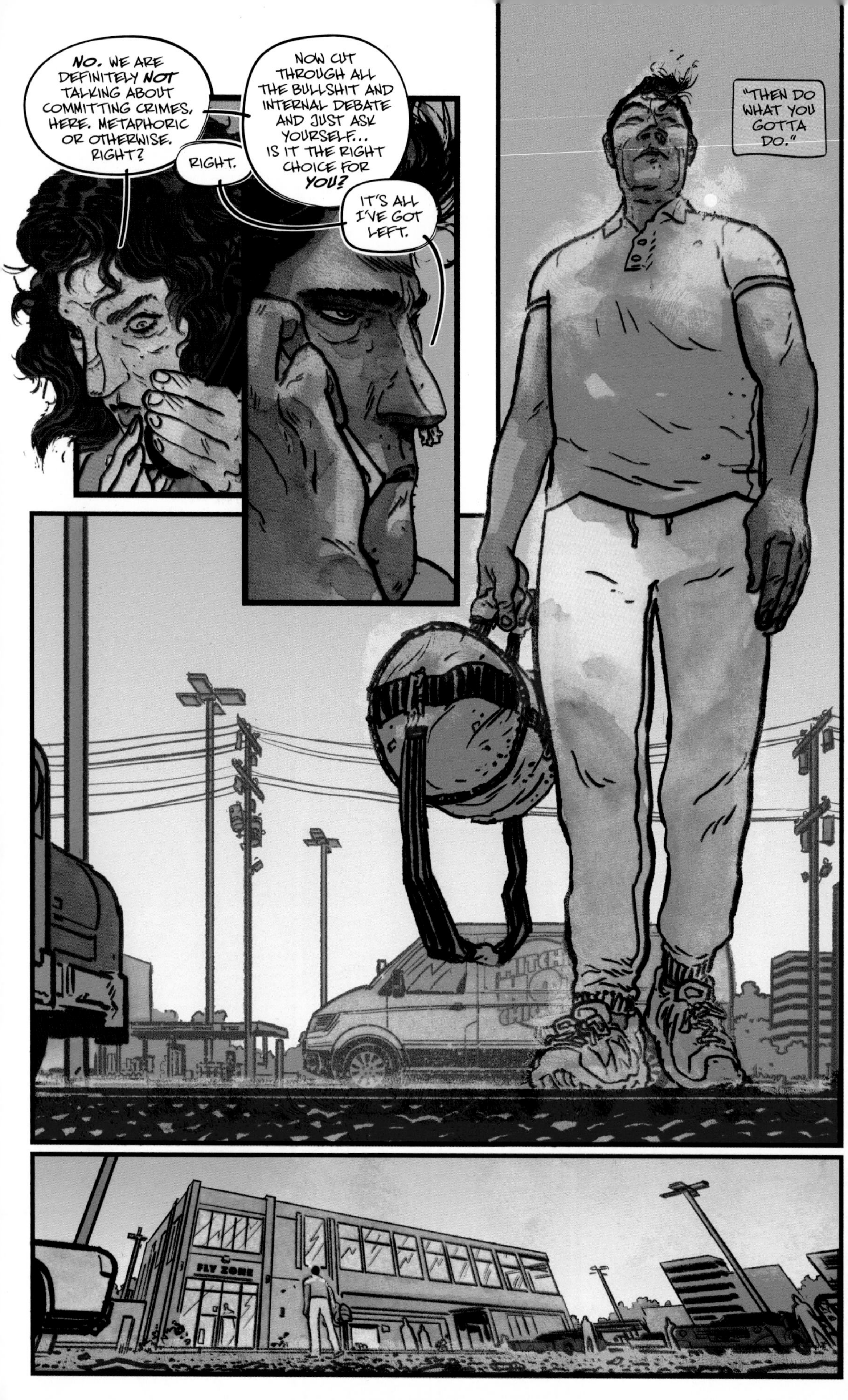

NO. WE ARE DEFINITELY NOT TALKING ABOUT COMMITTING CRIMES, HERE. METAPHORIC OR OTHERWISE. RIGHT?
RIGHT.
NOW CUT THROUGH ALL THE BULLSHIT AND INTERNAL DEBATE AND JUST ASK YOURSELF... IS IT THE RIGHT CHOICE FOR YOU?
IT'S ALL I'VE GOT LEFT.
"THEN DO WHAT YOU GOTTA DO."
FLY ZONE

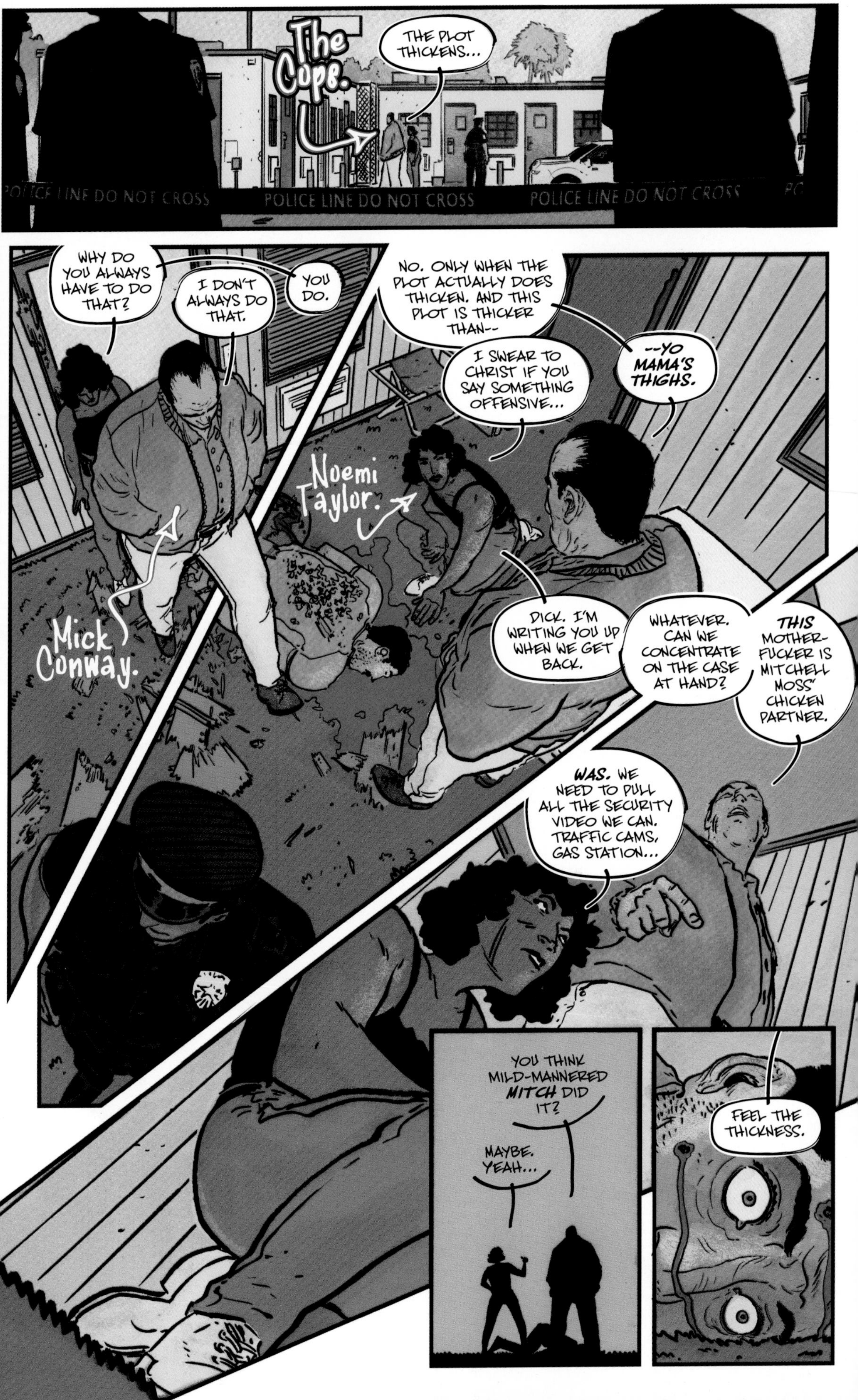
The Cops.
THE PLOT THICKENS...
POLICE LINE DO NOT CROSS
WHY DO YOU ALWAYS HAVE TO DO THAT?
I DON'T ALWAYS DO THAT.
YOU DO.
Mick Conway.
NO. ONLY WHEN THE PLOT ACTUALLY DOES THICKEN. AND THIS PLOT IS THICKER THAN--
I SWEAR TO CHRIST IF YOU SAY SOMETHING OFFENSIVE...
--YO MAMA'S THIGHS.
Noemi Taylor.
DICK. I'M WRITING YOU UP WHEN WE GET BACK.
WHATEVER. CAN WE CONCENTRATE ON THE CASE AT HAND?
THIS MOTHER-FUCKER IS MITCHELL MOSS' CHICKEN PARTNER.
WAS. WE NEED TO PULL ALL THE SECURITY VIDEO WE CAN. TRAFFIC CAMS, GAS STATION...
YOU THINK MILD-MANNERED MITCH DID IT?
MAYBE. YEAH...
FEEL THE THICKNESS.

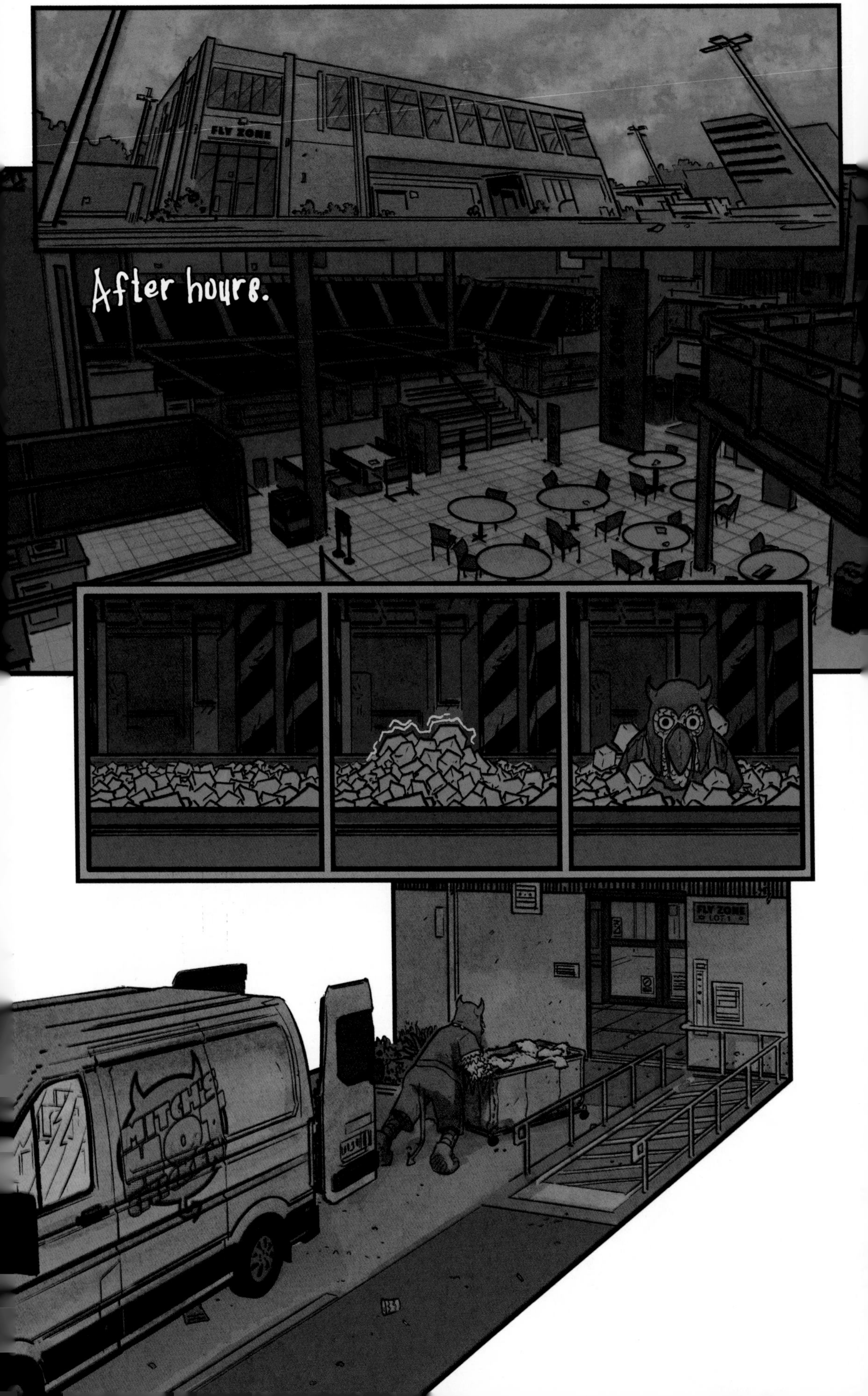
FLY ZONE
After hours.
FLY ZONE
LOT 1
MITCH'S

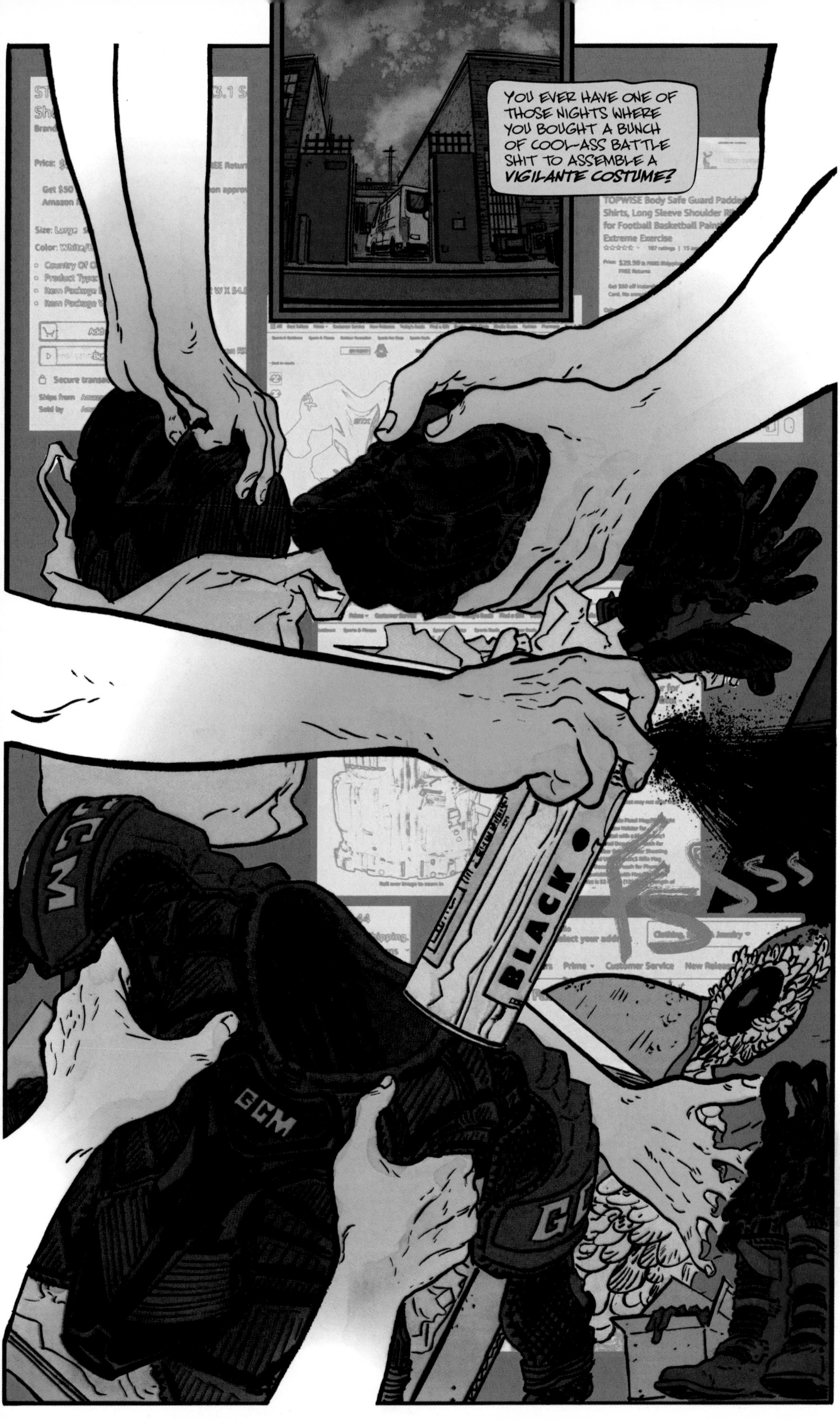
YOU EVER HAVE ONE OF THOSE NIGHTS WHERE YOU BOUGHT A BUNCH OF COOL-ASS BATTLE SHIT TO ASSEMBLE A *VIGILANTE COSTUME?*
BLACK
CCM

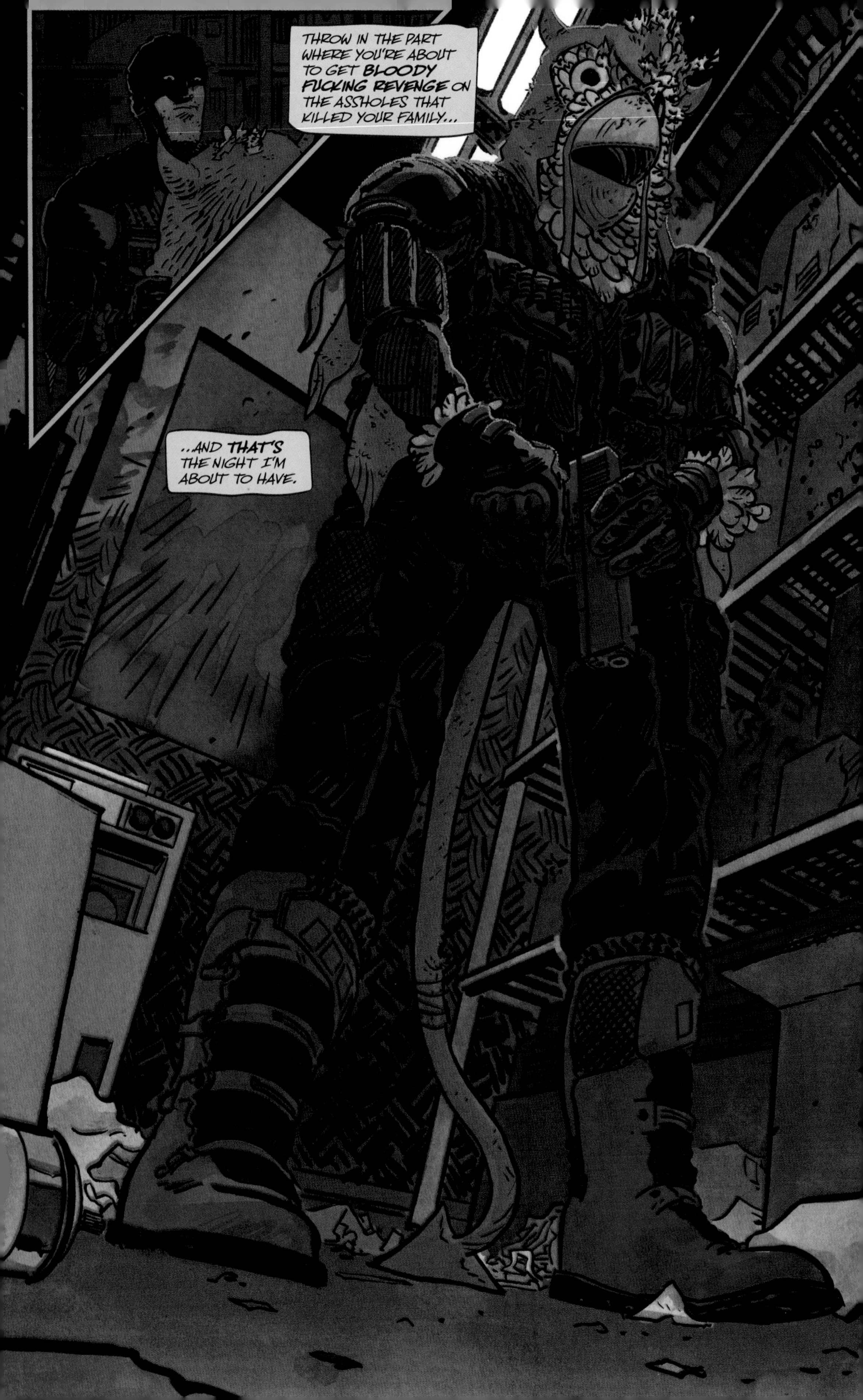
THROW IN THE PART WHERE YOU'RE ABOUT TO GET BLOODY FUCKING REVENGE ON THE ASSHOLES THAT KILLED YOUR FAMILY...
...AND THAT'S THE NIGHT I'M ABOUT TO HAVE.

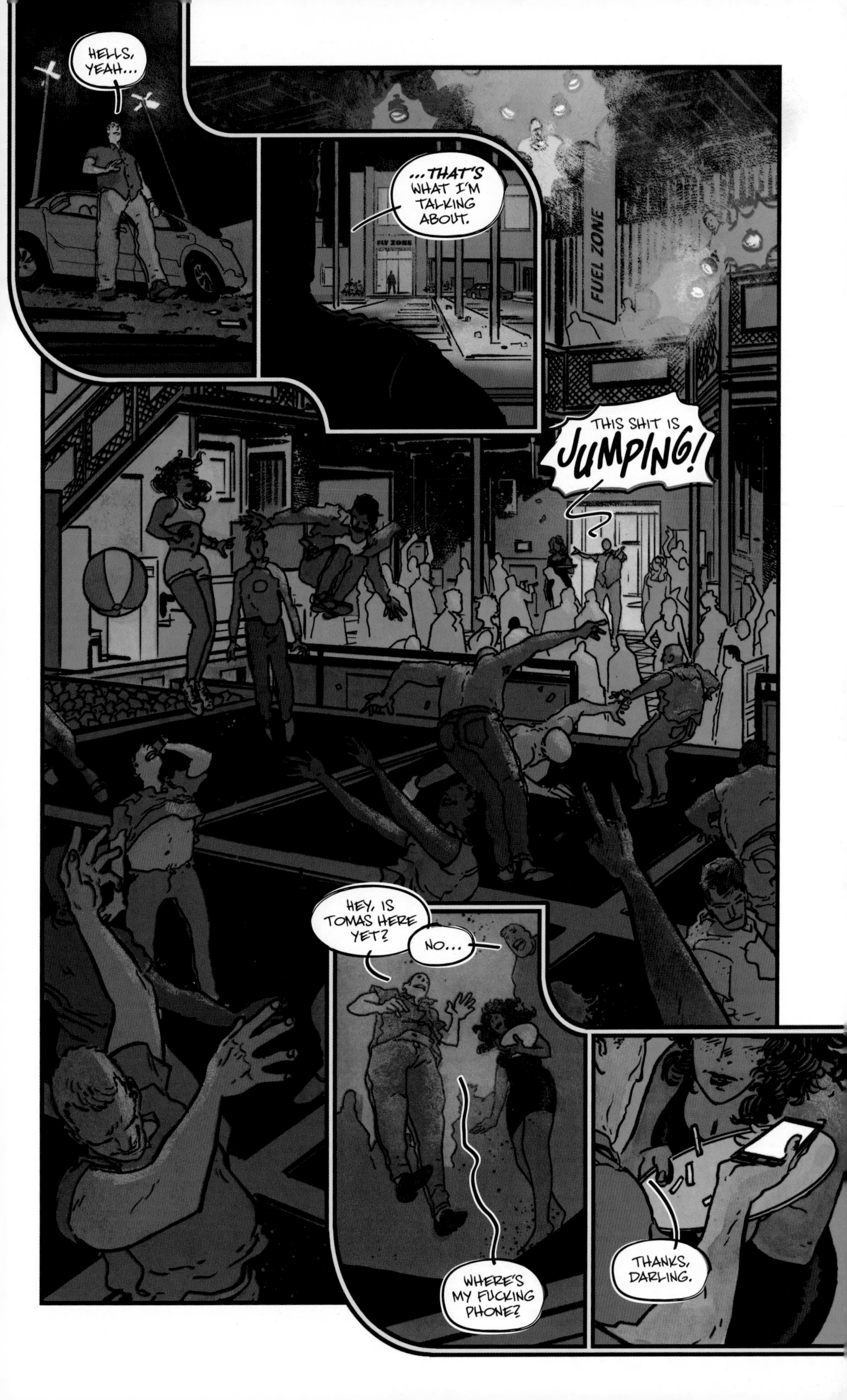
HELLS, YEAH...
...THAT'S WHAT I'M TALKING ABOUT.
FUEL ZONE
THIS SHIT IS JUMPING!
HEY, IS TOMAS HERE YET?
NO...
WHERE'S MY FUCKING PHONE?
THANKS, DARLING.

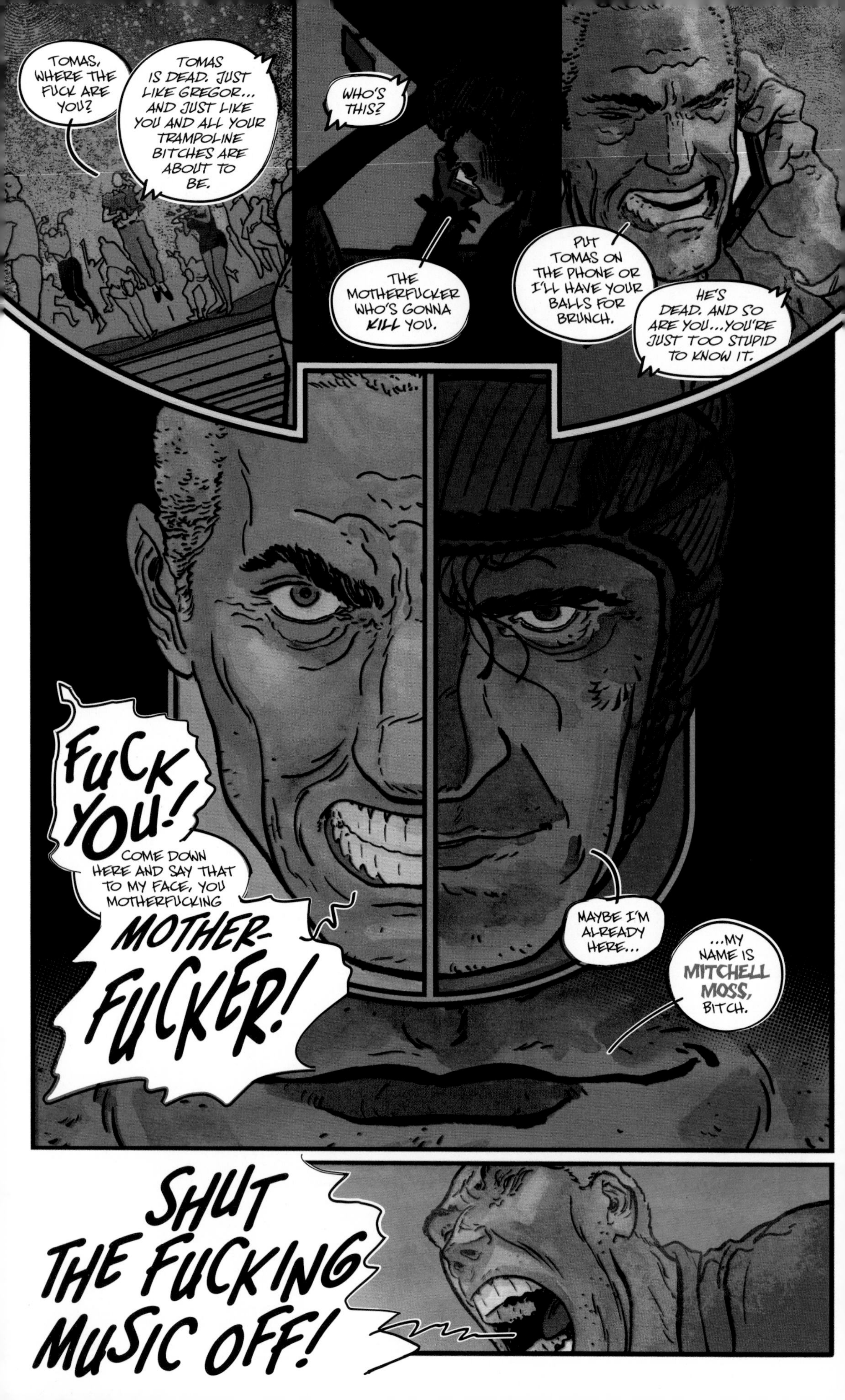
TOMAS, WHERE THE FUCK ARE YOU?
TOMAS IS DEAD. JUST LIKE GREGOR... AND JUST LIKE YOU AND ALL YOUR TRAMPOLINE BITCHES ARE ABOUT TO BE.
WHO'S THIS?
THE MOTHERFUCKER WHO'S GONNA KILL YOU.
PUT TOMAS ON THE PHONE OR I'LL HAVE YOUR BALLS FOR BRUNCH.
HE'S DEAD. AND SO ARE YOU...YOU'RE JUST TOO STUPID TO KNOW IT.
FUCK YOU! COME DOWN HERE AND SAY THAT TO MY FACE, YOU MOTHERFUCKING MOTHER-FUCKER!
MAYBE I'M ALREADY HERE...
...MY NAME IS MITCHELL MOSS, BITCH.
SHUT THE FUCKING MUSIC OFF!

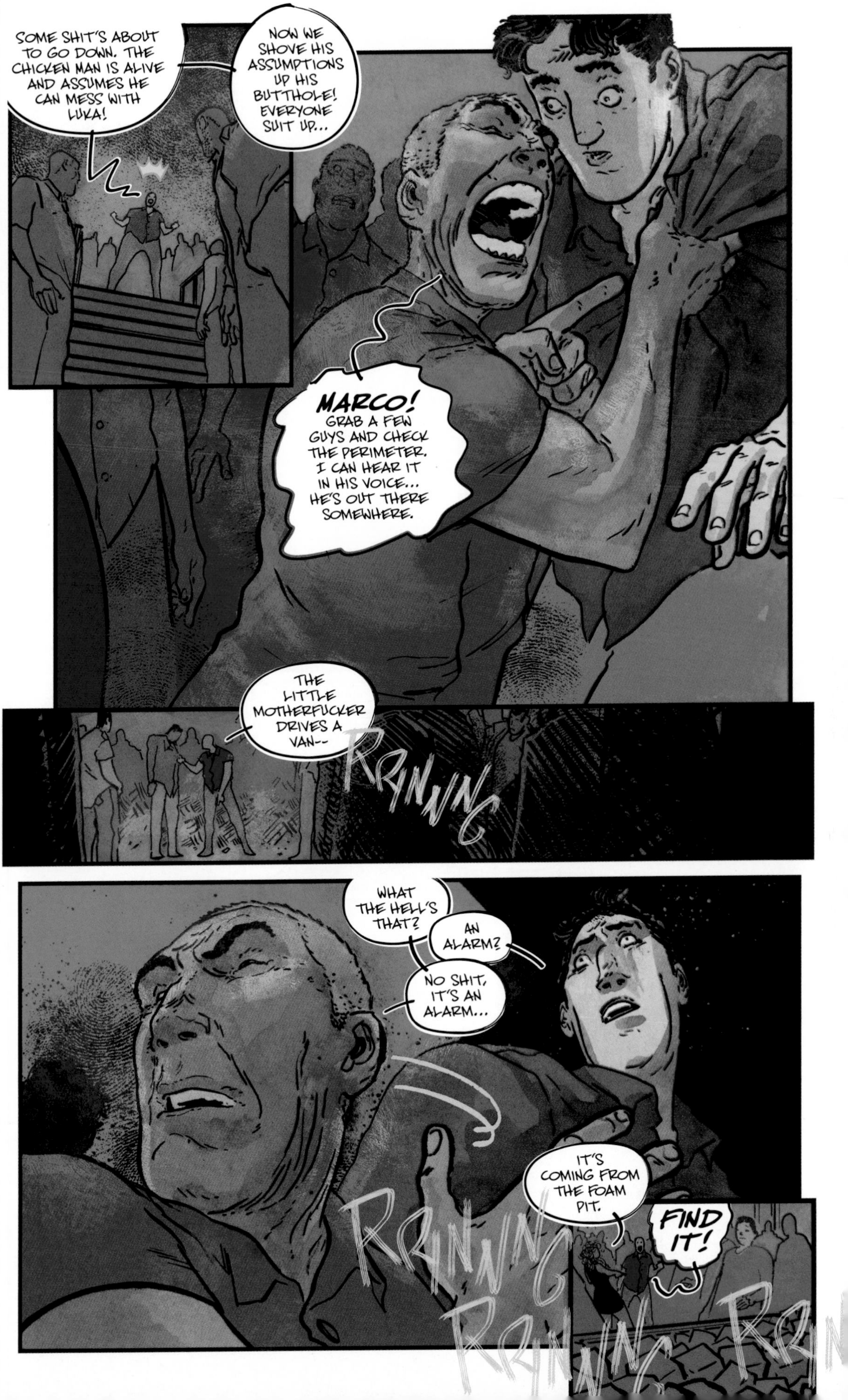

SOME SHIT'S ABOUT TO GO DOWN. THE CHICKEN MAN IS ALIVE AND ASSUMES HE CAN MESS WITH LUKA!
NOW WE SHOVE HIS ASSUMPTIONS UP HIS BUTTHOLE! EVERYONE SUIT UP...
MARCO! GRAB A FEW GUYS AND CHECK THE PERIMETER. I CAN HEAR IT IN HIS VOICE... HE'S OUT THERE SOMEWHERE.
THE LITTLE MOTHERFUCKER DRIVES A VAN--
RRINNNG
WHAT THE HELL'S THAT?
AN ALARM?
NO SHIT, IT'S AN ALARM...
IT'S COMING FROM THE FOAM PIT.
FIND IT!
RRINNNG
RRINNNG

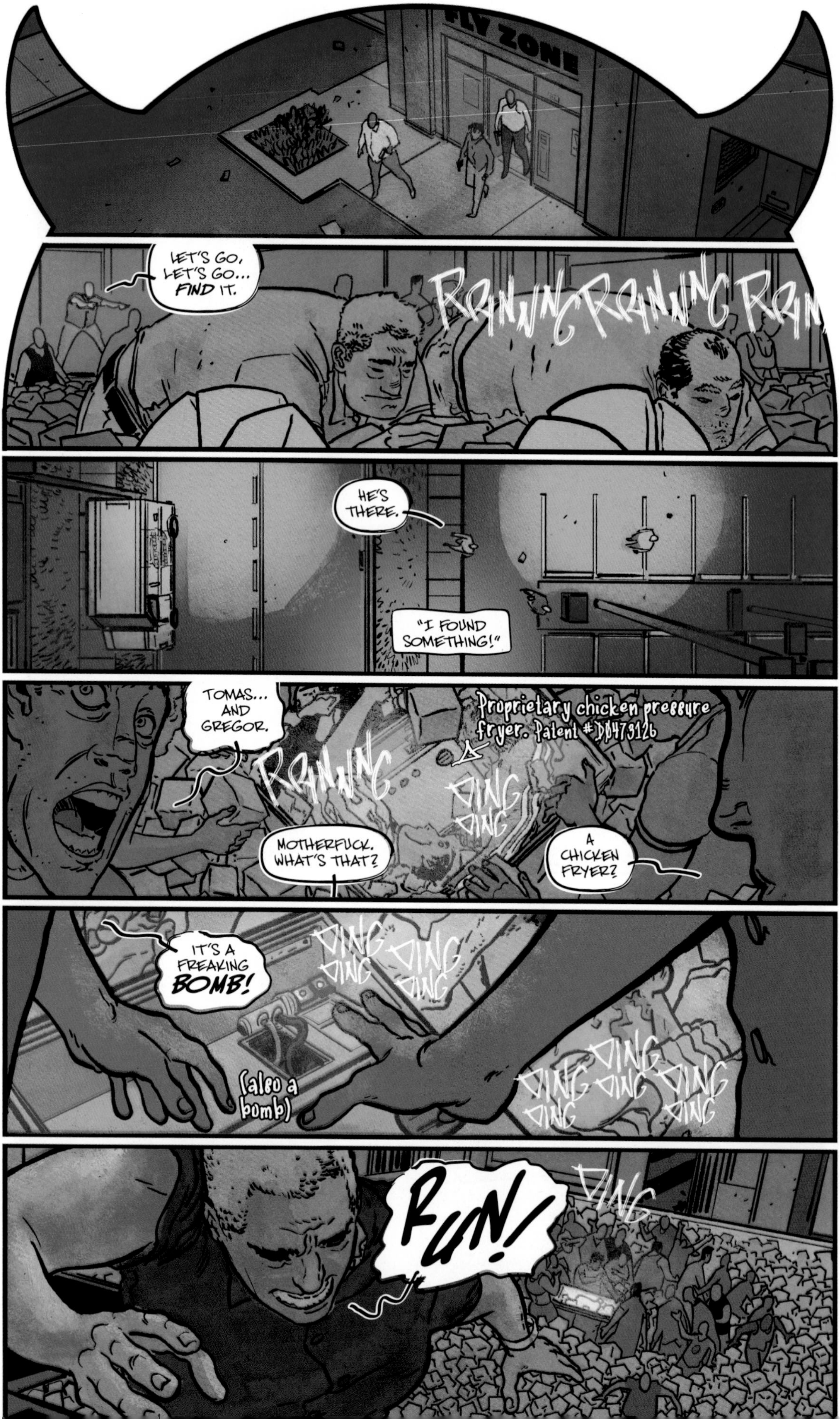
FLY ZONE
LET'S GO, LET'S GO... FIND IT.
RRINNNG RRINNNG RRIN
HE'S THERE.
"I FOUND SOMETHING!"
TOMAS... AND GREGOR.
Proprietary chicken pressure fryer. Patent #D047912b
RRINNNG
DING DING
MOTHERFUCK. WHAT'S THAT?
A CHICKEN FRYER?
IT'S A FREAKING BOMB!
DING DING DING DING
(also a bomb)
DING DING DING DING DING DING
RUN!
DING

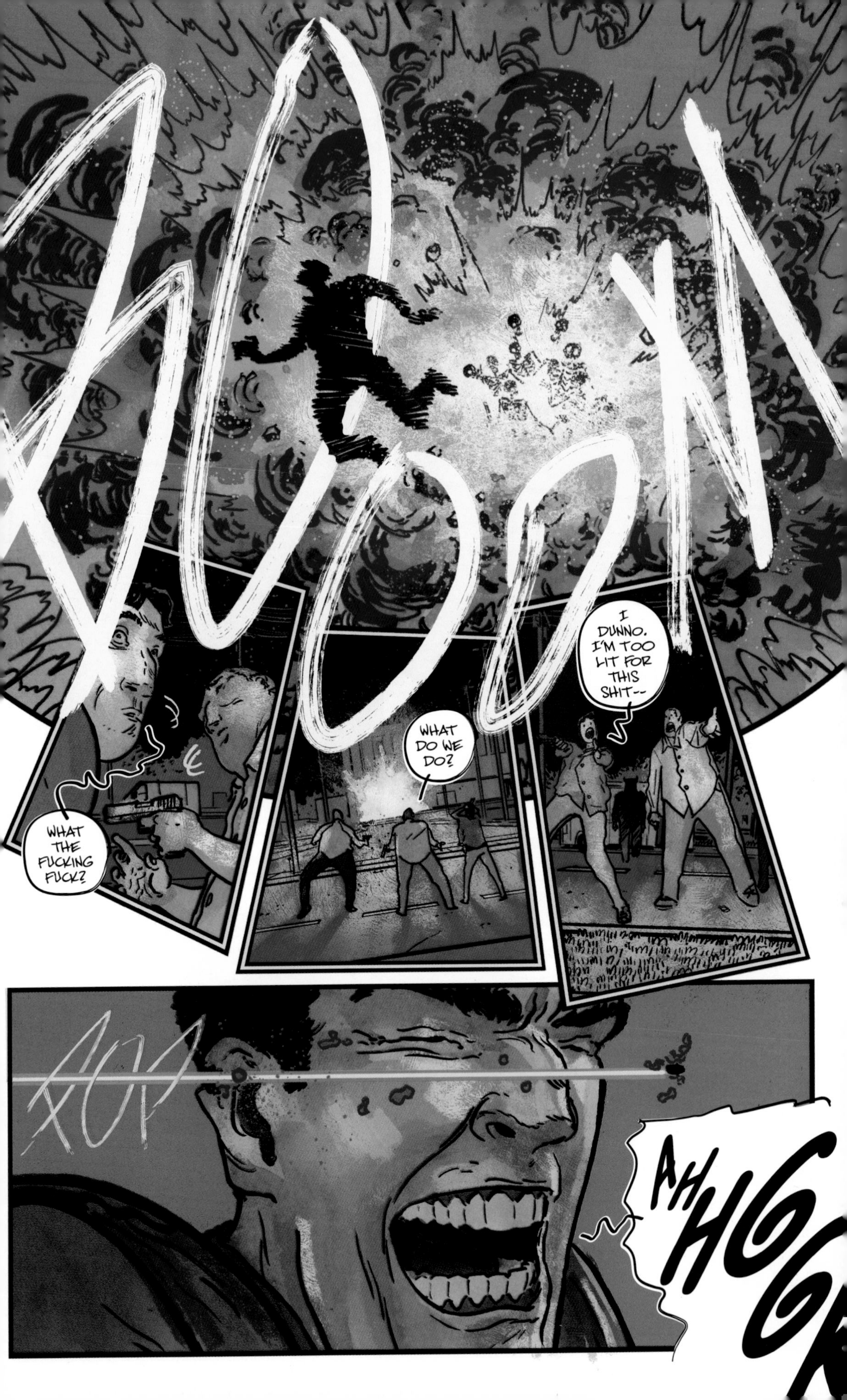
WHAT THE FUCKING FUCK?
WHAT DO WE DO?
I DUNNO. I'M TOO LIT FOR THIS SHIT--
POP

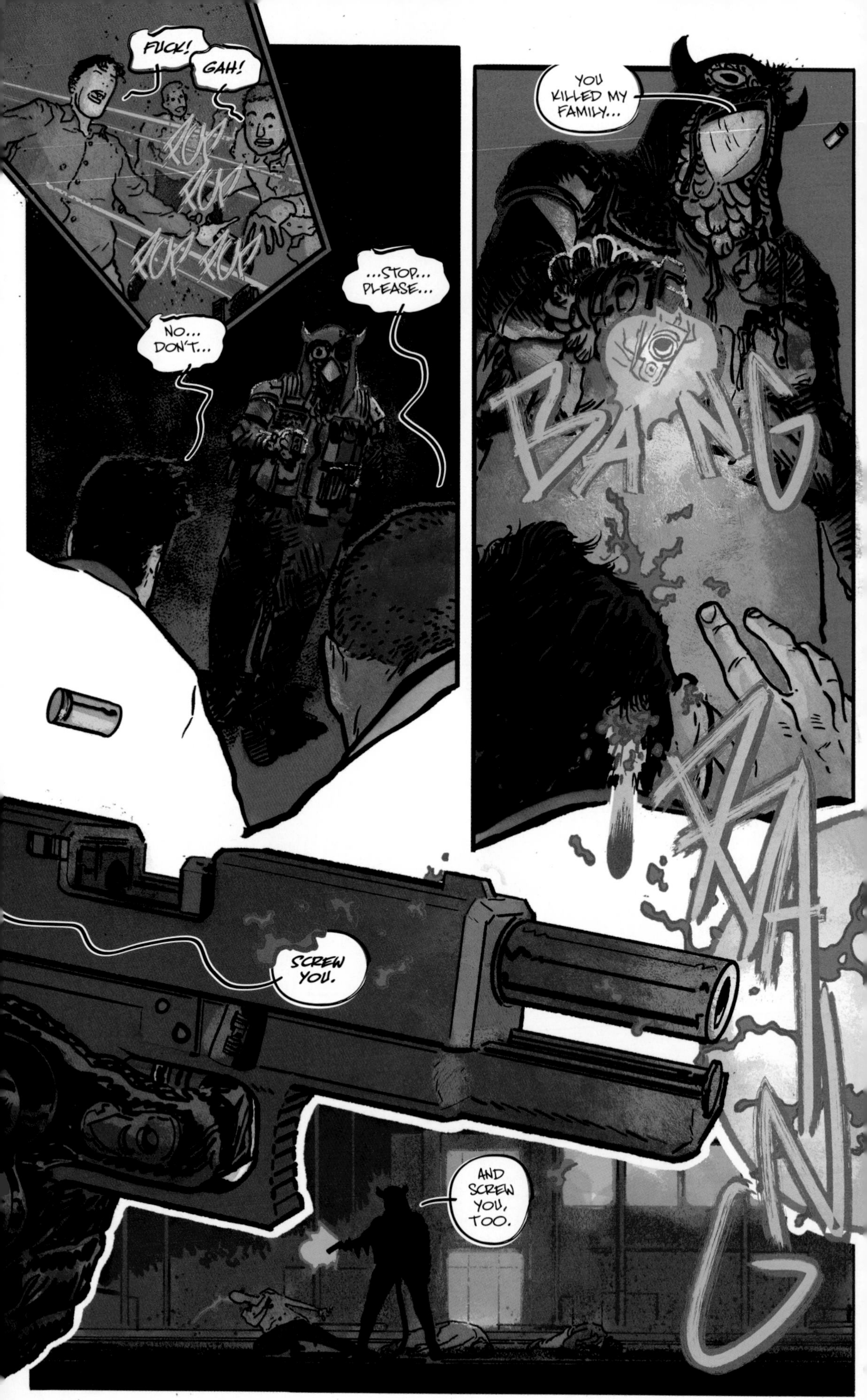
FUCK!
GAH!
POP POP
POP POP POP
...STOP... PLEASE...
NO... DON'T...
YOU KILLED MY FAMILY...
BANG
SCREW YOU.
BANG
AND SCREW YOU, TOO.

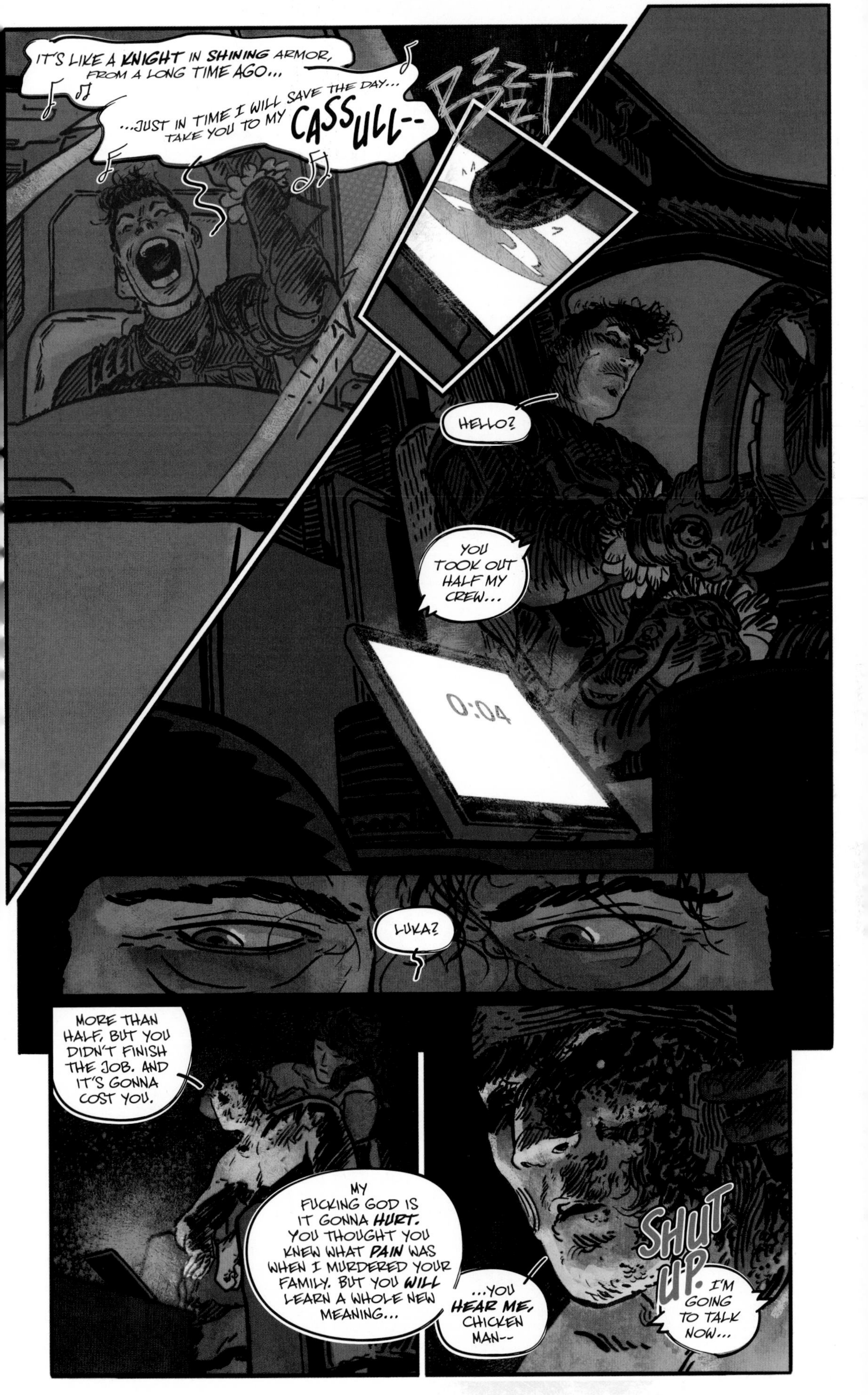
IT'S LIKE A KNIGHT IN SHINING ARMOR, FROM A LONG TIME AGO...
...JUST IN TIME I WILL SAVE THE DAY... TAKE YOU TO MY CASSULL--
BZZZT
HELLO?
YOU TOOK OUT HALF MY CREW...
0:04
LUKA?
MORE THAN HALF, BUT YOU DIDN'T FINISH THE JOB. AND IT'S GONNA COST YOU.
MY FUCKING GOD IS IT GONNA HURT. YOU THOUGHT YOU KNEW WHAT PAIN WAS WHEN I MURDERED YOUR FAMILY. BUT YOU WILL LEARN A WHOLE NEW MEANING...
...YOU HEAR ME, CHICKEN MAN--
SHUT UP.
I'M GOING TO TALK NOW...

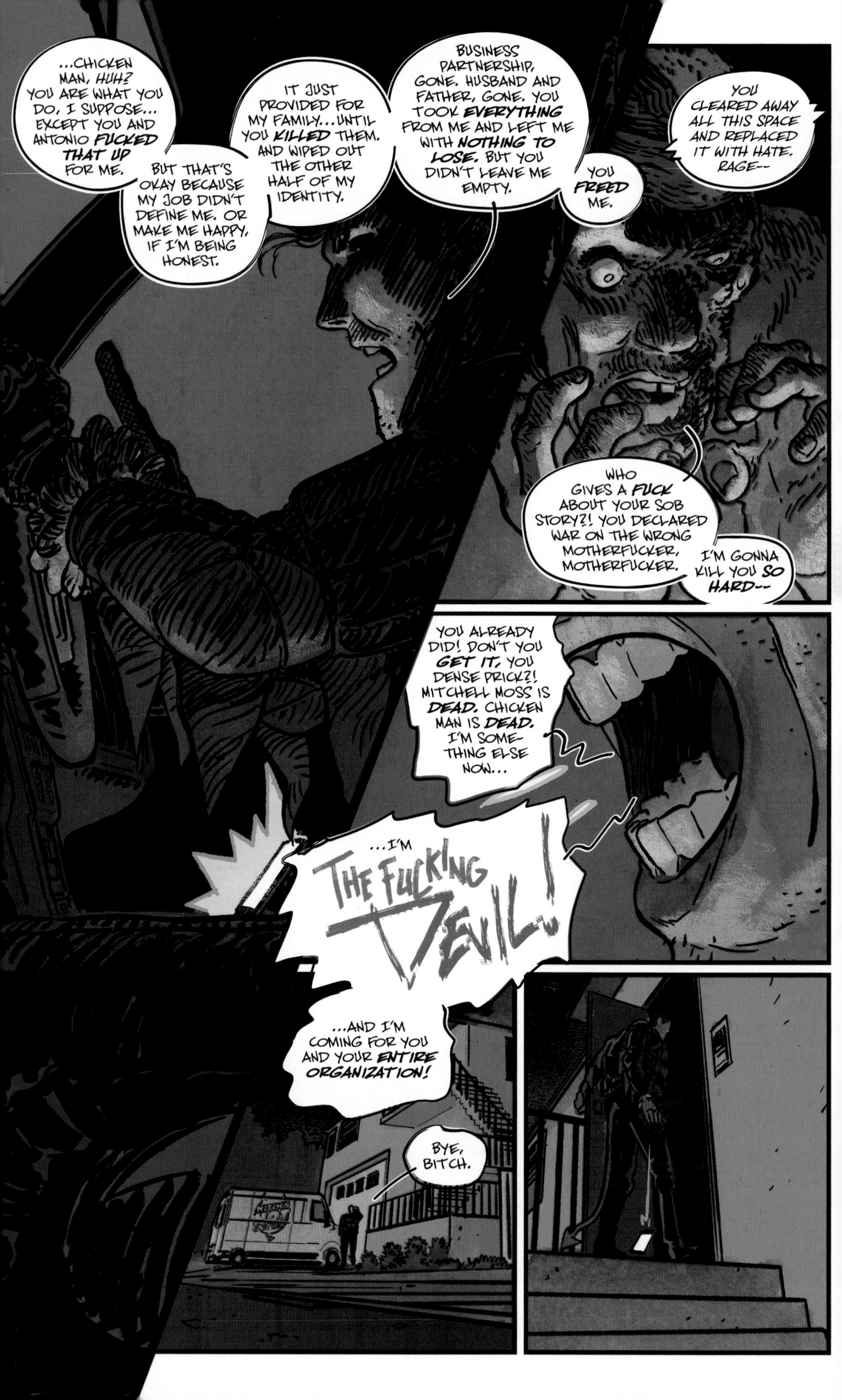

...CHICKEN MAN, HUH? YOU ARE WHAT YOU DO, I SUPPOSE... EXCEPT YOU AND ANTONIO FUCKED THAT UP FOR ME.
BUT THAT'S OKAY BECAUSE MY JOB DIDN'T DEFINE ME. OR MAKE ME HAPPY, IF I'M BEING HONEST.
IT JUST PROVIDED FOR MY FAMILY...UNTIL YOU KILLED THEM. AND WIPED OUT THE OTHER HALF OF MY IDENTITY.
BUSINESS PARTNERSHIP, GONE. HUSBAND AND FATHER, GONE. YOU TOOK EVERYTHING FROM ME AND LEFT ME WITH NOTHING TO LOSE. BUT YOU DIDN'T LEAVE ME EMPTY.
YOU FREED ME.
YOU CLEARED AWAY ALL THIS SPACE AND REPLACED IT WITH HATE. RAGE--
WHO GIVES A FUCK ABOUT YOUR SOB STORY?! YOU DECLARED WAR ON THE WRONG MOTHERFUCKER, MOTHERFUCKER.
I'M GONNA KILL YOU SO HARD--
YOU ALREADY DID! DON'T YOU GET IT, YOU DENSE PRICK?! MITCHELL MOSS IS DEAD. CHICKEN MAN IS DEAD. I'M SOMETHING ELSE NOW...
...I'M THE FUCKING DEVIL!
...AND I'M COMING FOR YOU AND YOUR ENTIRE ORGANIZATION!
BYE, BITCH.

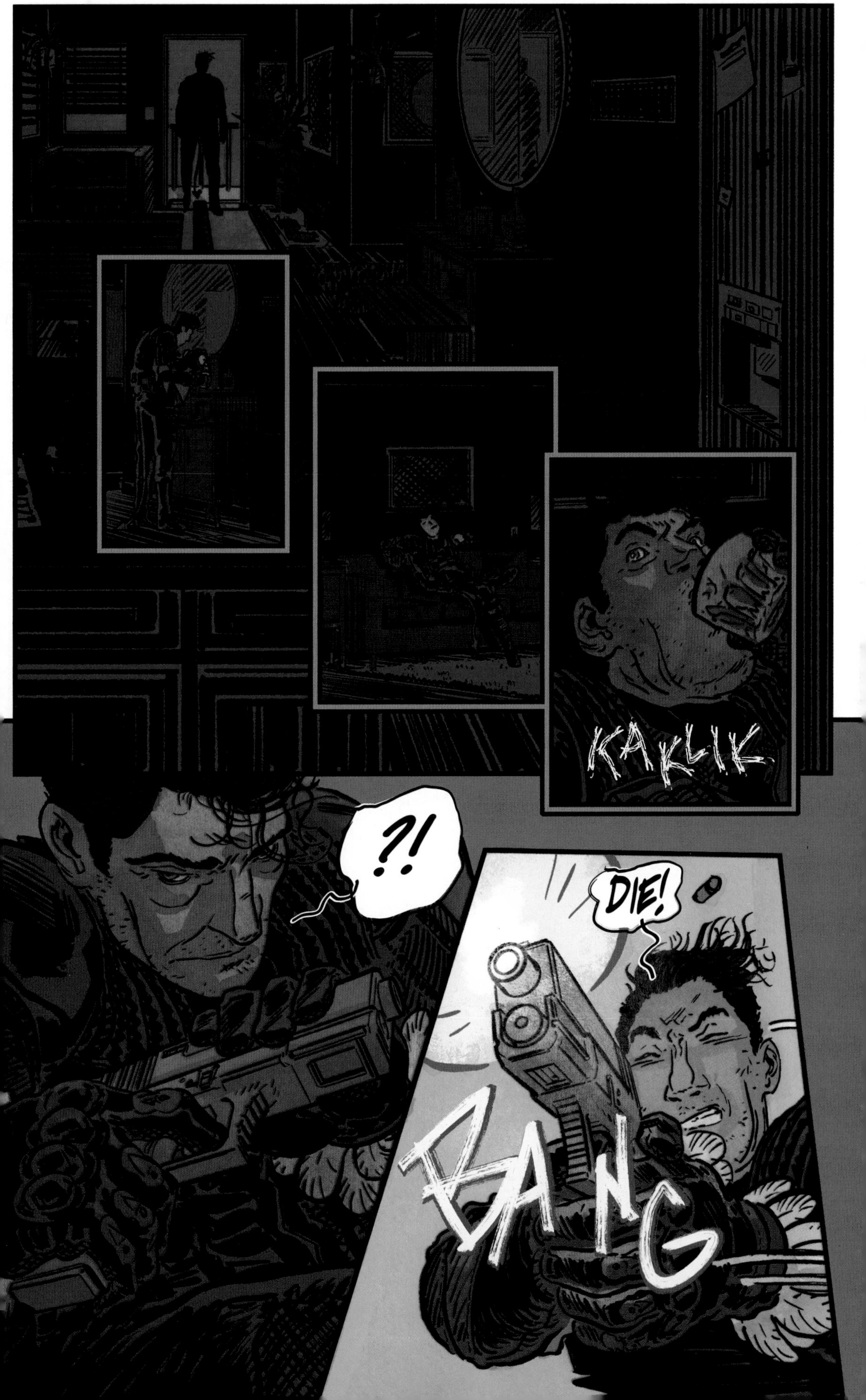

KAKLIK
?!
DIE!
BANG

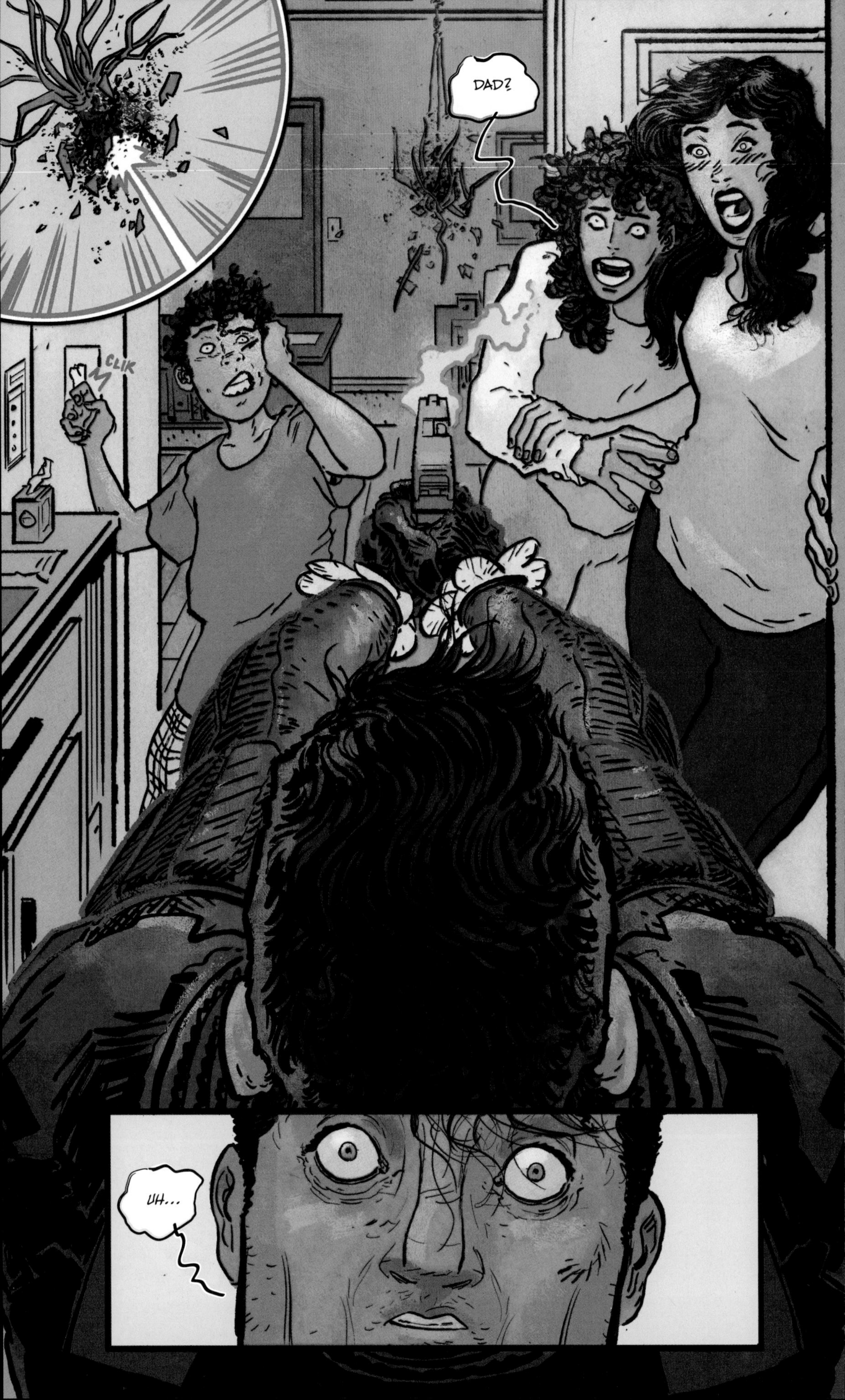
DAD?
CLIK
UH...

4

THE CHICKEN IS IN THE DETAILS

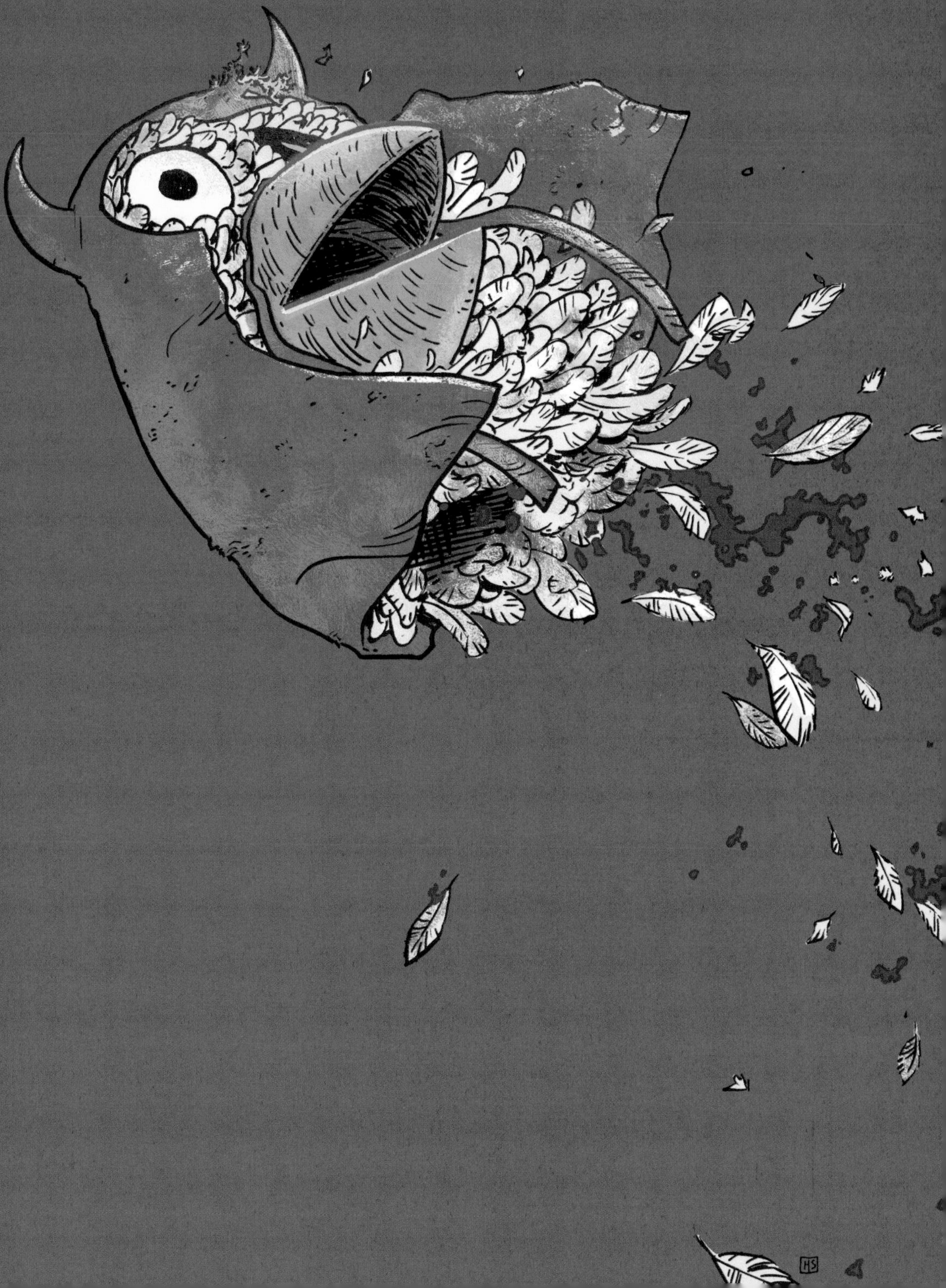
HS

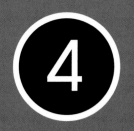

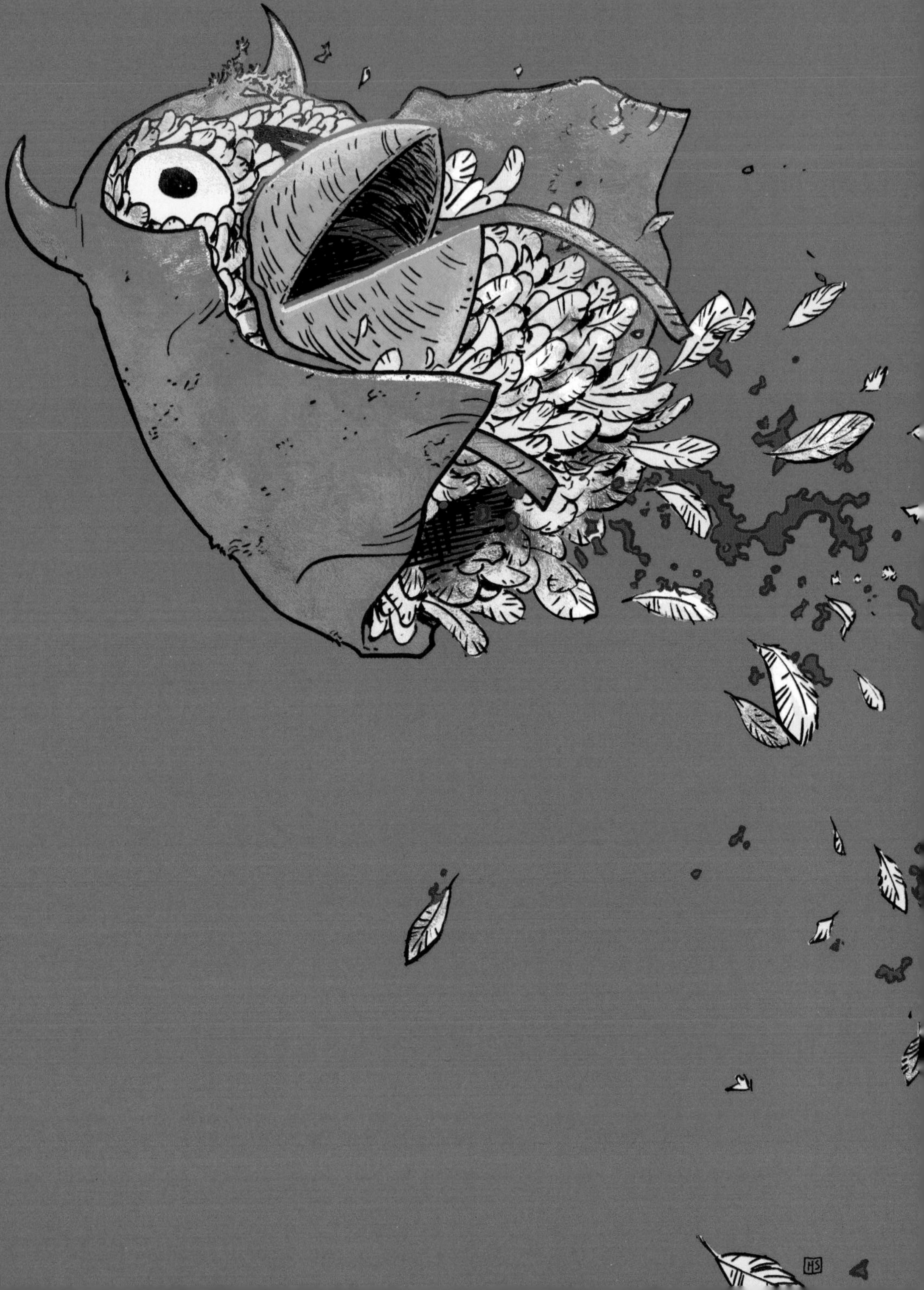

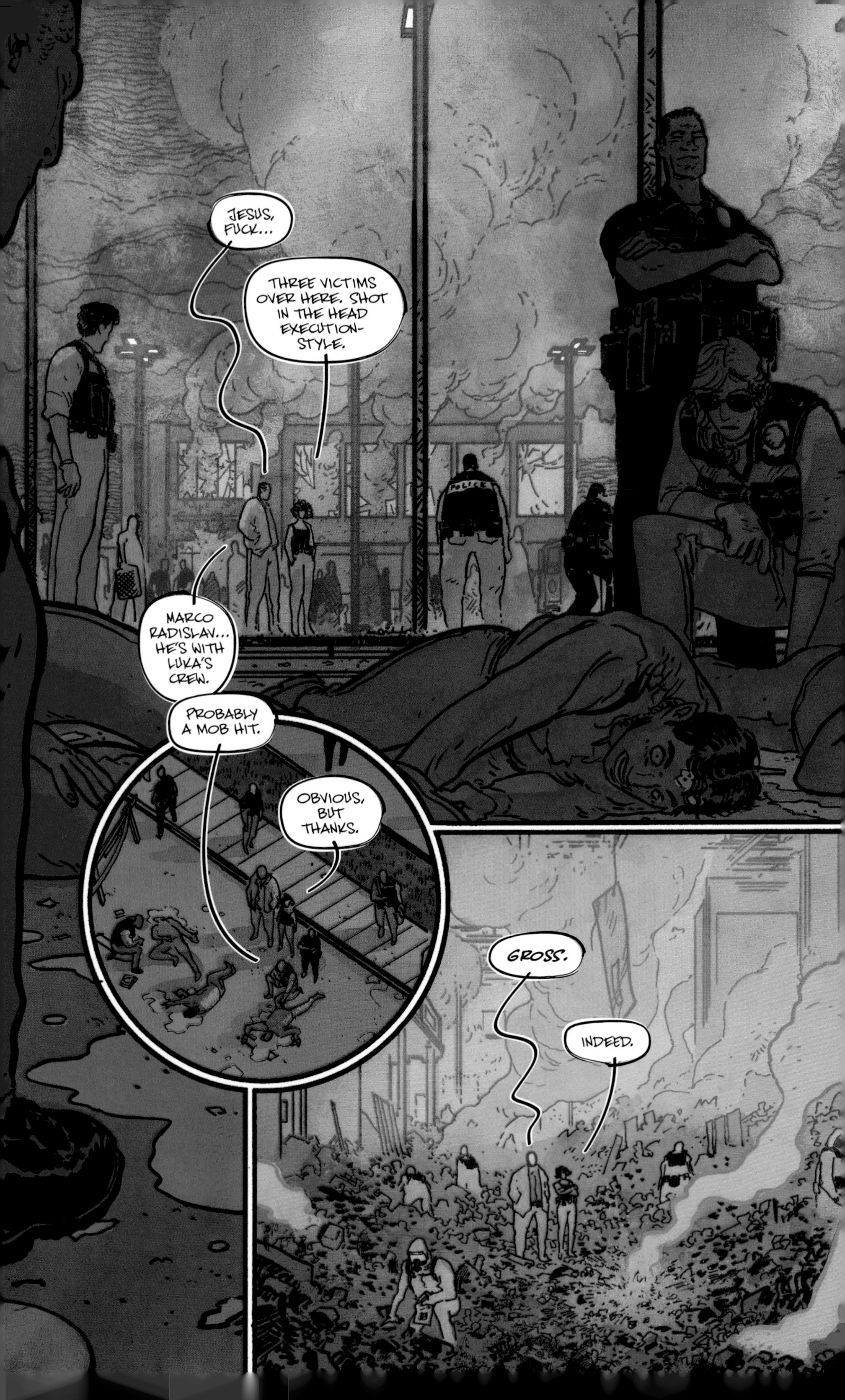
JESUS, FUCK...
THREE VICTIMS OVER HERE. SHOT IN THE HEAD EXECUTION-STYLE.
MARCO RADISLAV... HE'S WITH LUKA'S CREW.
PROBABLY A MOB HIT.
OBVIOUS, BUT THANKS.
GROSS.
INDEED.

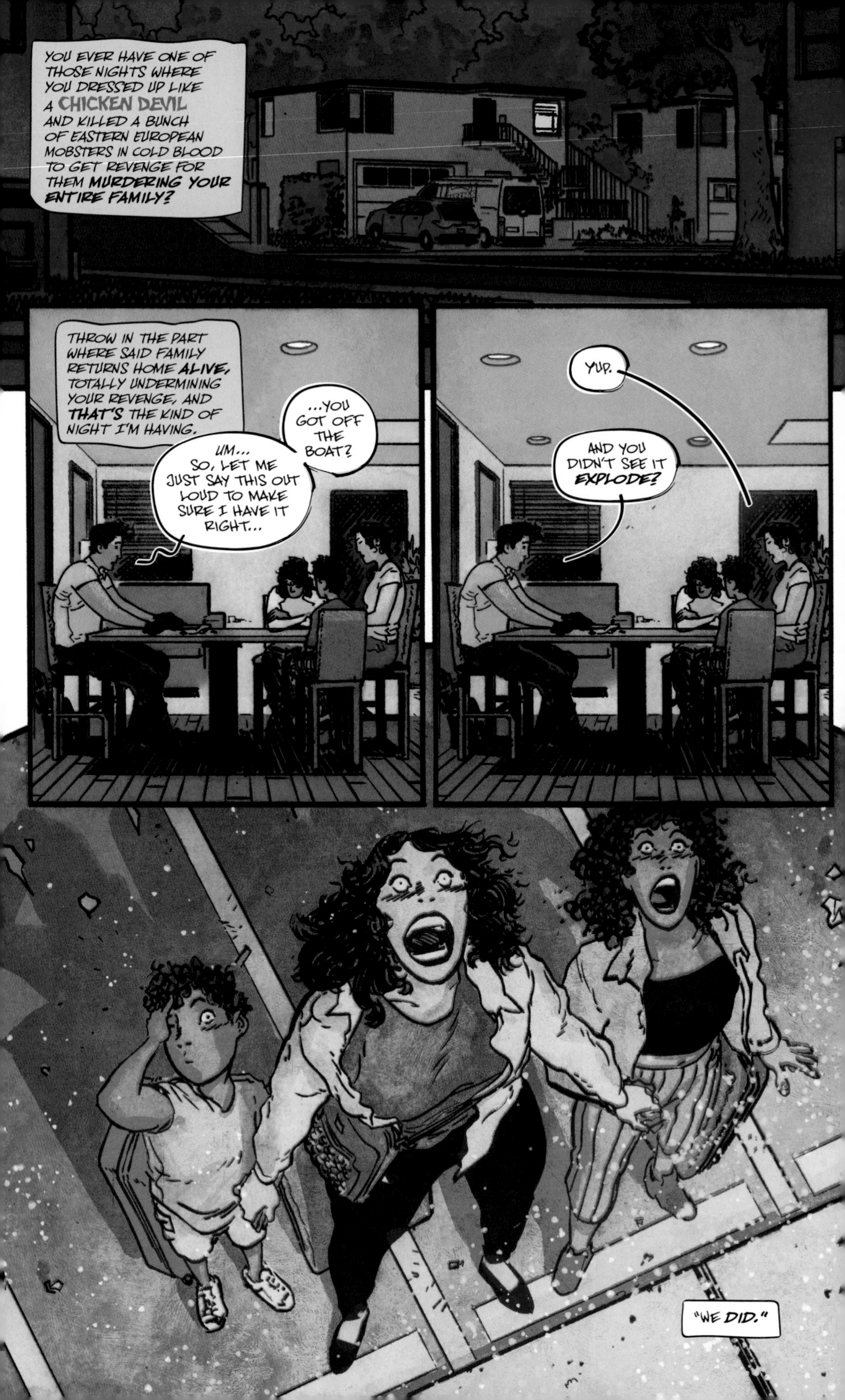
YOU EVER HAVE ONE OF THOSE NIGHTS WHERE YOU DRESSED UP LIKE A CHICKEN DEVIL AND KILLED A BUNCH OF EASTERN EUROPEAN MOBSTERS IN COLD BLOOD TO GET REVENGE FOR THEM MURDERING YOUR ENTIRE FAMILY?
THROW IN THE PART WHERE SAID FAMILY RETURNS HOME ALIVE, TOTALLY UNDERMINING YOUR REVENGE, AND THAT'S THE KIND OF NIGHT I'M HAVING.
UM... SO, LET ME JUST SAY THIS OUT LOUD TO MAKE SURE I HAVE IT RIGHT...
...YOU GOT OFF THE BOAT?
YUP.
AND YOU DIDN'T SEE IT EXPLODE?
"WE DID."

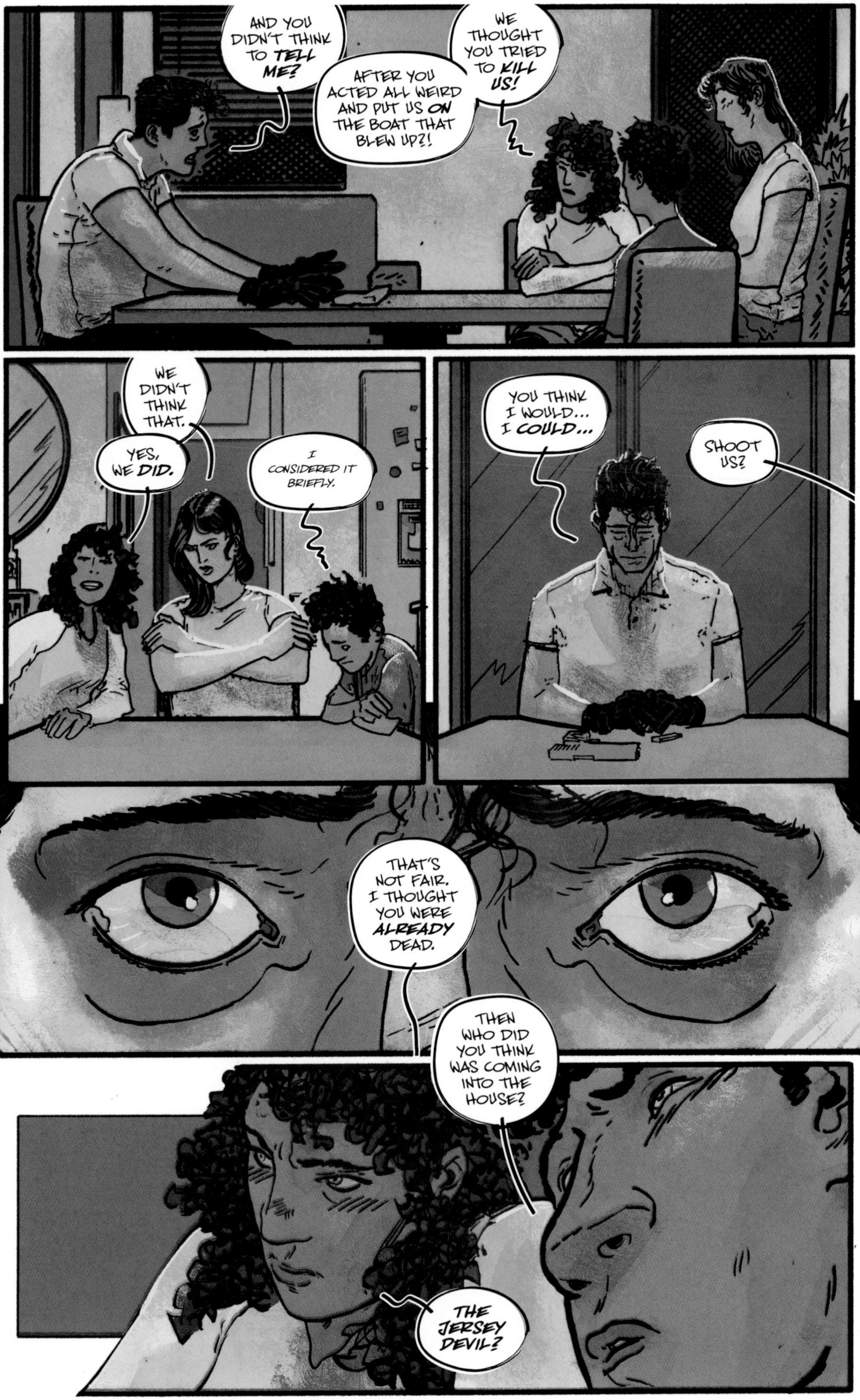
AND YOU DIDN'T THINK TO TELL ME?
AFTER YOU ACTED ALL WEIRD AND PUT US ON THE BOAT THAT BLEW UP?!
WE THOUGHT YOU TRIED TO KILL US!
WE DIDN'T THINK THAT.
YES, WE DID.
I CONSIDERED IT BRIEFLY.
YOU THINK I WOULD... I COULD...
SHOOT US?
THAT'S NOT FAIR. I THOUGHT YOU WERE ALREADY DEAD.
THEN WHO DID YOU THINK WAS COMING INTO THE HOUSE?
THE JERSEY DEVIL?

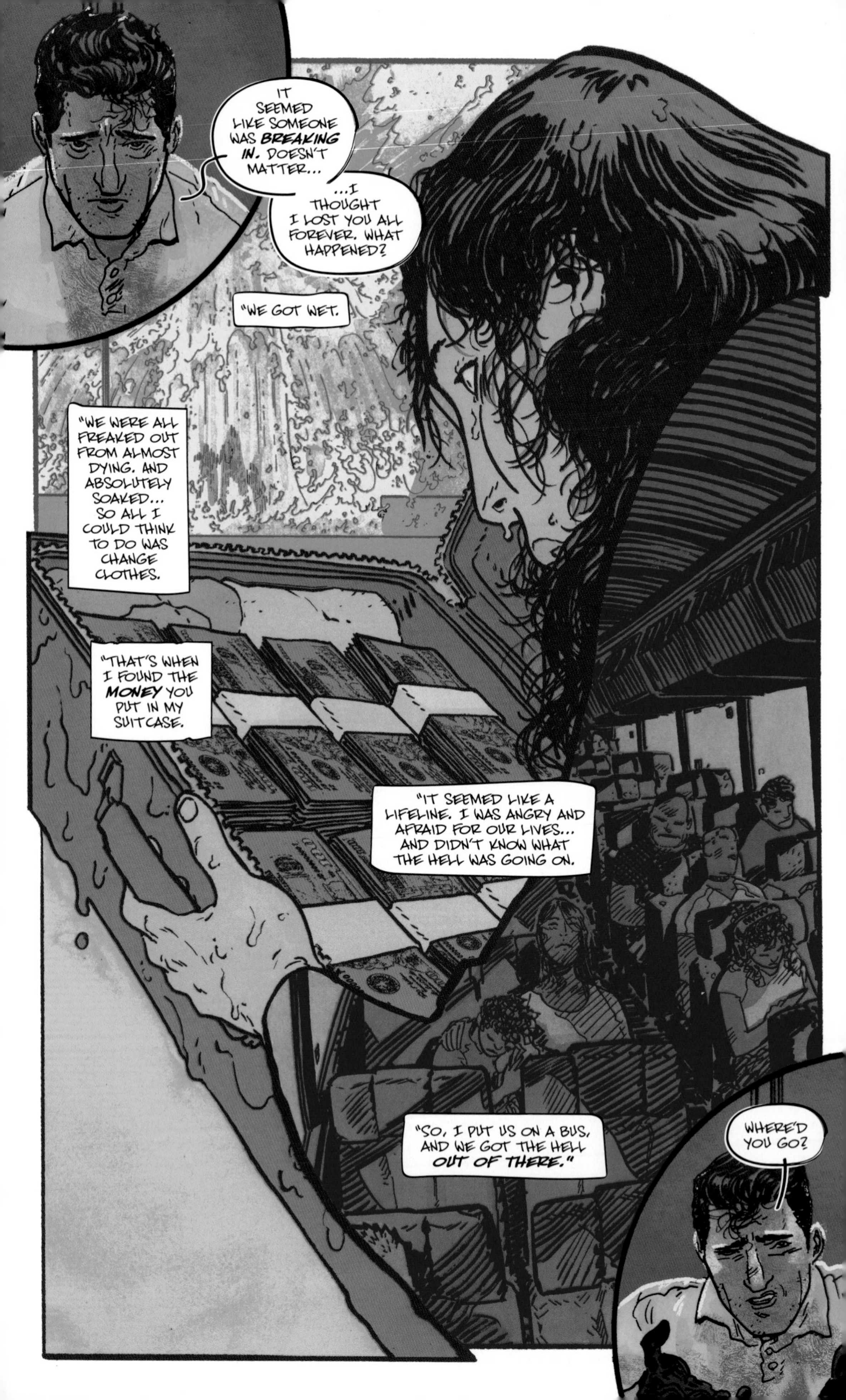
IT SEEMED LIKE SOMEONE WAS BREAKING IN. DOESN'T MATTER...
...I THOUGHT I LOST YOU ALL FOREVER. WHAT HAPPENED?
"WE GOT WET.
"WE WERE ALL FREAKED OUT FROM ALMOST DYING. AND ABSOLUTELY SOAKED... SO ALL I COULD THINK TO DO WAS CHANGE CLOTHES.
"THAT'S WHEN I FOUND THE MONEY YOU PUT IN MY SUITCASE.
"IT SEEMED LIKE A LIFELINE. I WAS ANGRY AND AFRAID FOR OUR LIVES... AND DIDN'T KNOW WHAT THE HELL WAS GOING ON.
"SO, I PUT US ON A BUS, AND WE GOT THE HELL OUT OF THERE."
WHERE'D YOU GO?

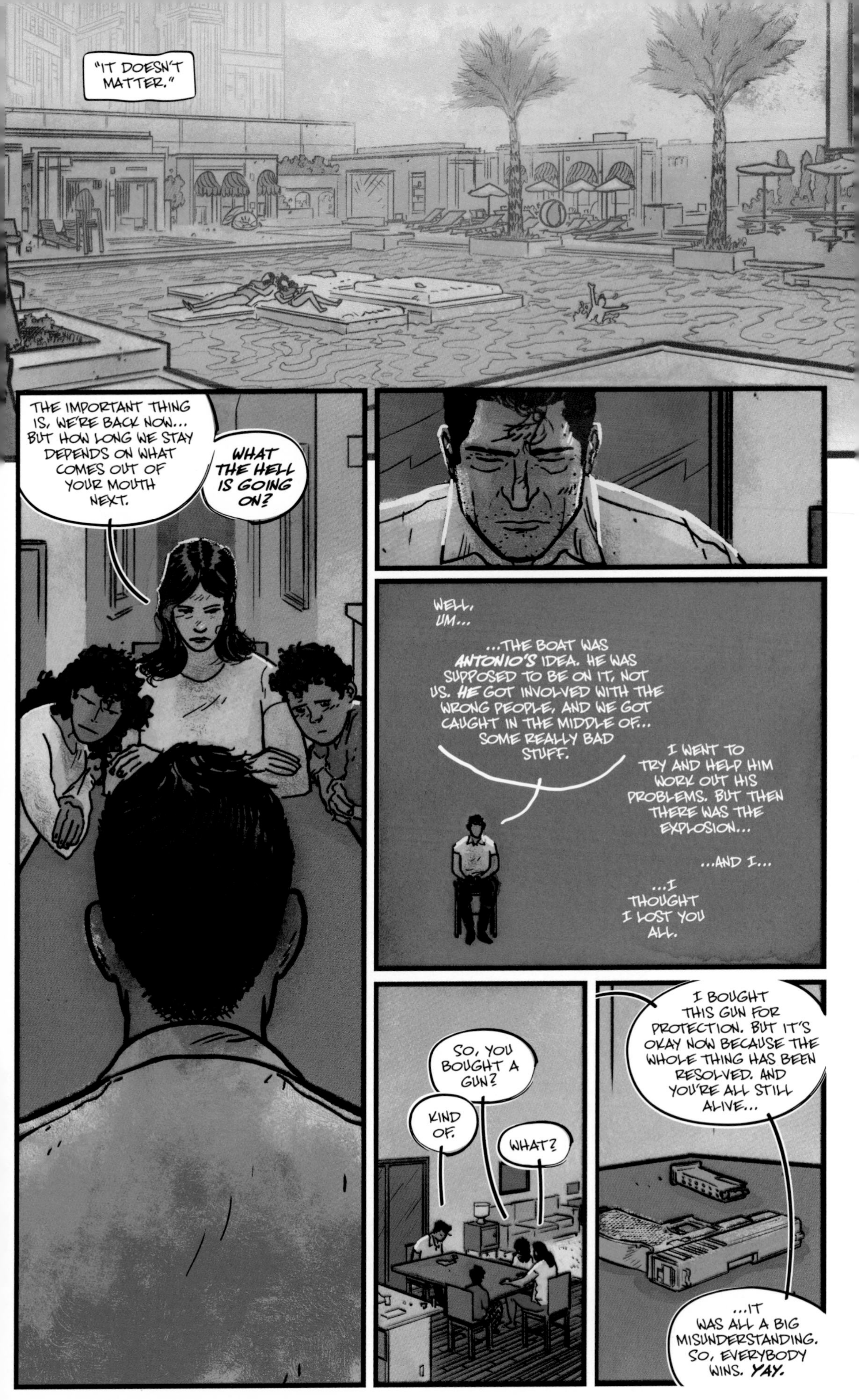

"IT DOESN'T MATTER."
THE IMPORTANT THING IS, WE'RE BACK NOW... BUT HOW LONG WE STAY DEPENDS ON WHAT COMES OUT OF YOUR MOUTH NEXT.
WHAT THE HELL IS GOING ON?
WELL, UM...
...THE BOAT WAS ANTONIO'S IDEA. HE WAS SUPPOSED TO BE ON IT, NOT US. HE GOT INVOLVED WITH THE WRONG PEOPLE, AND WE GOT CAUGHT IN THE MIDDLE OF... SOME REALLY BAD STUFF.
I WENT TO TRY AND HELP HIM WORK OUT HIS PROBLEMS. BUT THEN THERE WAS THE EXPLOSION...
...AND I...
...I THOUGHT I LOST YOU ALL.
SO, YOU BOUGHT A GUN?
KIND OF.
WHAT?
I BOUGHT THIS GUN FOR PROTECTION. BUT IT'S OKAY NOW BECAUSE THE WHOLE THING HAS BEEN RESOLVED. AND YOU'RE ALL STILL ALIVE...
...IT WAS ALL A BIG MISUNDERSTANDING. SO, EVERYBODY WINS. YAY.

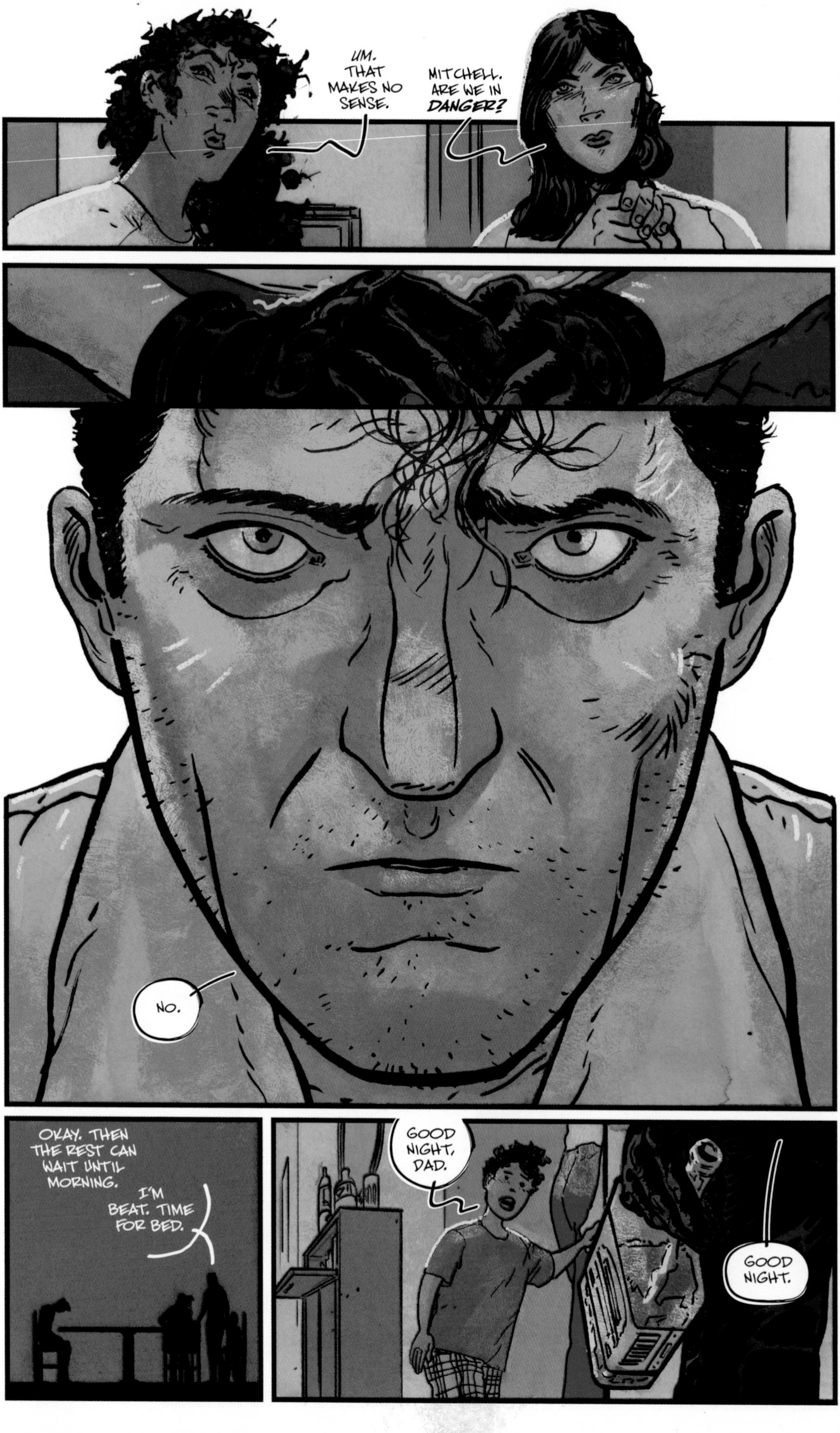
UM. THAT MAKES NO SENSE.
MITCHELL. ARE WE IN DANGER?
NO.
OKAY. THEN THE REST CAN WAIT UNTIL MORNING.
I'M BEAT. TIME FOR BED.
GOOD NIGHT, DAD.
GOOD NIGHT.

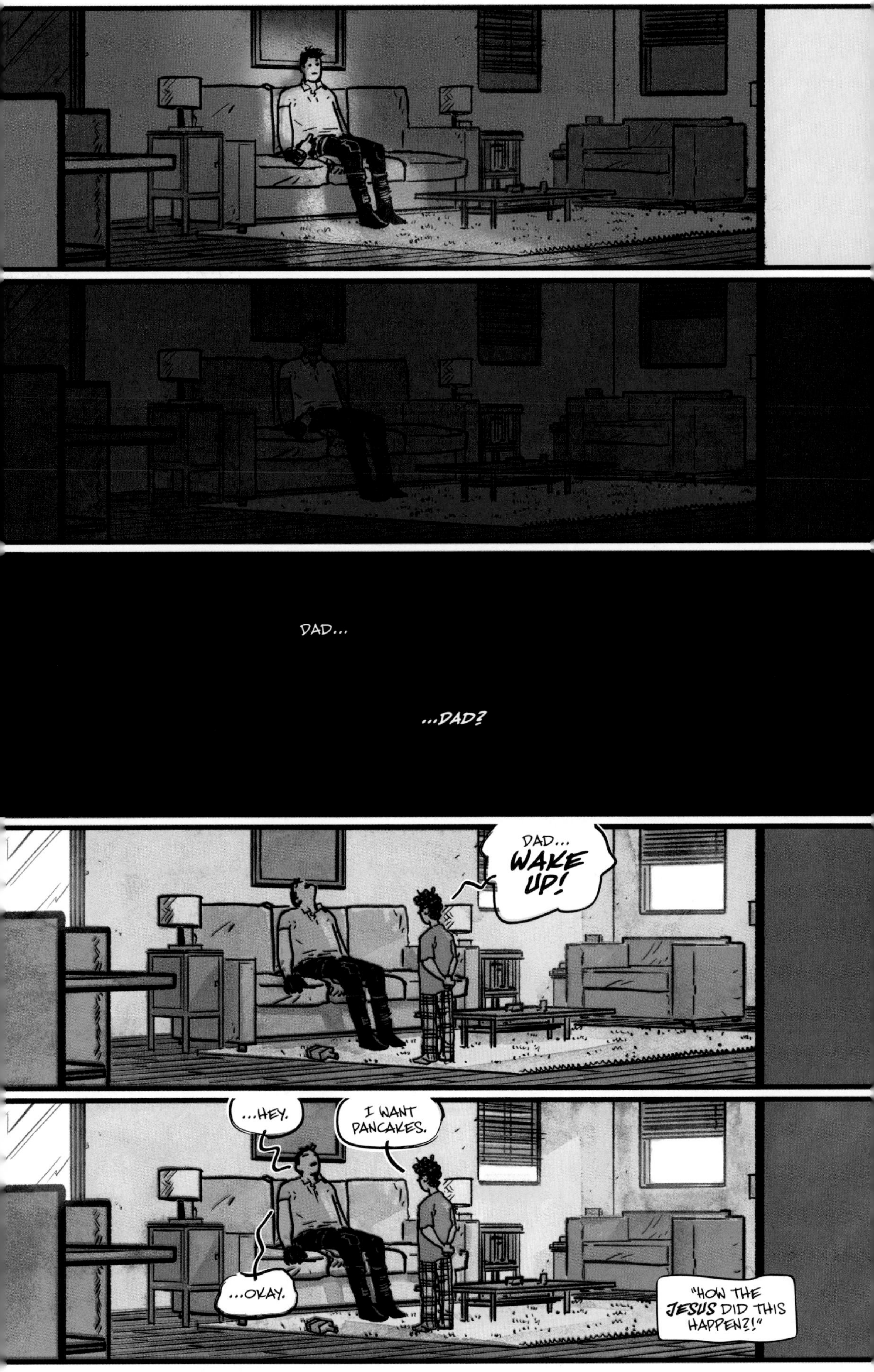
DAD...
...DAD?
DAD... WAKE UP!
...HEY.
I WANT PANCAKES.
...OKAY.
"HOW THE JESUS DID THIS HAPPEN?!"

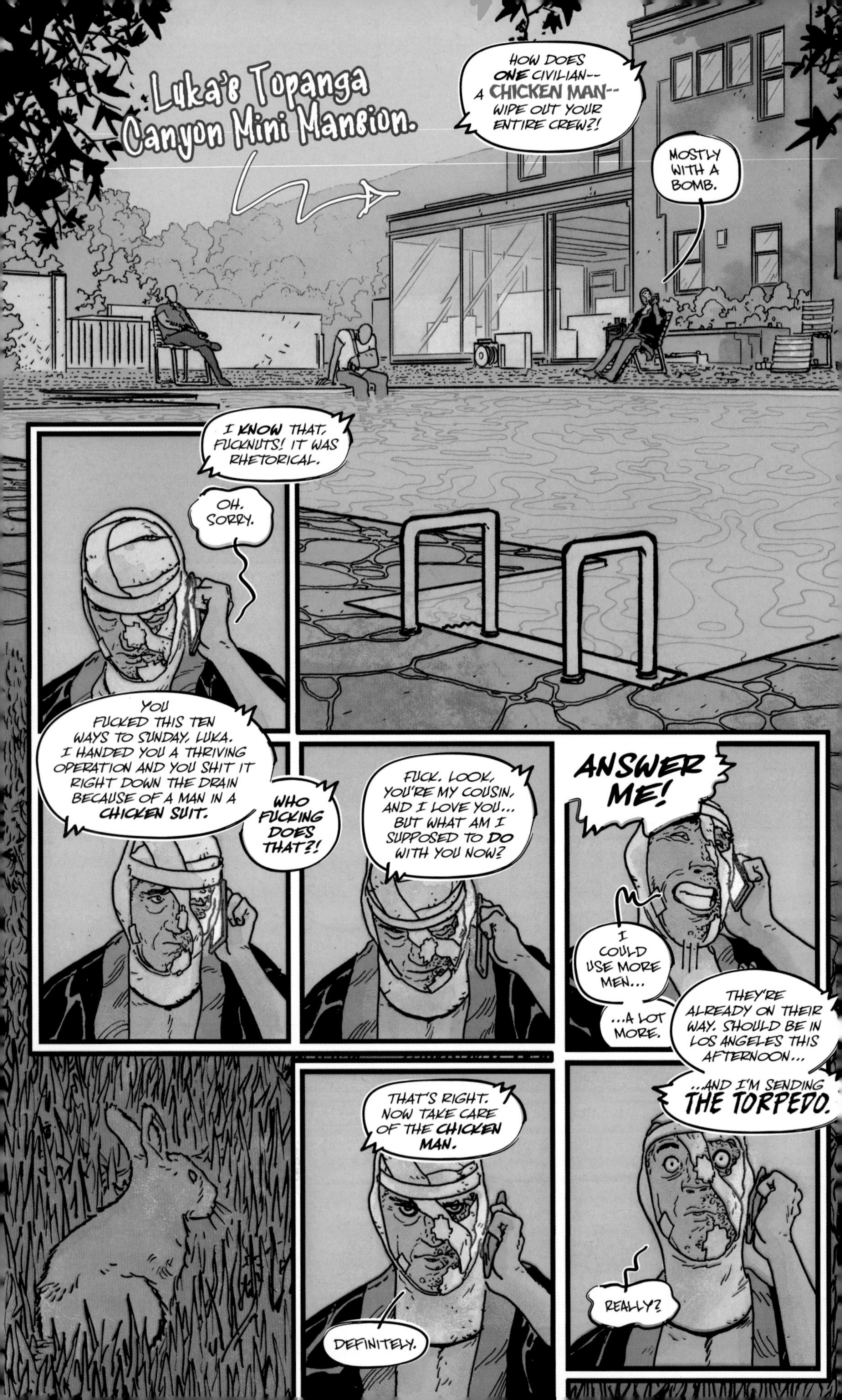

Luka's Topanga Canyon Mini Mansion.
HOW DOES ONE CIVILIAN-- A CHICKEN MAN-- WIPE OUT YOUR ENTIRE CREW?!
MOSTLY WITH A BOMB.
I KNOW THAT, FUCKNUTS! IT WAS RHETORICAL.
OH. SORRY.
YOU FUCKED THIS TEN WAYS TO SUNDAY, LUKA. I HANDED YOU A THRIVING OPERATION AND YOU SHIT IT RIGHT DOWN THE DRAIN BECAUSE OF A MAN IN A CHICKEN SUIT.
WHO FUCKING DOES THAT?!
FUCK. LOOK, YOU'RE MY COUSIN, AND I LOVE YOU... BUT WHAT AM I SUPPOSED TO DO WITH YOU NOW?
ANSWER ME!
I COULD USE MORE MEN...
...A LOT MORE.
THEY'RE ALREADY ON THEIR WAY. SHOULD BE IN LOS ANGELES THIS AFTERNOON...
...AND I'M SENDING THE TORPEDO.
REALLY?
THAT'S RIGHT. NOW TAKE CARE OF THE CHICKEN MAN.
DEFINITELY.

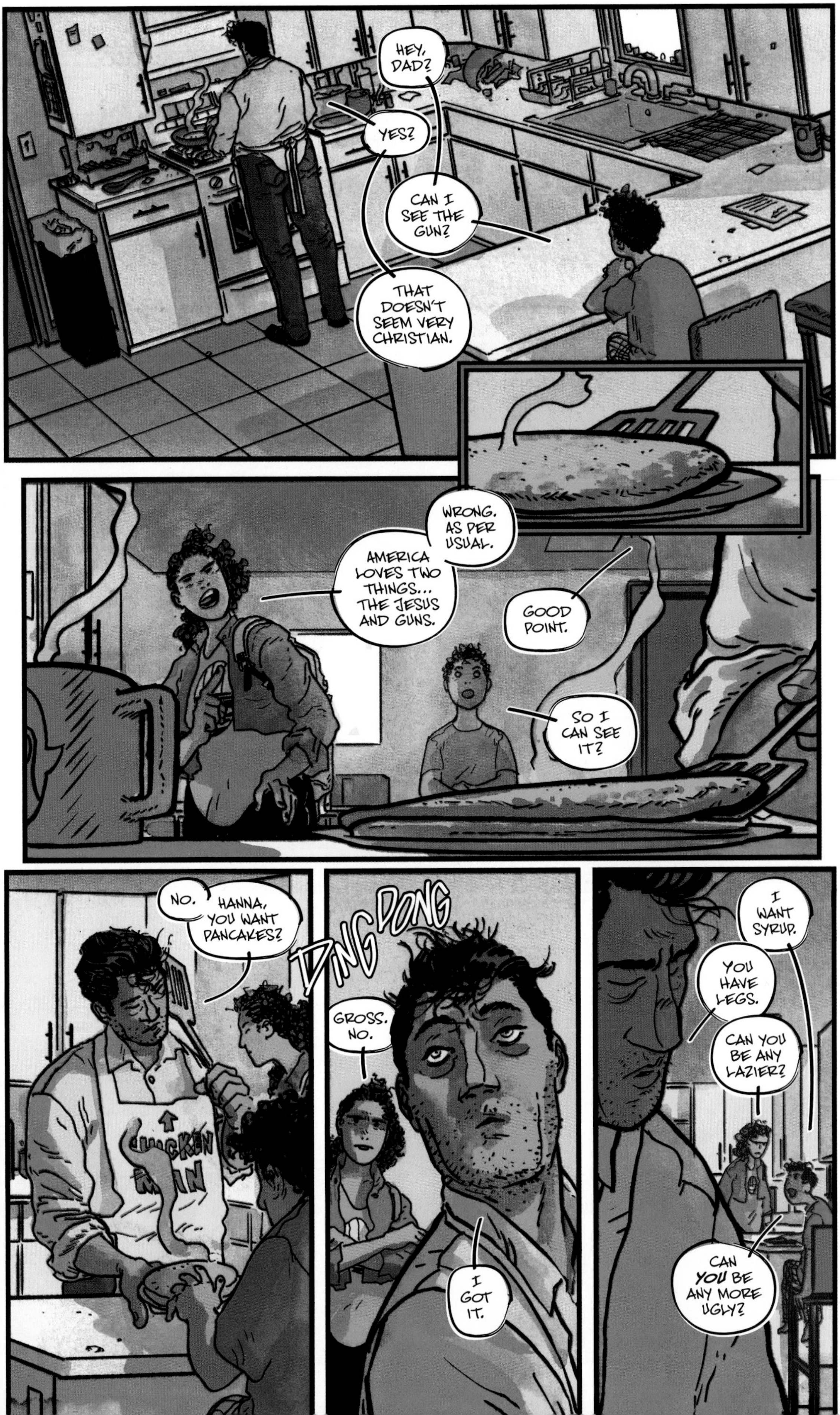

HEY, DAD?
YES?
CAN I SEE THE GUN?
THAT DOESN'T SEEM VERY CHRISTIAN.
WRONG. AS PER USUAL.
AMERICA LOVES TWO THINGS... THE JESUS AND GUNS.
GOOD POINT.
SO I CAN SEE IT?
NO.
HANNA, YOU WANT PANCAKES?
GROSS. NO.
DING DONG
I GOT IT.
I WANT SYRUP.
YOU HAVE LEGS.
CAN YOU BE ANY LAZIER?
CAN YOU BE ANY MORE UGLY?

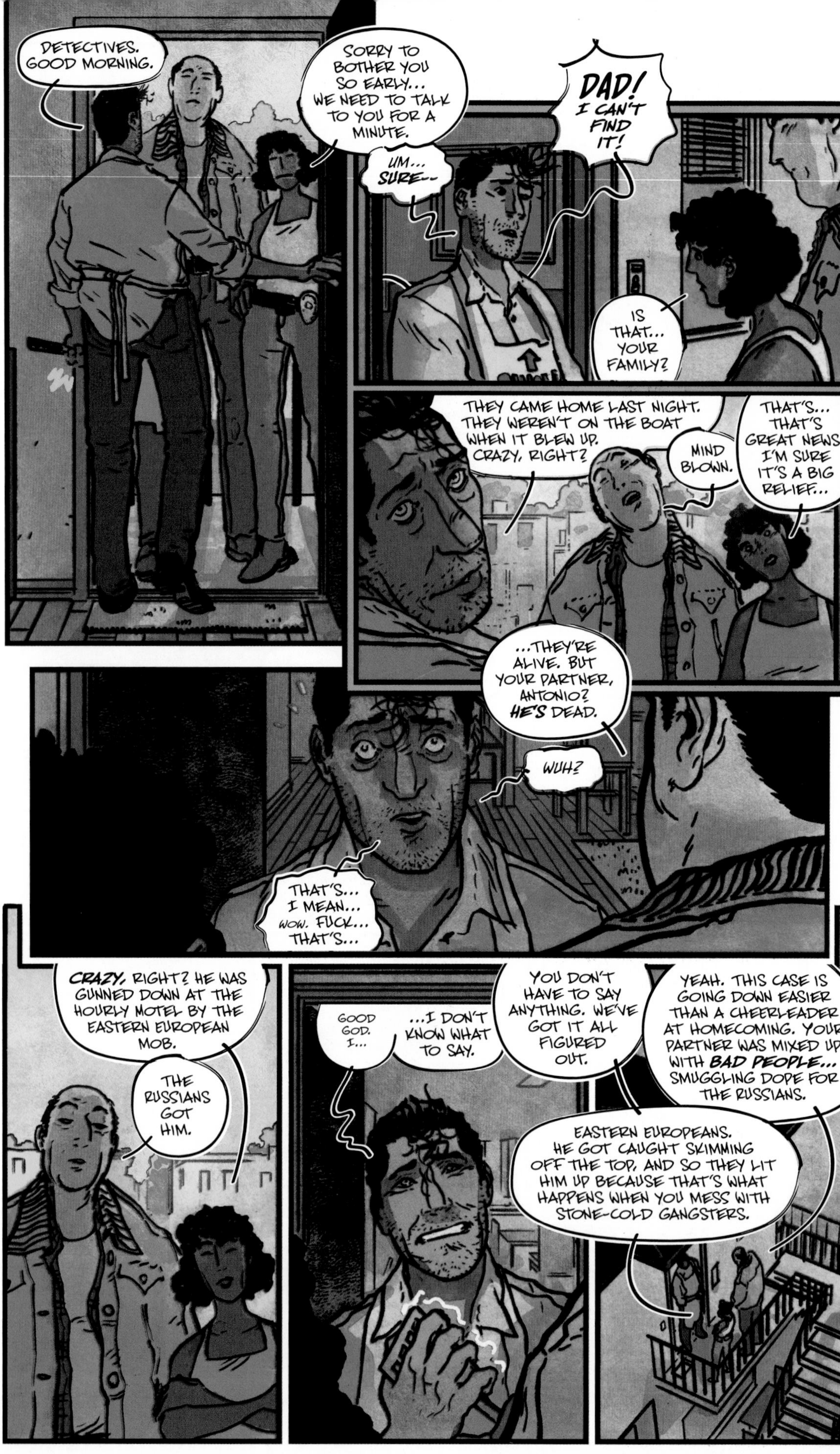

DETECTIVES. GOOD MORNING.
SORRY TO BOTHER YOU SO EARLY... WE NEED TO TALK TO YOU FOR A MINUTE.
UM... SURE...
DAD! I CAN'T FIND IT!
IS THAT... YOUR FAMILY?
THEY CAME HOME LAST NIGHT. THEY WEREN'T ON THE BOAT WHEN IT BLEW UP. CRAZY, RIGHT?
MIND BLOWN.
THAT'S... THAT'S GREAT NEWS. I'M SURE IT'S A BIG RELIEF...
...THEY'RE ALIVE. BUT YOUR PARTNER, ANTONIO? HE'S DEAD.
WUH?
THAT'S... I MEAN... WOW. FUCK... THAT'S...
CRAZY, RIGHT? HE WAS GUNNED DOWN AT THE HOURLY MOTEL BY THE EASTERN EUROPEAN MOB.
THE RUSSIANS GOT HIM.
GOOD GOD. I...
...I DON'T KNOW WHAT TO SAY.
YOU DON'T HAVE TO SAY ANYTHING. WE'VE GOT IT ALL FIGURED OUT.
YEAH. THIS CASE IS GOING DOWN EASIER THAN A CHEERLEADER AT HOMECOMING. YOUR PARTNER WAS MIXED UP WITH BAD PEOPLE... SMUGGLING DOPE FOR THE RUSSIANS.
EASTERN EUROPEANS. HE GOT CAUGHT SKIMMING OFF THE TOP, AND SO THEY LIT HIM UP BECAUSE THAT'S WHAT HAPPENS WHEN YOU MESS WITH STONE-COLD GANGSTERS.

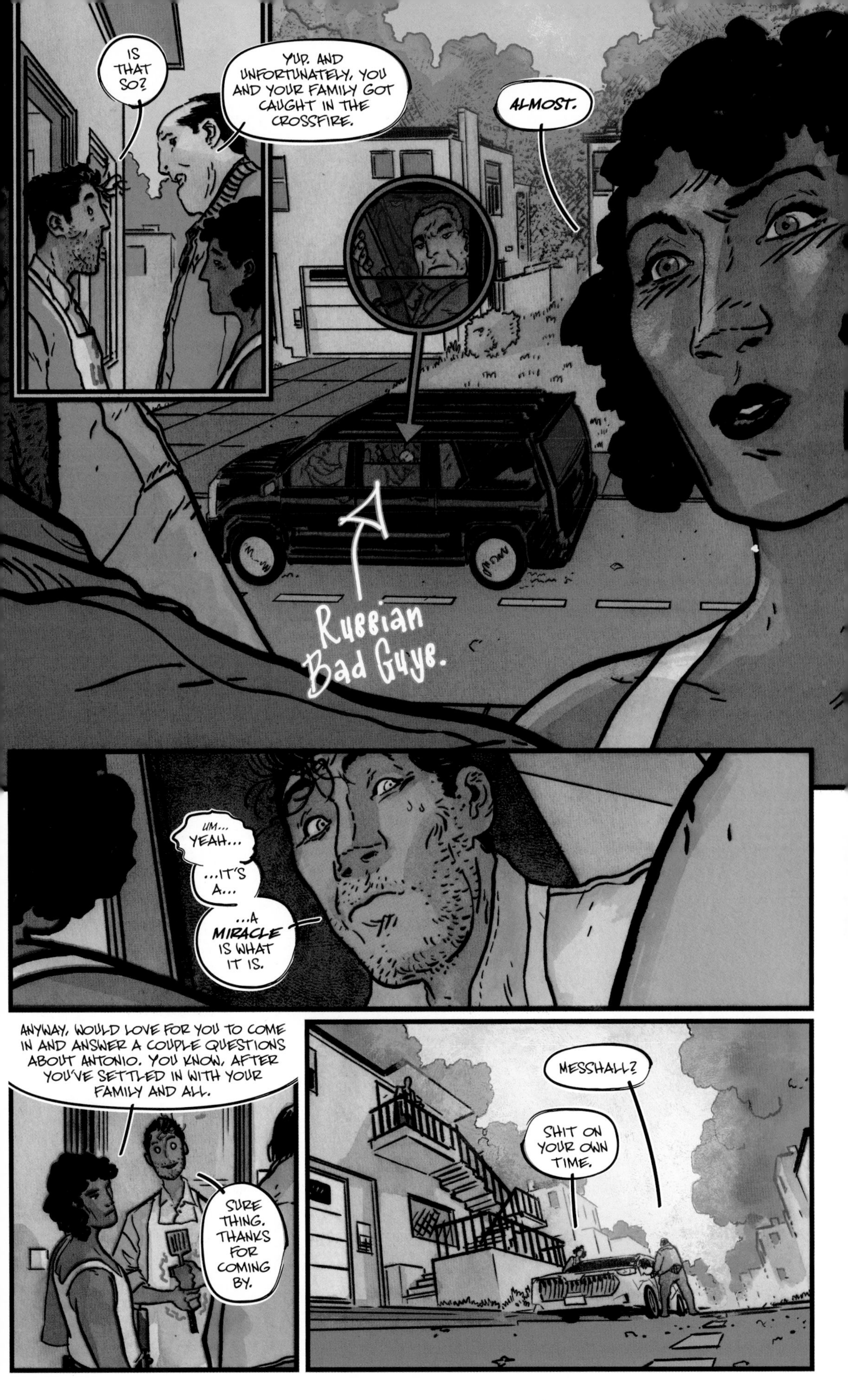
IS THAT SO?
YUP. AND UNFORTUNATELY, YOU AND YOUR FAMILY GOT CAUGHT IN THE CROSSFIRE.
ALMOST.
Russian Bad Guys.
UM... YEAH...
...IT'S A...
...A MIRACLE IS WHAT IT IS.
ANYWAY, WOULD LOVE FOR YOU TO COME IN AND ANSWER A COUPLE QUESTIONS ABOUT ANTONIO. YOU KNOW, AFTER YOU'VE SETTLED IN WITH YOUR FAMILY AND ALL.
SURE THING. THANKS FOR COMING BY.
MESSHALL?
SHIT ON YOUR OWN TIME.

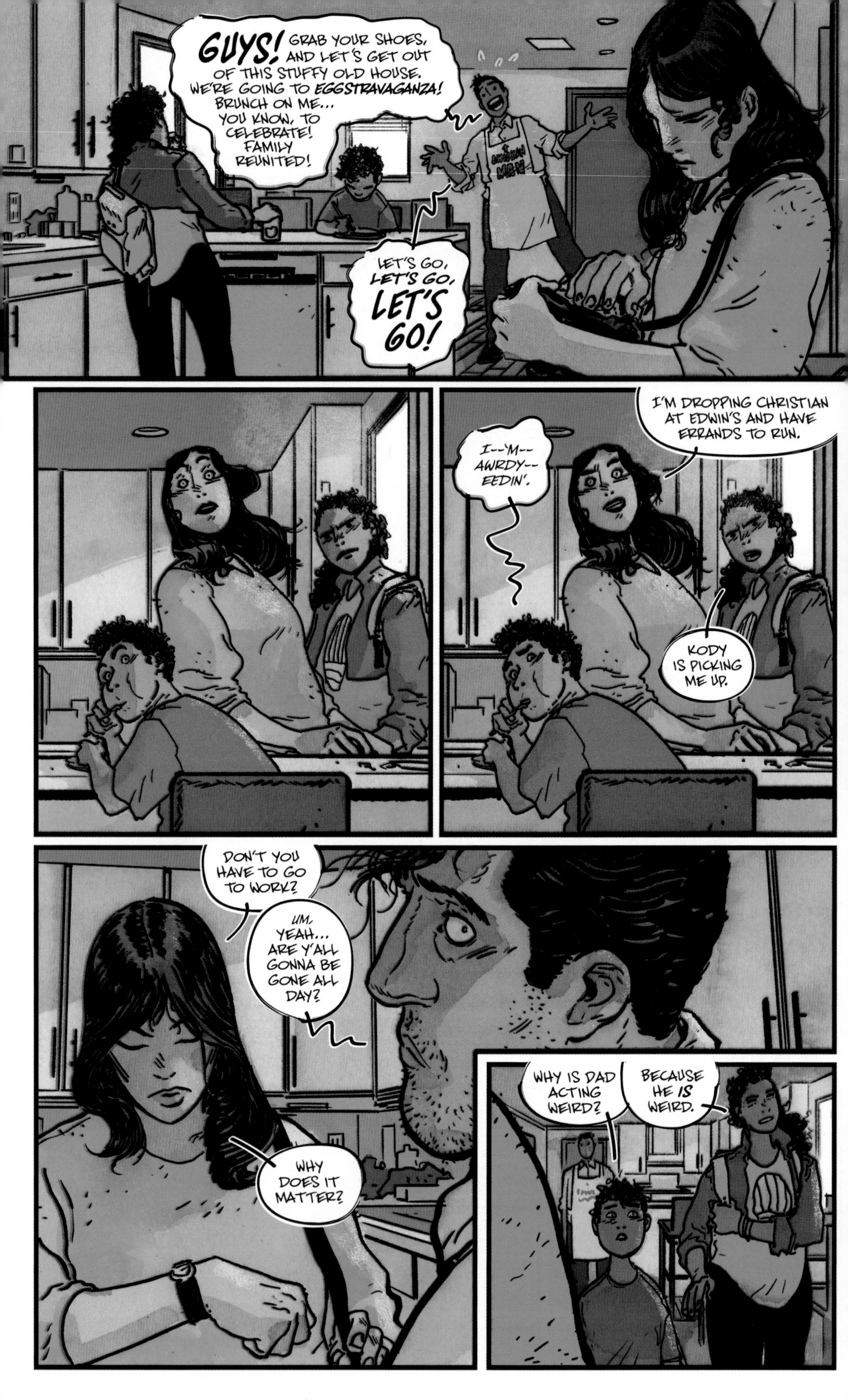
GUYS! GRAB YOUR SHOES, AND LET'S GET OUT OF THIS STUFFY OLD HOUSE. WE'RE GOING TO EGGSTRAVAGANZA! BRUNCH ON ME... YOU KNOW, TO CELEBRATE! FAMILY REUNITED!
LET'S GO, LET'S GO, LET'S GO!
I--'M-- AWRDY-- EEDIN'.
I'M DROPPING CHRISTIAN AT EDWIN'S AND HAVE ERRANDS TO RUN.
KODY IS PICKING ME UP.
DON'T YOU HAVE TO GO TO WORK?
UM, YEAH... ARE Y'ALL GONNA BE GONE ALL DAY?
WHY DOES IT MATTER?
WHY IS DAD ACTING WEIRD?
BECAUSE HE IS WEIRD.

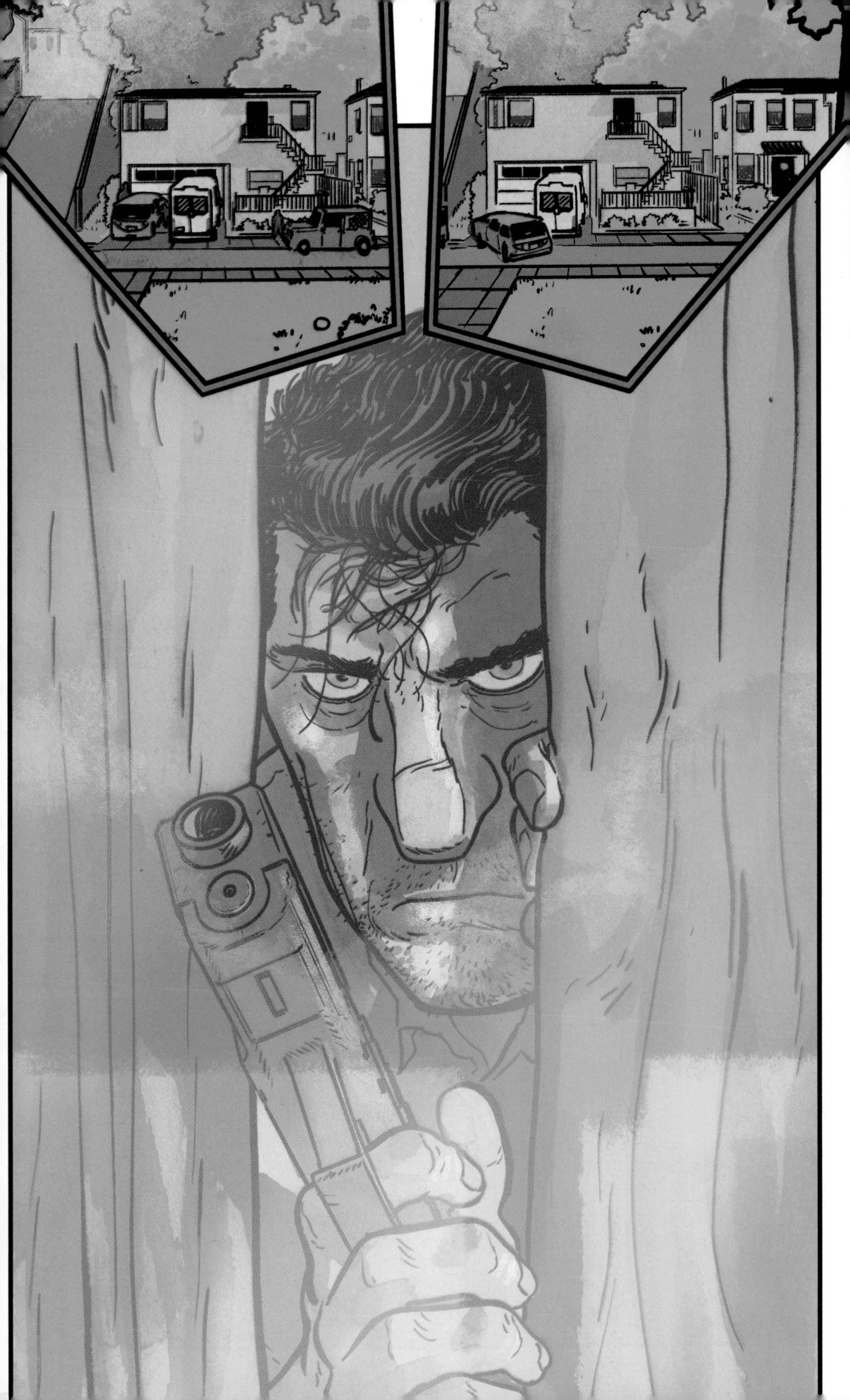

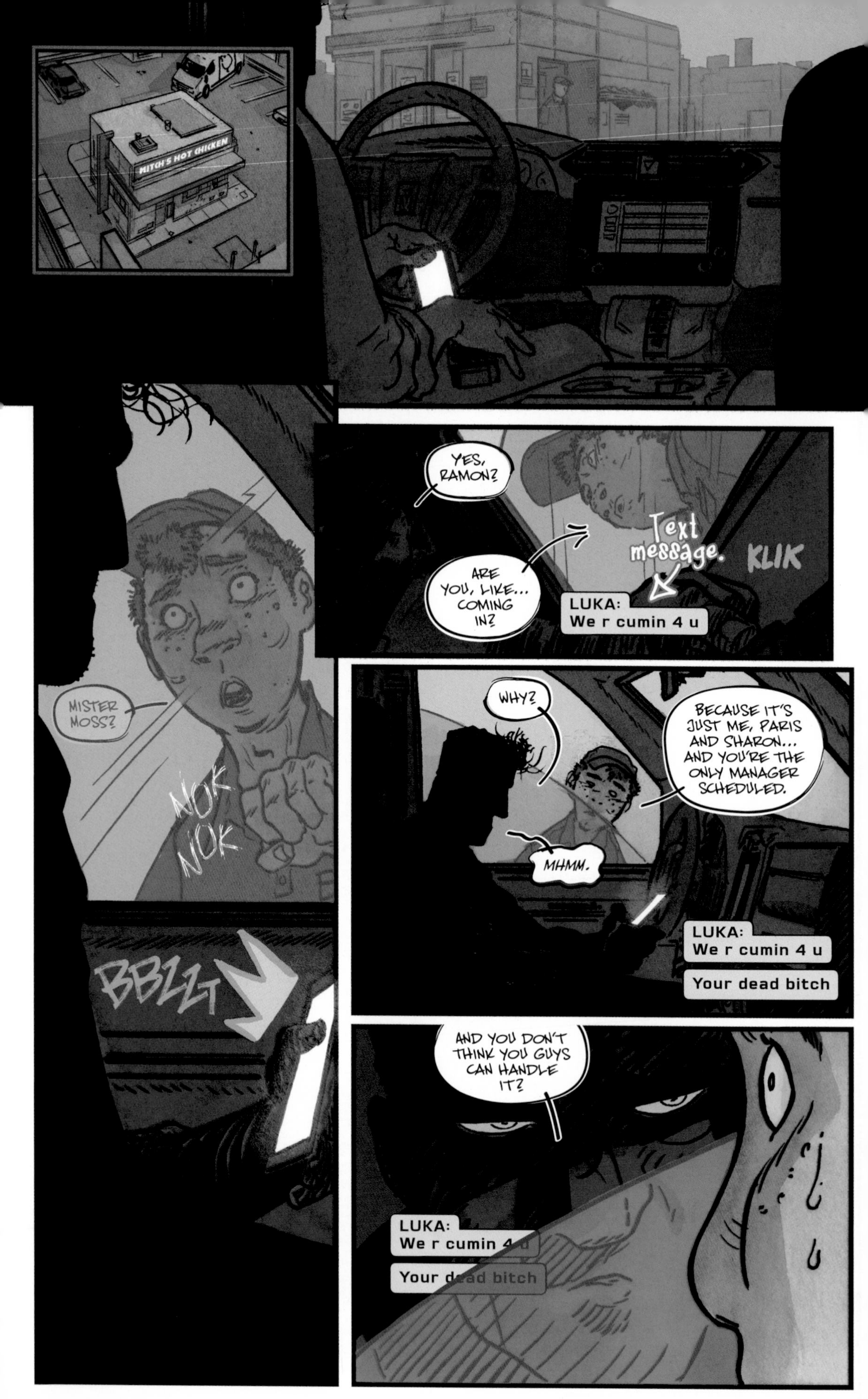
MITCH'S HOT CHICKEN
MISTER MOSS?
NOK NOK
BBZZT
YES, RAMON?
ARE YOU, LIKE... COMING IN?
Text message.
KLIK
LUKA: We r cumin 4 u
WHY?
BECAUSE IT'S JUST ME, PARIS AND SHARON... AND YOU'RE THE ONLY MANAGER SCHEDULED.
MHMM.
LUKA: We r cumin 4 u
Your dead bitch
AND YOU DON'T THINK YOU GUYS CAN HANDLE IT?
LUKA: We r cumin 4 u
Your dead bitch

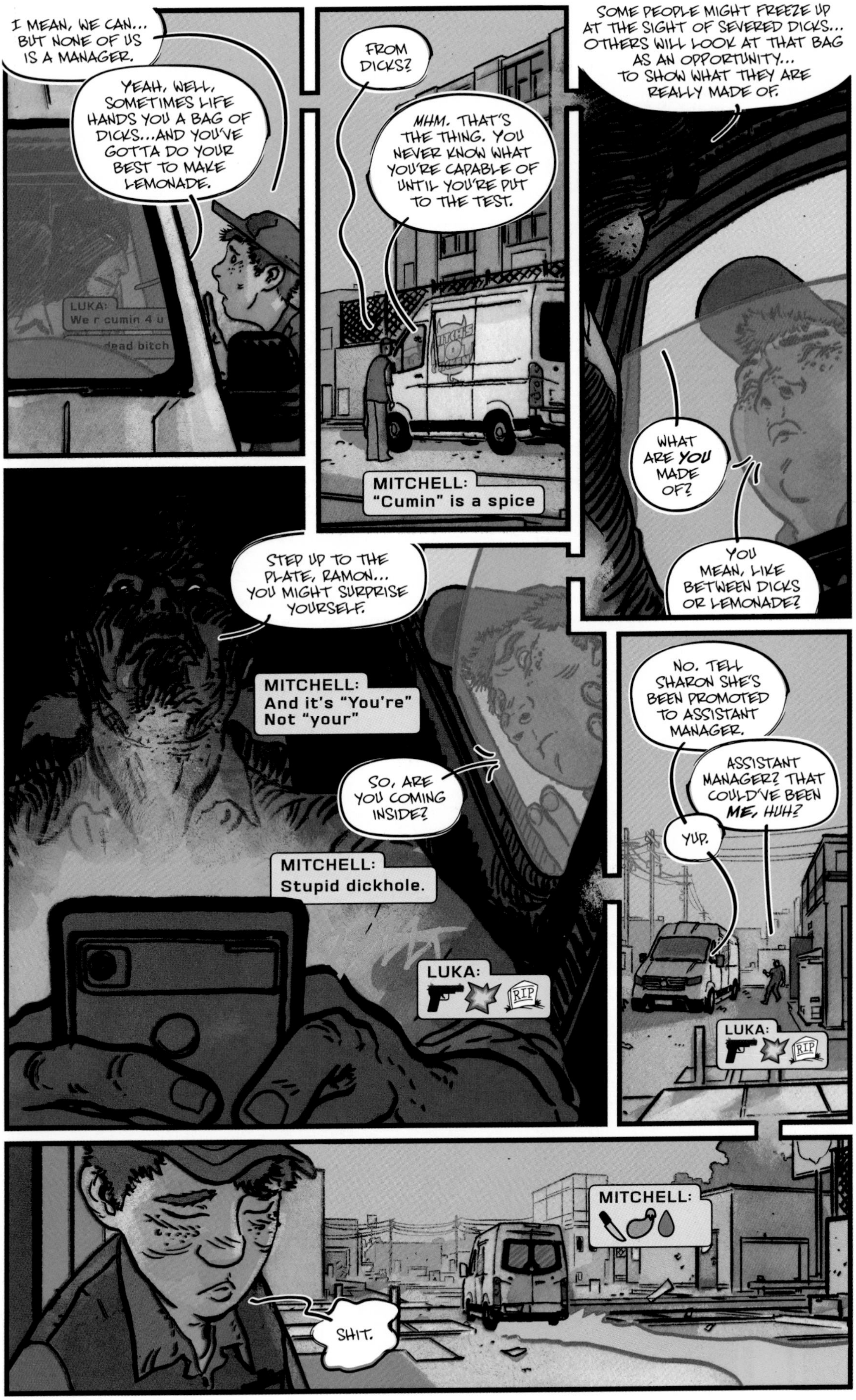
I MEAN, WE CAN... BUT NONE OF US IS A MANAGER.
YEAH, WELL, SOMETIMES LIFE HANDS YOU A BAG OF DICKS...AND YOU'VE GOTTA DO YOUR BEST TO MAKE LEMONADE.
LUKA:
We r cumin 4 u
dead bitch
FROM DICKS?
MHM. THAT'S THE THING. YOU NEVER KNOW WHAT YOU'RE CAPABLE OF UNTIL YOU'RE PUT TO THE TEST.
MITCHELL:
"Cumin" is a spice
SOME PEOPLE MIGHT FREEZE UP AT THE SIGHT OF SEVERED DICKS... OTHERS WILL LOOK AT THAT BAG AS AN OPPORTUNITY... TO SHOW WHAT THEY ARE REALLY MADE OF.
WHAT ARE *YOU* MADE OF?
YOU MEAN, LIKE BETWEEN DICKS OR LEMONADE?
STEP UP TO THE PLATE, RAMON... YOU MIGHT SURPRISE YOURSELF.
MITCHELL:
And it's "You're" Not "your"
SO, ARE YOU COMING INSIDE?
MITCHELL:
Stupid dickhole.
LUKA:
RIP
NO. TELL SHARON SHE'S BEEN PROMOTED TO ASSISTANT MANAGER.
ASSISTANT MANAGER? THAT COULD'VE BEEN *ME*, HUH?
YUP.
LUKA:
RIP
MITCHELL:
SHIT.

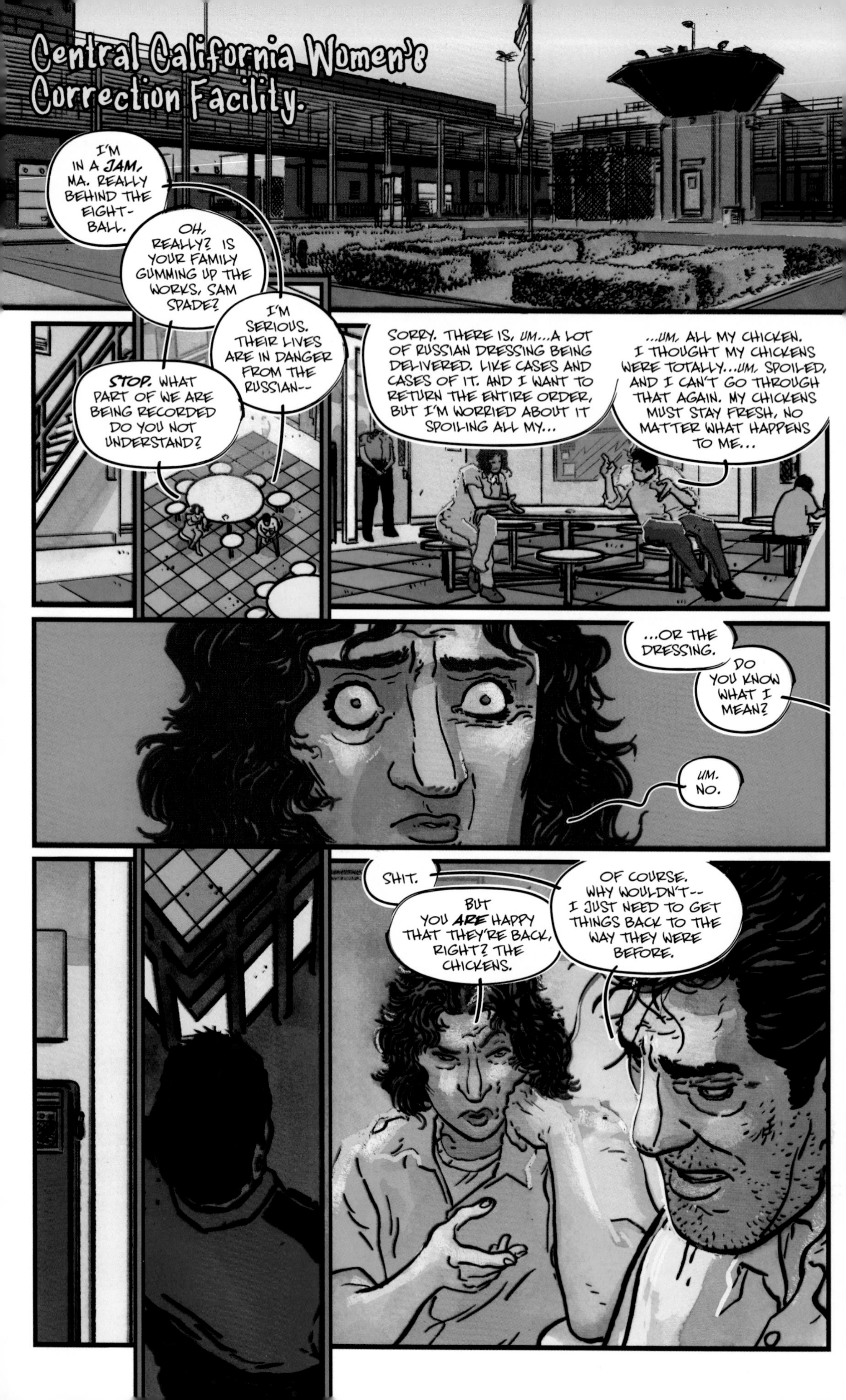
Central California Women's Correction Facility.
I'M IN A JAM, MA. REALLY BEHIND THE EIGHT-BALL.
OH, REALLY? IS YOUR FAMILY GUMMING UP THE WORKS, SAM SPADE?
I'M SERIOUS. THEIR LIVES ARE IN DANGER FROM THE RUSSIAN--
STOP. WHAT PART OF WE ARE BEING RECORDED DO YOU NOT UNDERSTAND?
SORRY. THERE IS, UM...A LOT OF RUSSIAN DRESSING BEING DELIVERED. LIKE CASES AND CASES OF IT. AND I WANT TO RETURN THE ENTIRE ORDER, BUT I'M WORRIED ABOUT IT SPOILING ALL MY...
...UM, ALL MY CHICKEN. I THOUGHT MY CHICKENS WERE TOTALLY...UM, SPOILED, AND I CAN'T GO THROUGH THAT AGAIN. MY CHICKENS MUST STAY FRESH, NO MATTER WHAT HAPPENS TO ME...
...OR THE DRESSING.
DO YOU KNOW WHAT I MEAN?
UM. NO.
SHIT.
OF COURSE. WHY WOULDN'T-- I JUST NEED TO GET THINGS BACK TO THE WAY THEY WERE BEFORE.
BUT YOU ARE HAPPY THAT THEY'RE BACK, RIGHT? THE CHICKENS.

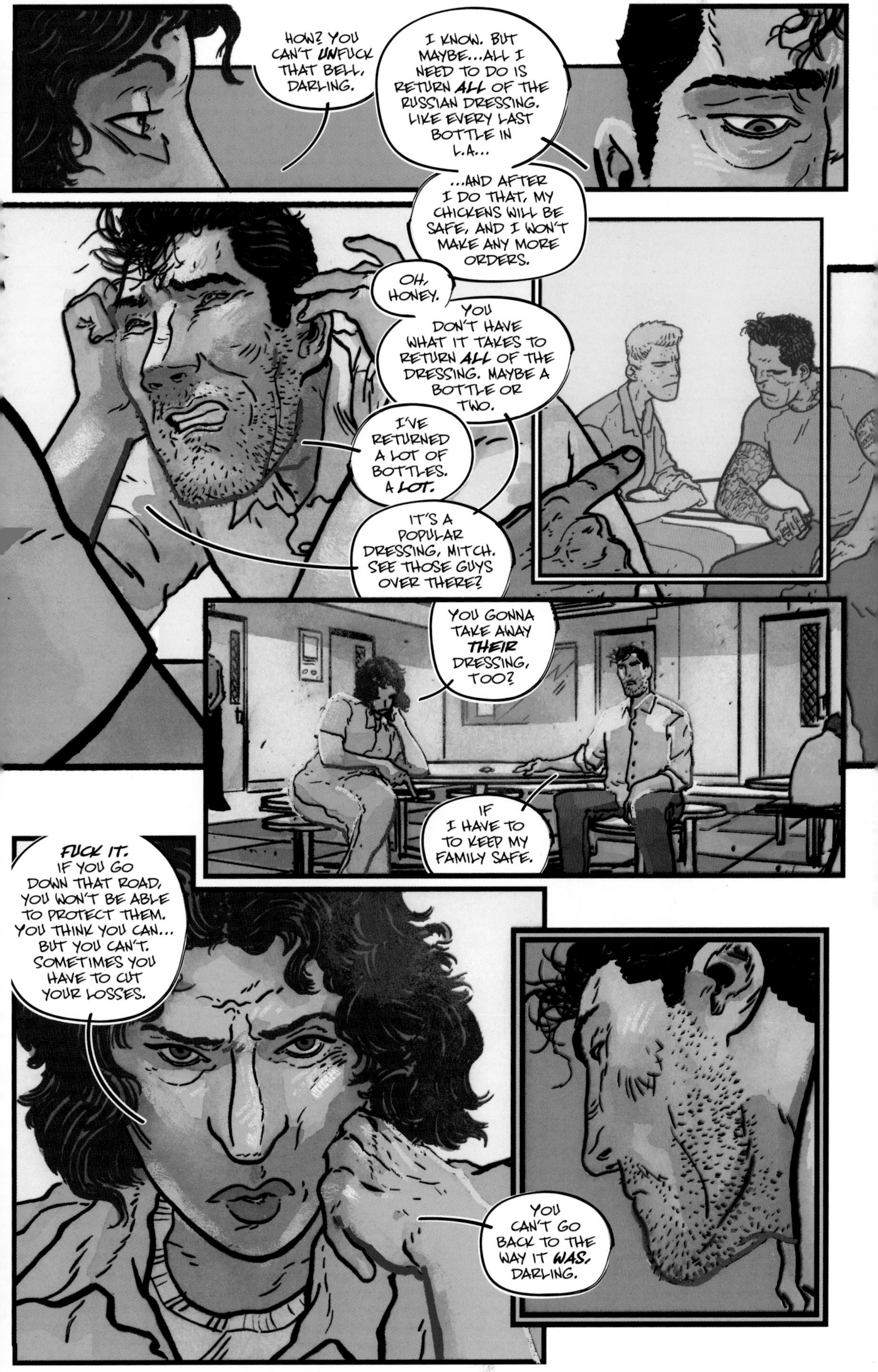

HOW? YOU CAN'T UNFUCK THAT BELL, DARLING.
I KNOW. BUT MAYBE...ALL I NEED TO DO IS RETURN ALL OF THE RUSSIAN DRESSING. LIKE EVERY LAST BOTTLE IN L.A...
...AND AFTER I DO THAT, MY CHICKENS WILL BE SAFE, AND I WON'T MAKE ANY MORE ORDERS.
OH, HONEY.
YOU DON'T HAVE WHAT IT TAKES TO RETURN ALL OF THE DRESSING. MAYBE A BOTTLE OR TWO.
I'VE RETURNED A LOT OF BOTTLES. A LOT.
IT'S A POPULAR DRESSING, MITCH. SEE THOSE GUYS OVER THERE?
YOU GONNA TAKE AWAY THEIR DRESSING, TOO?
IF I HAVE TO TO KEEP MY FAMILY SAFE.
FUCK IT. IF YOU GO DOWN THAT ROAD, YOU WON'T BE ABLE TO PROTECT THEM. YOU THINK YOU CAN... BUT YOU CAN'T. SOMETIMES YOU HAVE TO CUT YOUR LOSSES.
YOU CAN'T GO BACK TO THE WAY IT WAS, DARLING.

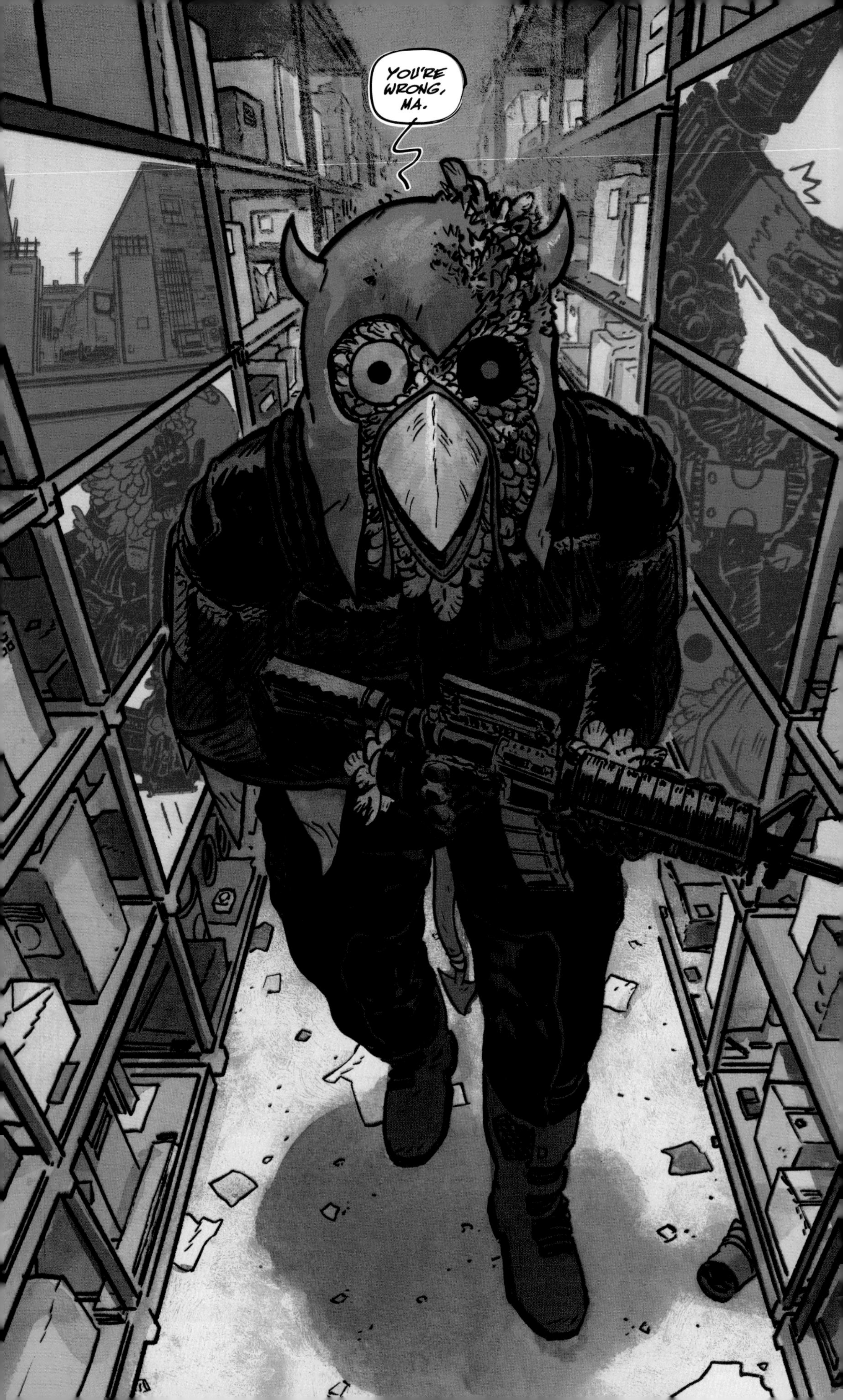
YOU'RE WRONG, MA.

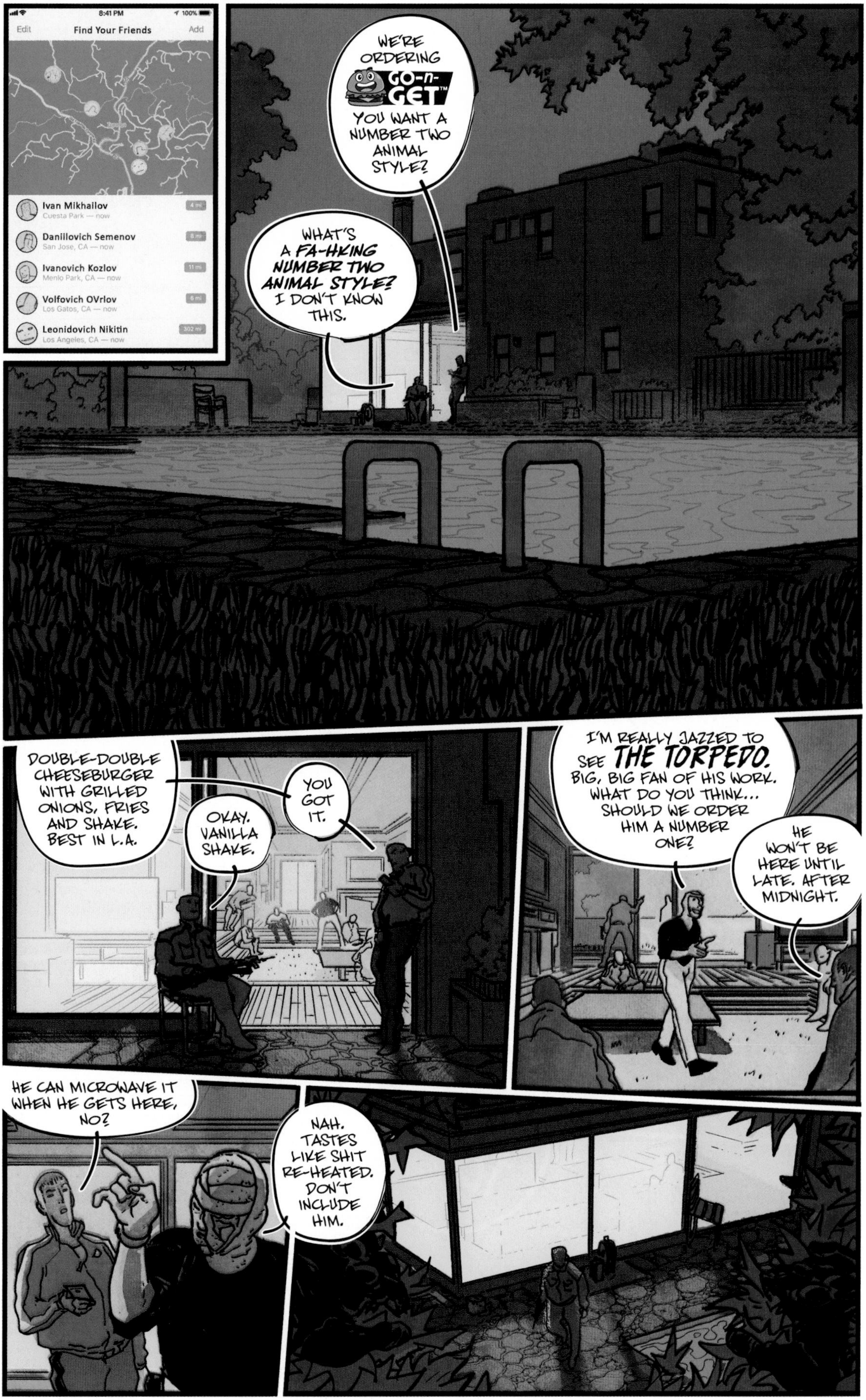
8:41 PM
100%
Edit
Find Your Friends
Add
Ivan Mikhailov
Cuesta Park — now
4 mi
Daniilovich Semenov
San Jose, CA — now
8 mi
Ivanovich Kozlov
Menlo Park, CA — now
11 mi
Volfovich OVrlov
Los Gatos, CA — now
6 mi
Leonidovich Nikitin
Los Angeles, CA — now
302 mi
WE'RE ORDERING GO-n-GET™ YOU WANT A NUMBER TWO ANIMAL STYLE?
WHAT'S A FA-HKING NUMBER TWO ANIMAL STYLE? I DON'T KNOW THIS.
DOUBLE-DOUBLE CHEESEBURGER WITH GRILLED ONIONS, FRIES AND SHAKE. BEST IN L.A.
YOU GOT IT.
OKAY. VANILLA SHAKE.
I'M REALLY JAZZED TO SEE THE TORPEDO. BIG, BIG FAN OF HIS WORK. WHAT DO YOU THINK... SHOULD WE ORDER HIM A NUMBER ONE?
HE WON'T BE HERE UNTIL LATE. AFTER MIDNIGHT.
HE CAN MICROWAVE IT WHEN HE GETS HERE, NO?
NAH. TASTES LIKE SHIT RE-HEATED. DON'T INCLUDE HIM.

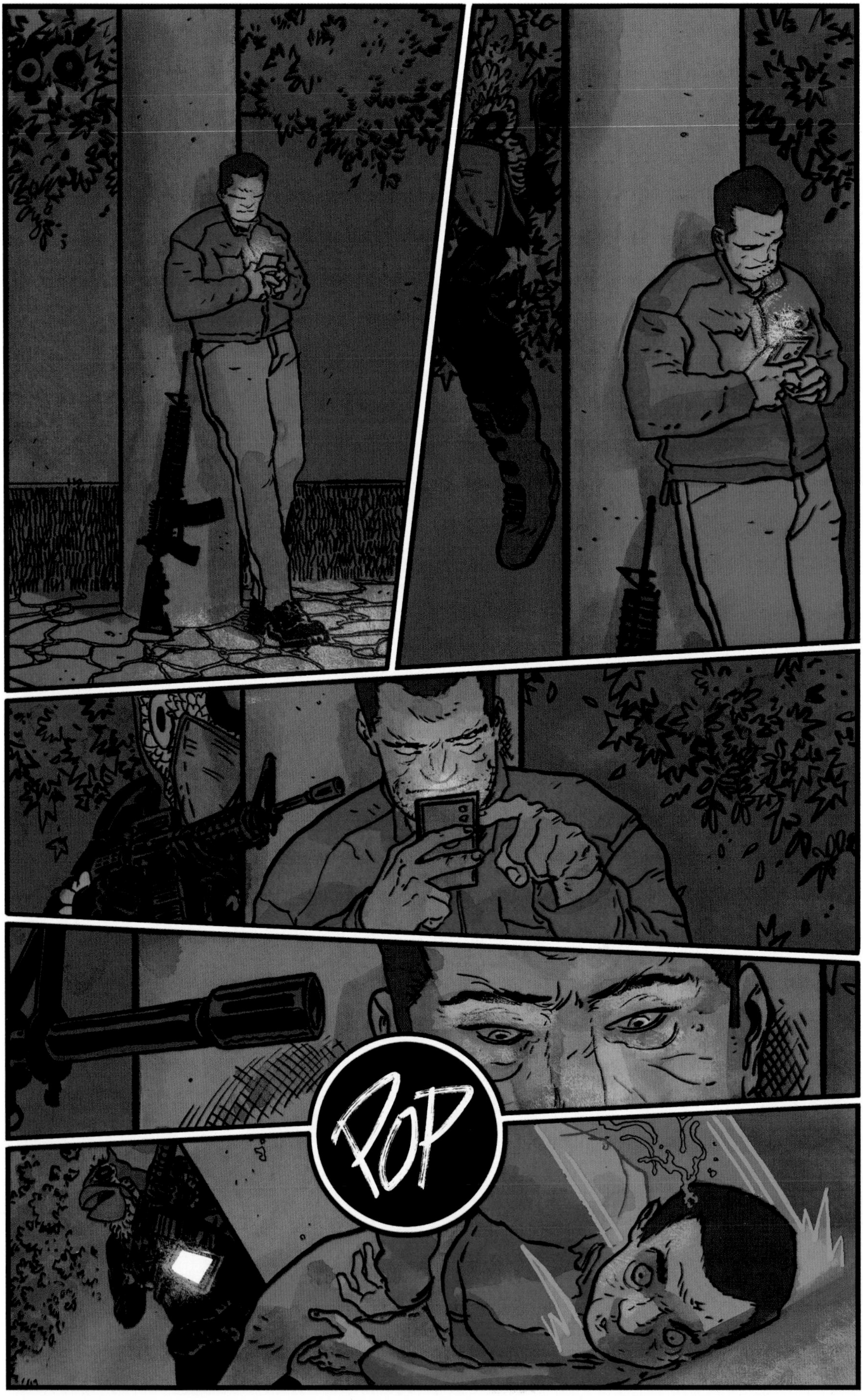
POP

SKLSK

KRASH

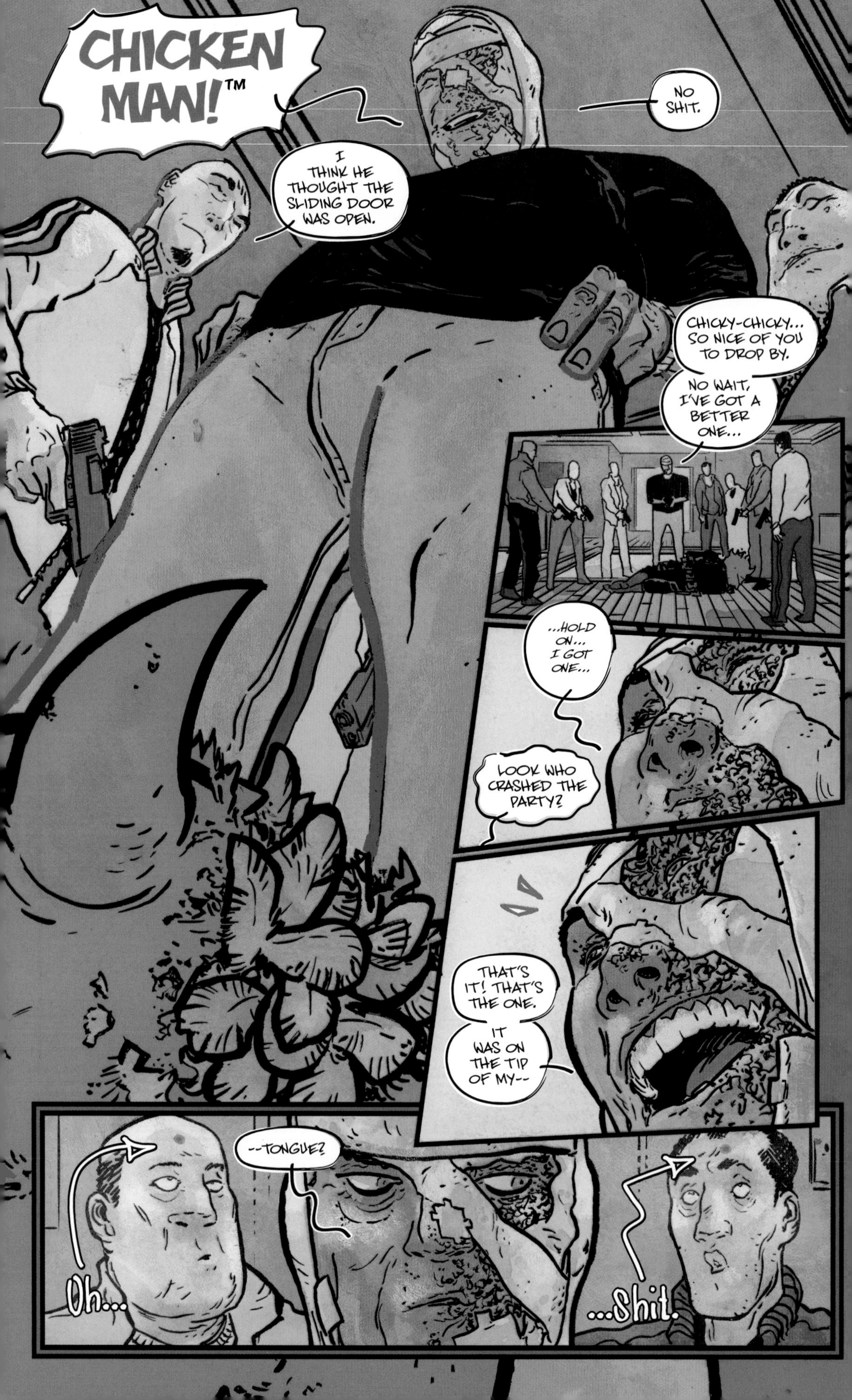
CHICKEN MAN!™
NO SHIT.
I THINK HE THOUGHT THE SLIDING DOOR WAS OPEN.
CHICKY-CHICKY... SO NICE OF YOU TO DROP BY.
NO WAIT, I'VE GOT A BETTER ONE...
...HOLD ON... I GOT ONE...
LOOK WHO CRASHED THE PARTY?
THAT'S IT! THAT'S THE ONE.
IT WAS ON THE TIP OF MY--
--TONGUE?
Oh...
...Shit.

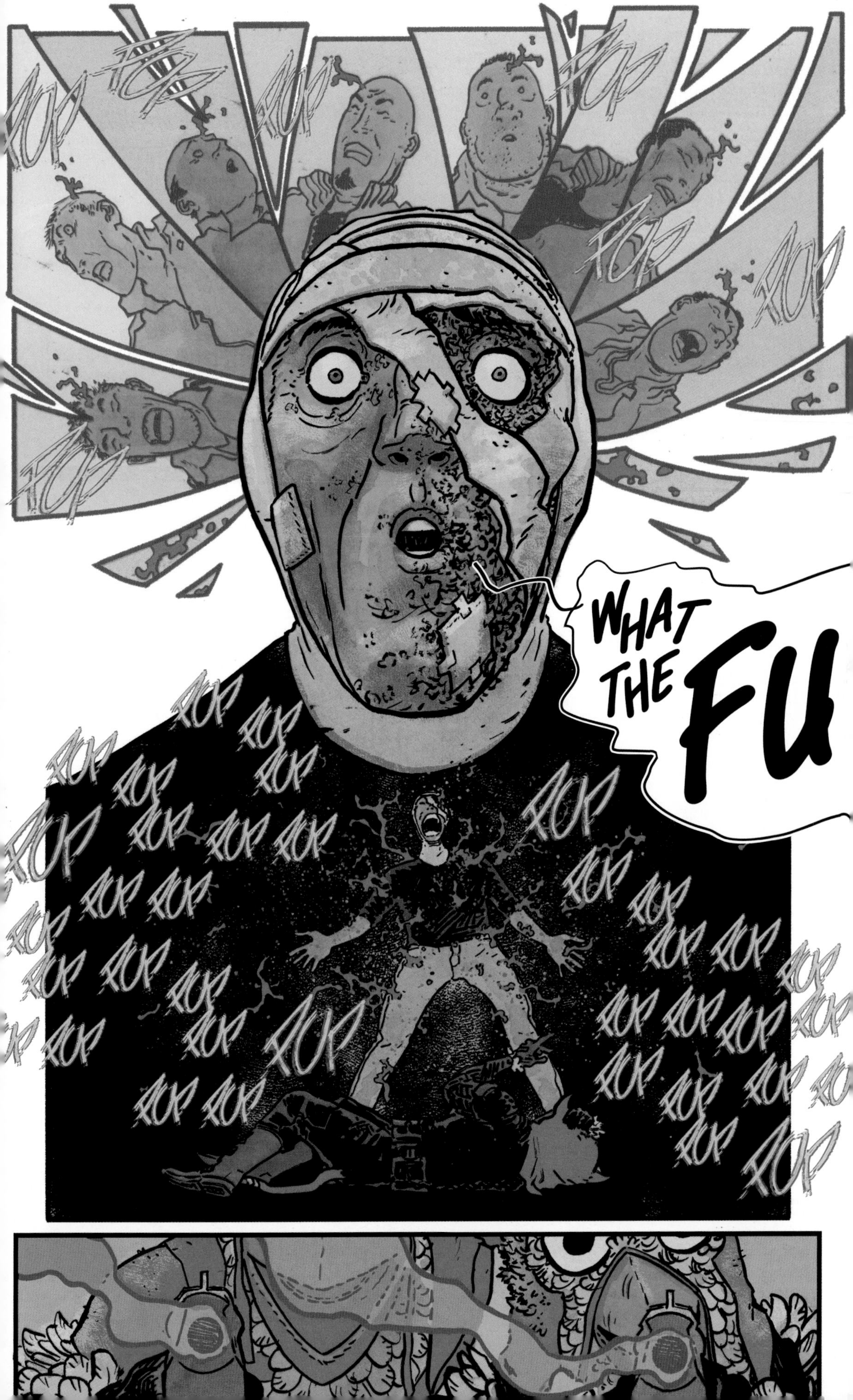
WHAT THE FU

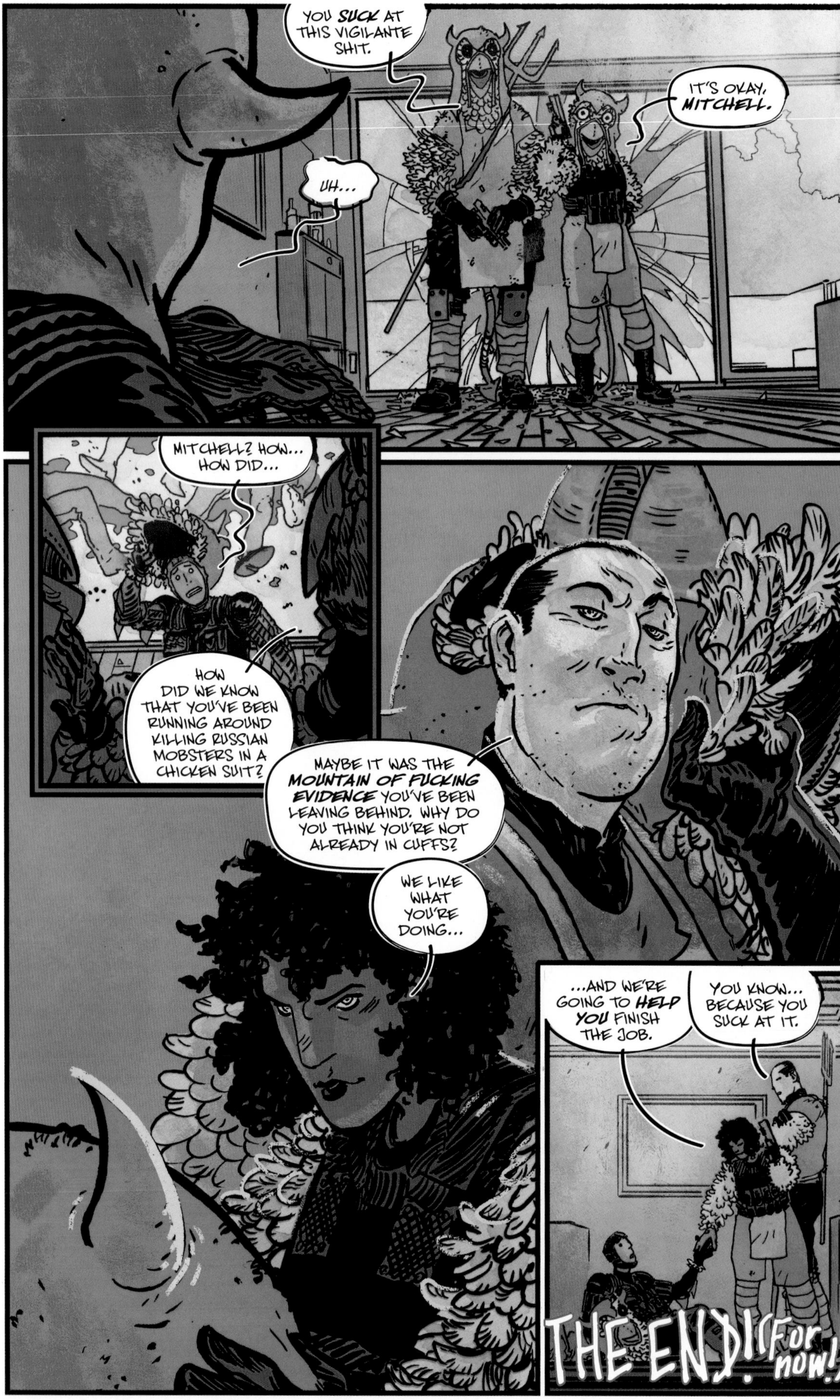
YOU SUCK AT THIS VIGILANTE SHIT.
IT'S OKAY, MITCHELL.
UH...
MITCHELL? HOW... HOW DID...
HOW DID WE KNOW THAT YOU'VE BEEN RUNNING AROUND KILLING RUSSIAN MOBSTERS IN A CHICKEN SUIT?
MAYBE IT WAS THE MOUNTAIN OF FUCKING EVIDENCE YOU'VE BEEN LEAVING BEHIND. WHY DO YOU THINK YOU'RE NOT ALREADY IN CUFFS?
WE LIKE WHAT YOU'RE DOING...
...AND WE'RE GOING TO HELP YOU FINISH THE JOB.
YOU KNOW... BECAUSE YOU SUCK AT IT.
THE END! (For now!)

CHICKEN DEVIL™

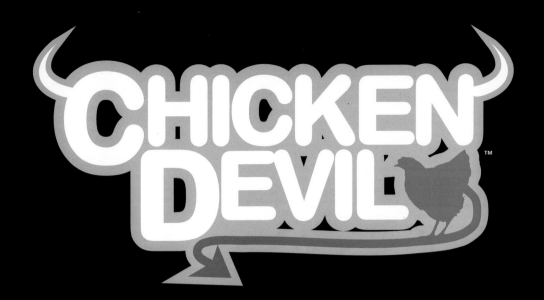

COVER GALLERY & EXTRAS

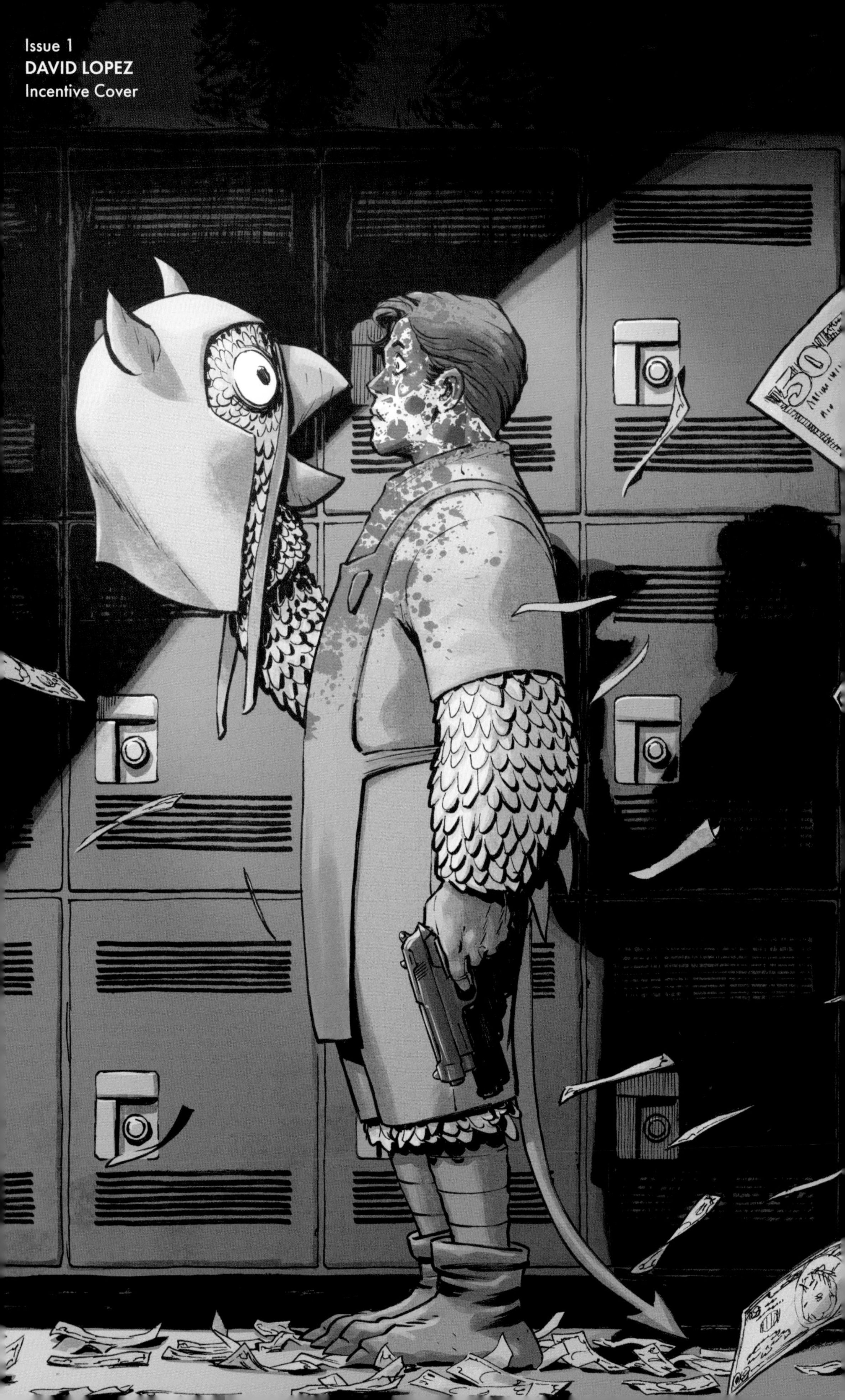

Issue 1
DAVID LOPEZ
Incentive Cover

Issue 1
HAYDEN SHERMAN
Mask Cover

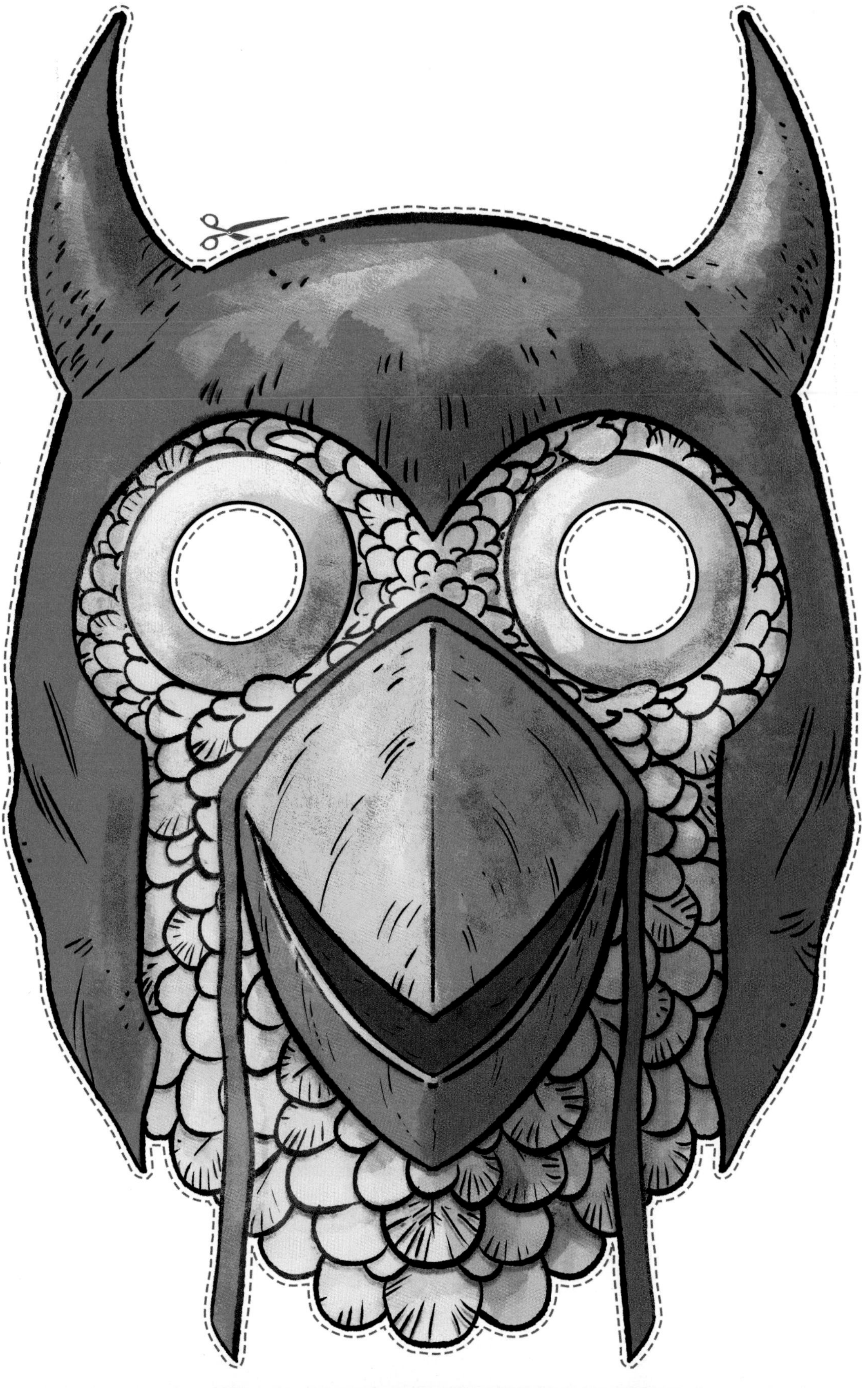

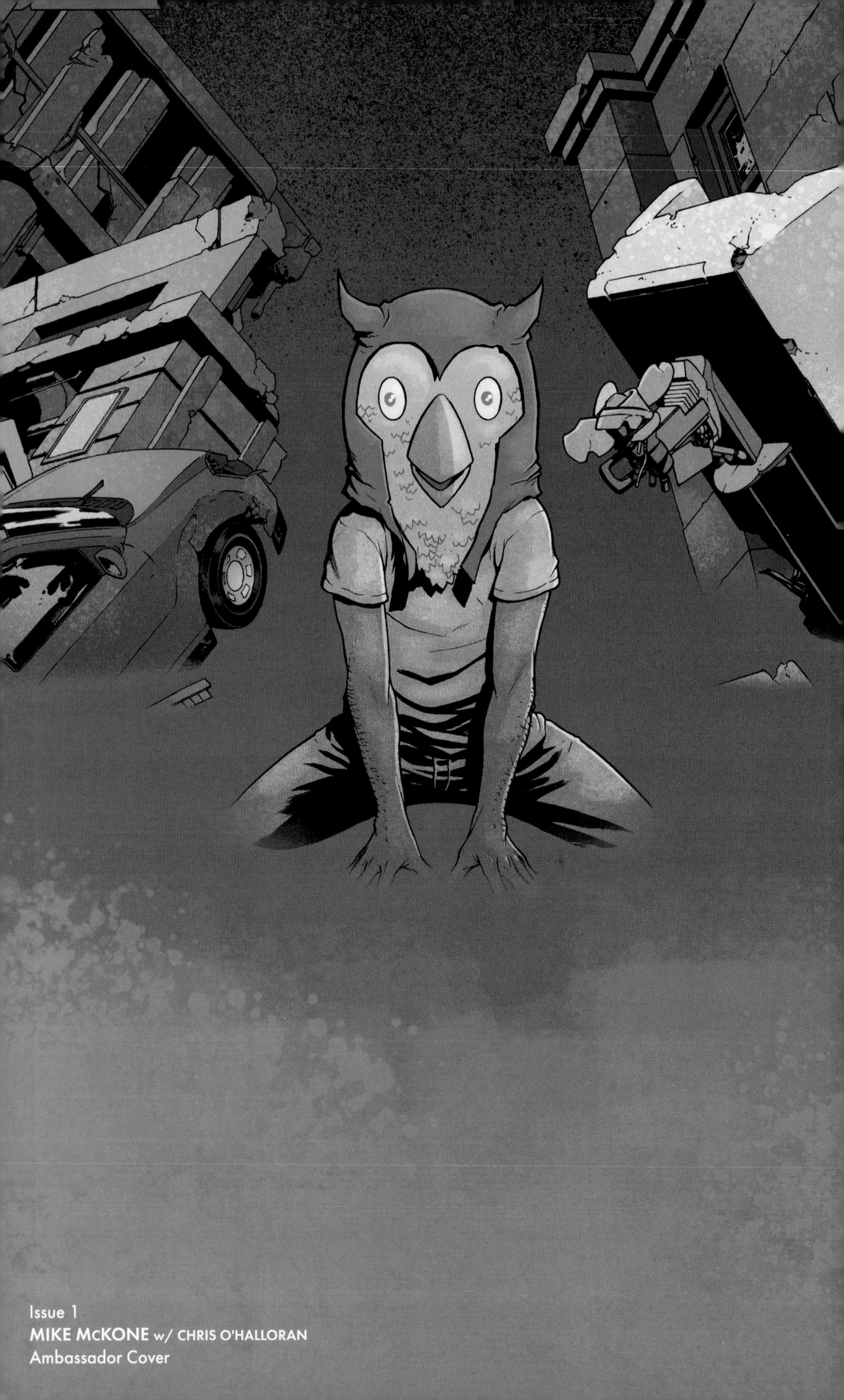

Issue 1
MIKE McKONE w/ CHRIS O'HALLORAN
Ambassador Cover

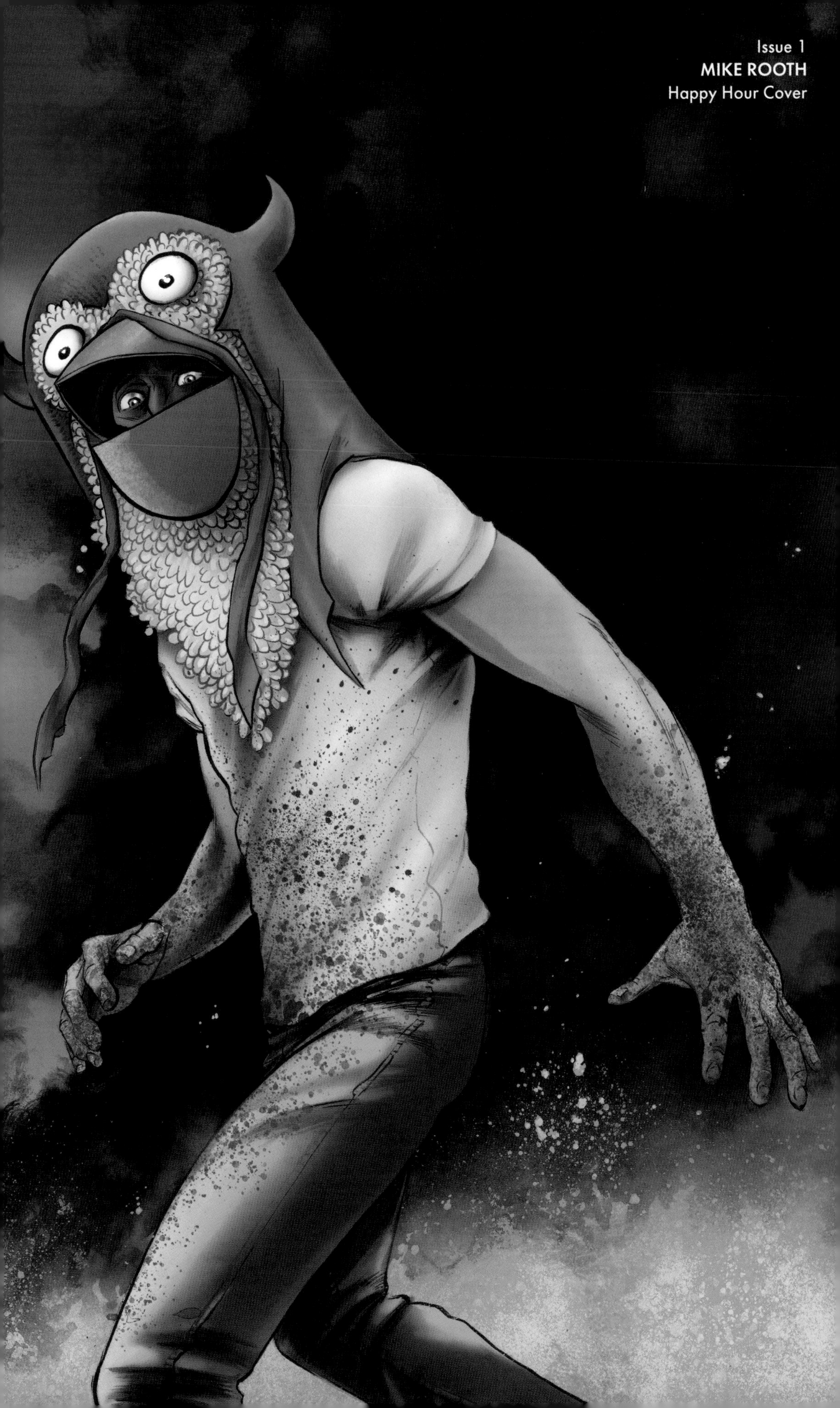

Issue 1
MIKE ROOTH
Happy Hour Cover

Issue 1
DAN PANOSIAN
NYCC & Baltimore Comic Con Exclsuive Cover

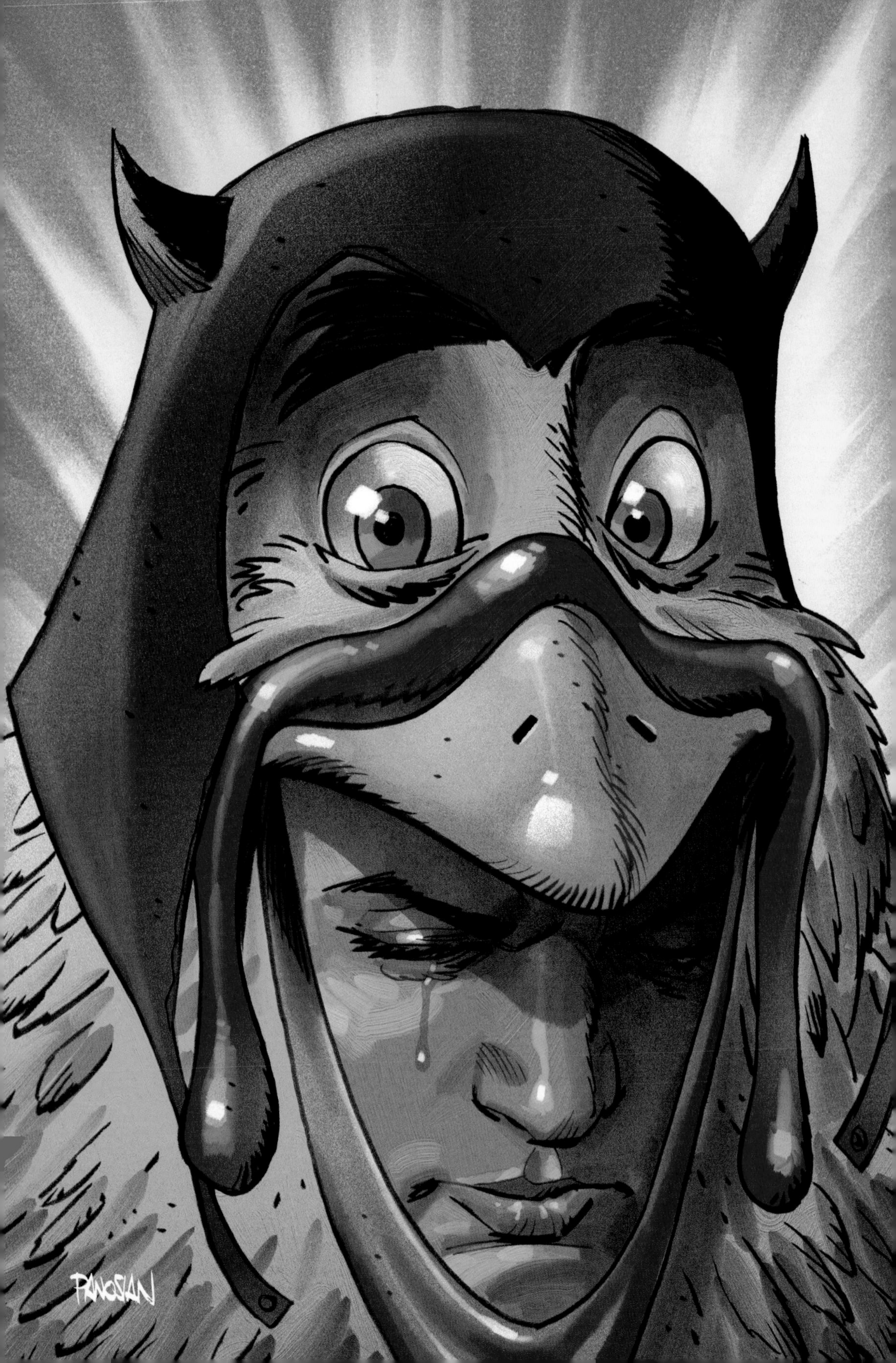
PANOSIAN

Issue 1

HUGH ROCKWOOD

Big Country Comics / Natdaddy Collectibles Variant Cover

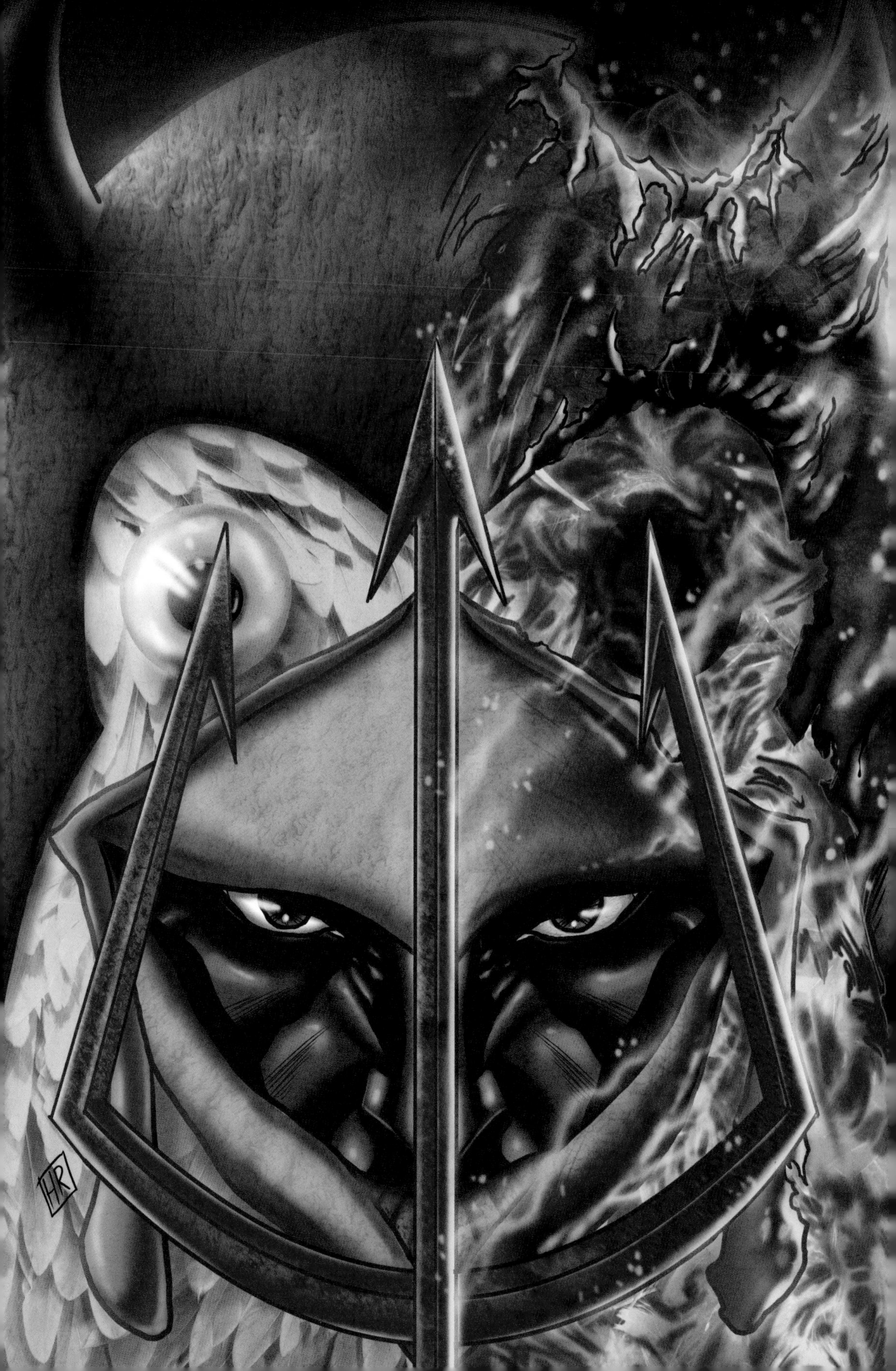

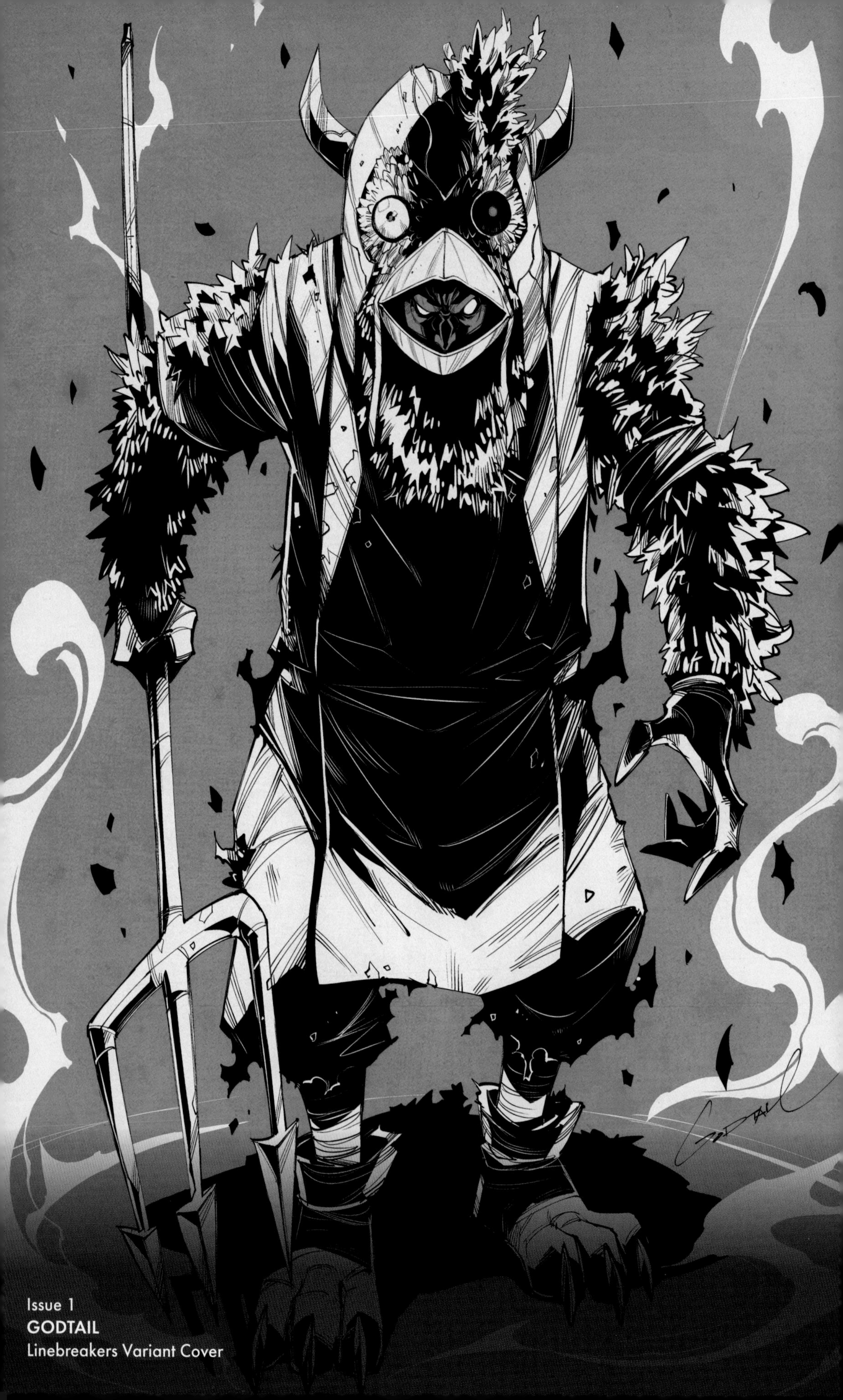

Issue 1
GODTAIL
Linebreakers Variant Cover

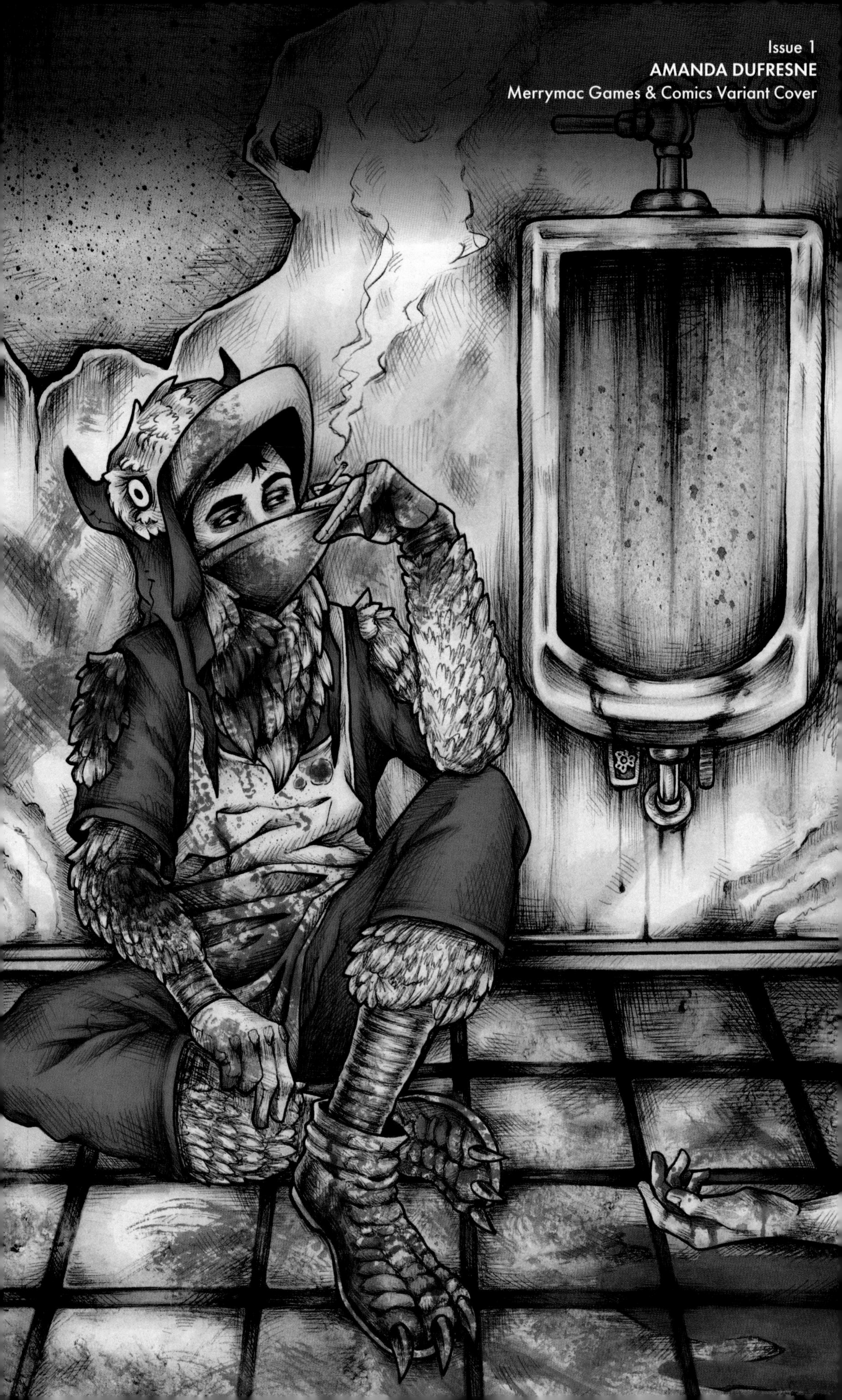

Issue 1
AMANDA DUFRESNE
Merrymac Games & Comics Variant Cover

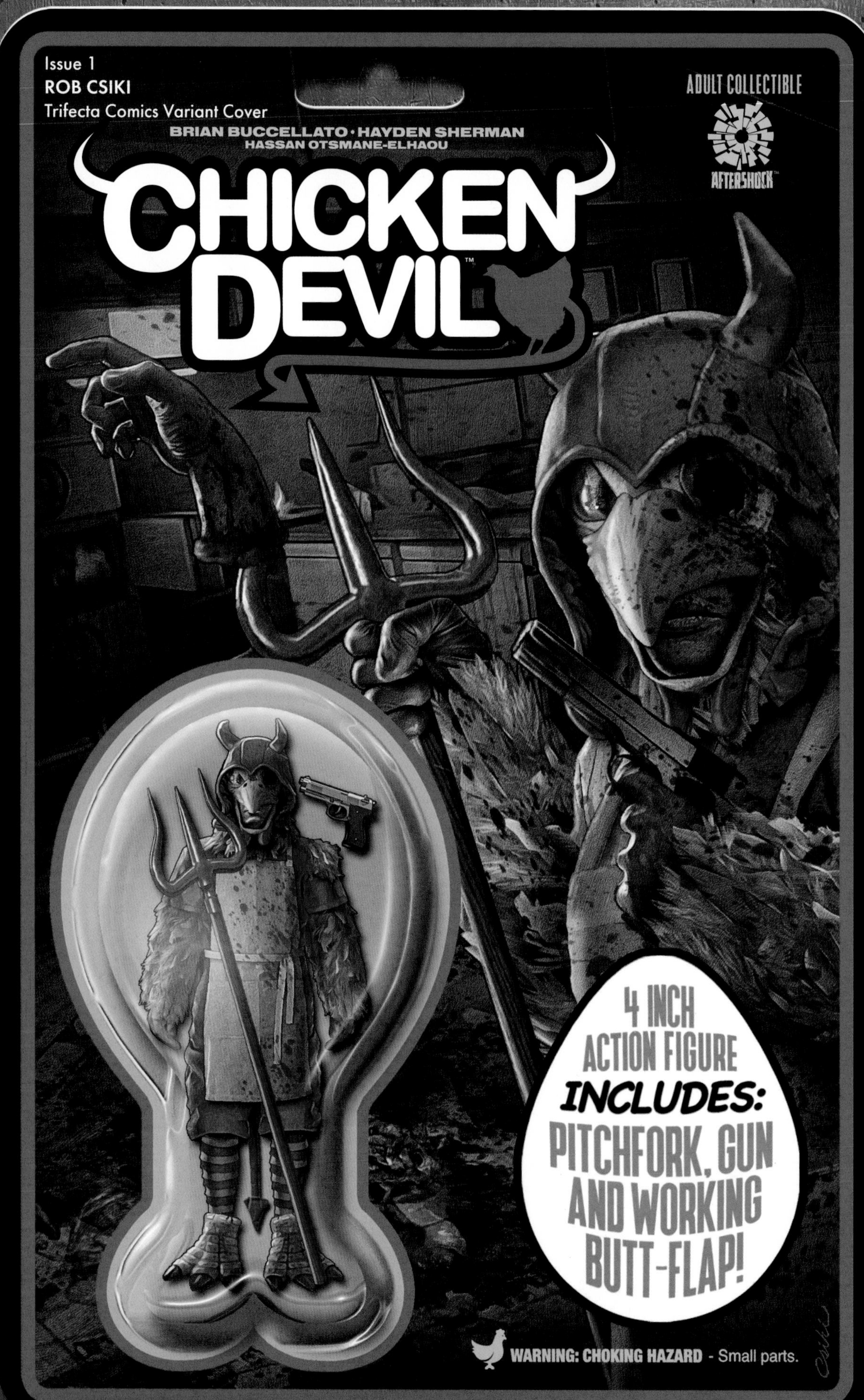
Issue 1
ROB CSIKI
Trifecta Comics Variant Cover
BRIAN BUCCELLATO · HAYDEN SHERMAN
HASSAN OTSMANE-ELHAOU
CHICKEN DEVIL™
ADULT COLLECTIBLE
AFTERSHOCK™
4 INCH
ACTION FIGURE
INCLUDES:
PITCHFORK, GUN
AND WORKING
BUTT-FLAP!
WARNING: CHOKING HAZARD - Small parts.

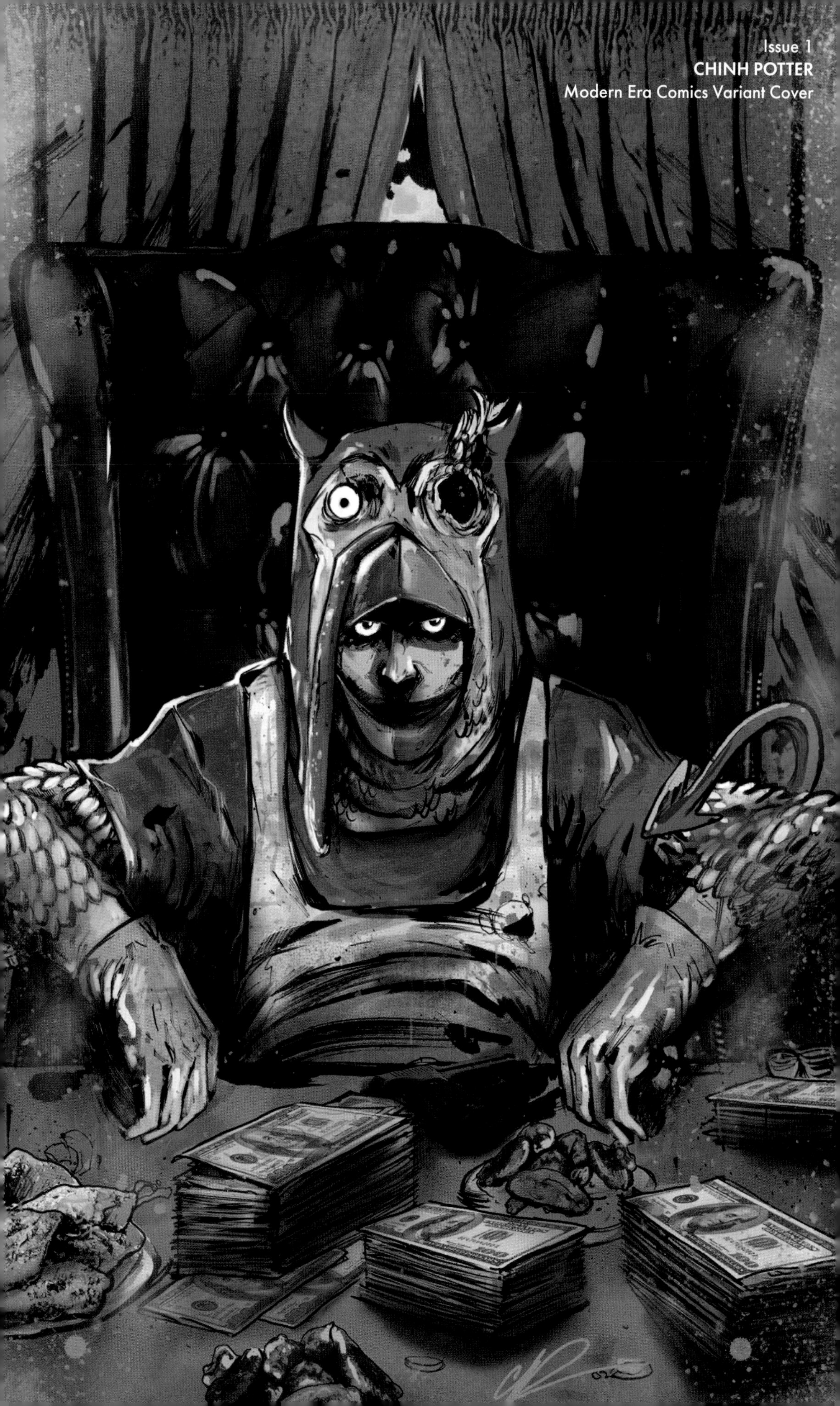
Issue 1
CHINH POTTER
Modern Era Comics Variant Cover

N-MITCH'S HOT CHICKEN-MITCH'S HOT CHICKEN-MITC
EN-MITCH'S HOT CHICKEN-MITCH'S HOT CHICKEN-MIT

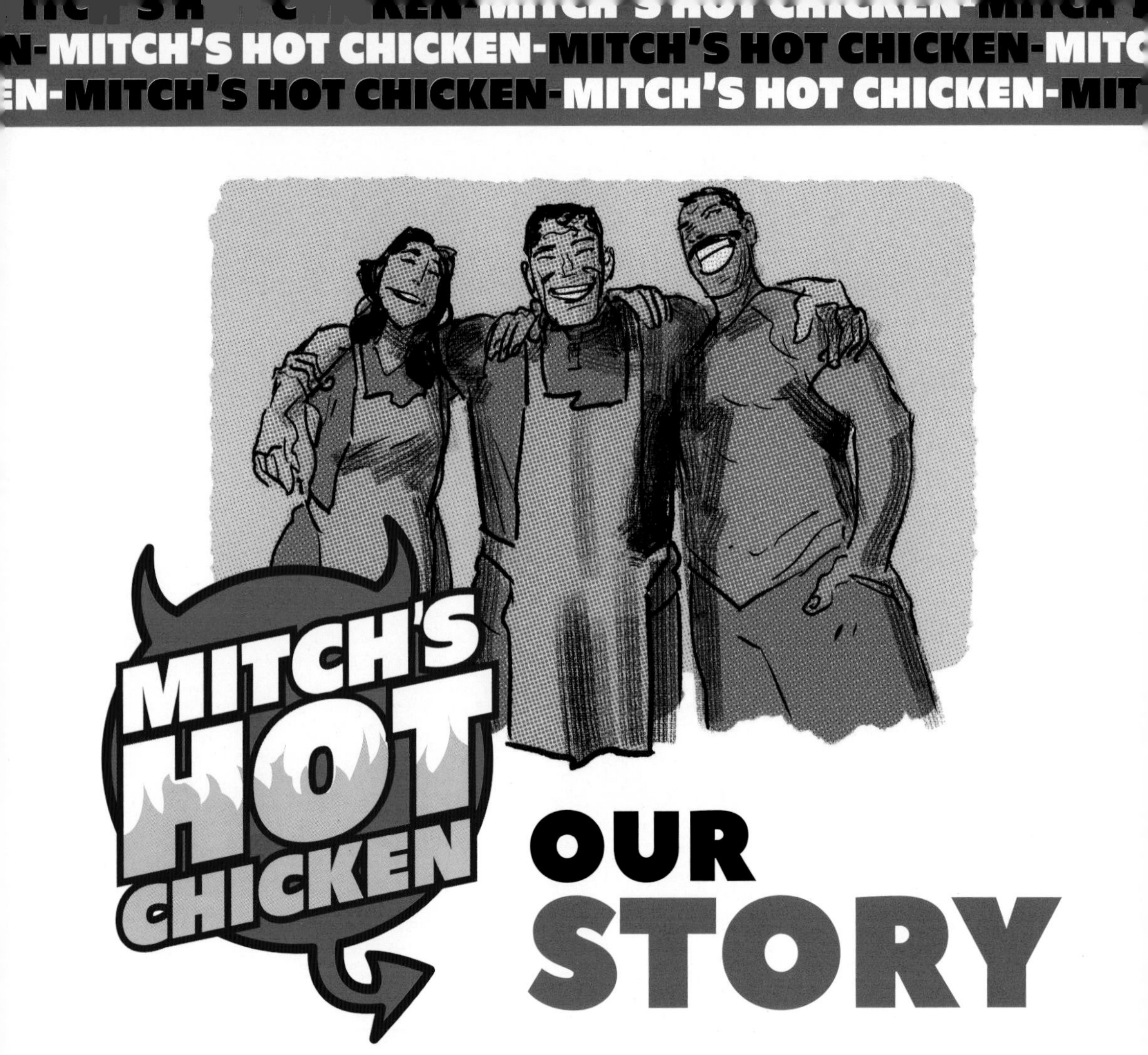

MITCH'S HOT CHICKEN

OUR STORY

MITCH'S HOT CHICKEN is the story of friendship, love and a fateful trip to Tennessee that led to the creation of Los Angeles' premiere hot chicken sandwich. MITCHELL MOSS grew up in the food scene. Not the Gordon Ramsey, Michelin star kind of dining. His path was the world of fast food, dive bars and hole-in-the-wall eating. Starting at fifteen, he worked at California favorites such as Go-n-Get Burger, Fatburger and The Pollo Brothers. There, he learned the ins and outs of fast food and the meaning of a hard day's work. But as great a proving ground as that was, he earned his stripes at the now-closed Hollywood AllStar Lanes Diner becoming the head chef at the age of 19 and creating his own contemporary menu by 21.

The young chef's good life became great in 2004 when Mitch met DENISE, a grad student tending bar at a Koreatown dive called K-Bar. She served him a criminally under-exposed kimchi chicken sandwich, which was the best he'd ever had up to that point. It was love at first sight—with her AND the sandwich. So, he made them both permanent fixtures in his life, taking a job as head chef and marrying Denise. And with the love of his life beside him, Mitchell turned the bar into a hip, multiple award-winning restaurant bar…

...AND BEGAN TO THINK ABOUT OPENING HIS OWN RESTAURANT.

The spark that would become MITCH'S HOT CHICKEN was lit at a 2010 restaurateur's conference in Nashville, Tennessee. An unexpected reunion with his childhood best friend, ANTONIO, turned into a vow of partnership by the end of the conference. But, wanting to work together is one thing—the all-important inspiration needed to turn it into a thriving business is another. Serendipitously for them, Antonio had his identity stolen on the last day and all his accounts were frozen. With no money or options, Mitchell stepped up to drive Antonio back to Los Angeles. On the way home, they stopped at a hole-in-the-wall hot chicken spot—whose name they will never admit —and were absolutely blown away by the Nashville hot chicken sandwich.

It was like a religious experience; after one bite they knew they had found their inspiration. Denise was on the next flight to meet them, and after a two-week tour of hot chicken joints from Nashville to Memphis, Mitchell perfected HIS signature version of the sandwich. For a moment there was talk of buying out K-Bar and introducing the sandwich there, but Denise would have none of it. This was their chance to do something special. The City of Angels needed Hot Chicken in their lives in a big way. Not as bar food, or at some gastropub—as quality sandwiches made quickly and affordably.

By the end of 2013, the original MITCH'S HOT CHICKEN food truck was born.

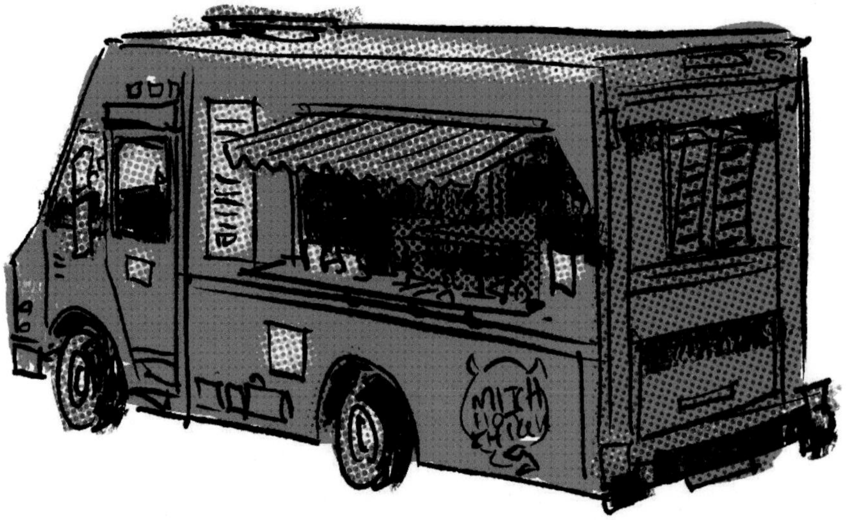
MITCH

Two years later they opened their first brick and mortar location and haven't looked back since. As of 2021 there are locations in Koreatown, Hollywood, Eagle Rock and Studio City, where life-mates Mitch, Denise, and Antonio continue to make the best hot chicken sandwiches in Los Angeles…and maybe the world.

One last bit of advice: If it's your first time, get THE MITCH. If it's your second, get THE K-TOWN. You won't be disappointed.

MITCH'S HOT CHICKEN-MITCH'S HOT CHICKEN-MITC
MITCH'S HOT CHICKEN-MITCH'S HOT CHICKEN-MIT

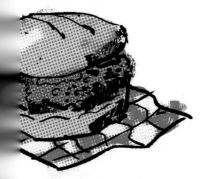

CHOOSE YOUR OWN HOT CHICKEN ADVENTURE

PICK YOUR PROTEIN & A HEAT LEVEL

THE MITCH $12
boneless breast, comeback sauce, sweet relish, honey drizzle, brioche bun

THE DENISE $12
boneless thigh, comeback sauce, spicy relish, American cheese, brioche bun

THE K-TOWN $12
boneless thigh, gochujang sauce, cucumber relish, kimchi, brioche bun

KETO STYLE $10
boneless breast. served with coleslaw & collard greens

MITCH NUGGETS $12
3 big tenders. served with Hawaiian roll & fries

DEVIL WINGS $10
5 wings served with Hawaiian roll & fries

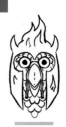

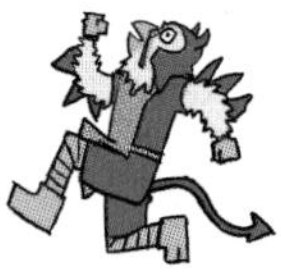

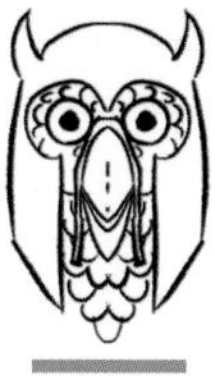

ANGEL STYLE
no heat

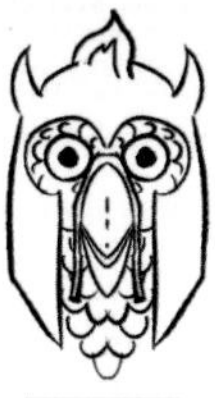

MILD
a lil heat

MEDIUM
a nice mouthy hotness

ANTONIO FRIES $12
thin cut, shaken with spicy mix, melted
American, sweet relish, comeback sauce

BORING FRIES $6
thin cut. salt and pepper. that's it.

SIDES & EXTRAS

COLLARD GREENS	$4
GLORIA'S MACARONI SALAD	$4
CHRISTIAN'S CUCUMBER SLAW	$4
KIMCHI	$3
COMEBACK SAUCE	$.50

DRINKS

ICED SWEET TEA	$2
SODAS	$2
WATERMELON JUICE	$2
LEMONADE	$2

HOT
serious mouth
fire

EXTRA HOT
wear gloves & don't
touch your face

**THE DEVIL MADE
ME DO IT**
hellishly hot

artist interview:
HAYDEN SHERMAN

AfterShock Comics: What were your influences behind the iconic Chicken Suit and overall look of CHICKEN DEVIL?

Hayden Sherman: Mick McMahon and Cam Kennedy's *Judge Dredd* work definitely factored into the feel of CHICKEN DEVIL for me. That look and feel is probably most evident in the look of Mitch's armored-up Devil suit. Otherwise, the chicken suit is 100% inspired by dorky lovable mascot costumes.

ASC: Do you have a favorite character? A favorite panel?

— ANTONIO

HS: My favorite character has gotta be Mitch. For me, he's just so neurotic and paranoid and in over his head from start to finish. He's a great guy to draw. Favorite panel has gotta go to the final shot of issue one. I have a lot of favorite moments throughout the rest of the book, but that whole page, with Mitch in the chicken mask freaking out over a dead body, fully set the tone for everything that followed.

ASC: What is your process when coming up with unique page layouts like those found throughout CHICKEN DEVIL?

DENISE-

HS: More than anything, I want to make pages that are fun, and a big part of that is finding different ways to arrange panels. Or different shapes for them to be, or not be, or whatever. So when I start laying out an issue, I usually try to find each page's focus and then more or less build each page around that. Of course, clarity of reading does have to take priority as much as possible. But if I know a character will be doing something BIG in a page, or a moment just really sticks out to me, I'm going to try and arrange the panelling to amplify that beat however I can. Which can lead to fun stuff!

ASC: Any advice for artists trying to break into the industry?

HS: Biggest thing: Keep making comics. Make a bunch of short stories, experiment with different settings, characters, genres, anything. And just keep making more from there. Post them online, submit them to competitions, submit them to publishers. Show them to anyone who'll look, but what's most important is that you've got the work to show.

ASC: What was the most challenging aspect for you when illustrating CHICKEN DEVIL?

HS: Coloring. This is the fifth book I've colored, but only the first book where I pushed for a more rendered out and painted approach. In the past, I'd try and skate by on limited color palettes and flats, but now I've fully painted this whole thing, and I'm really pleased with the result! It was real difficult though.

ASC: What's your go-to fast-food chain and order?

HS: Bacon cheeseburger. Doesn't matter where I am, I'm getting a bacon cheeseburger.

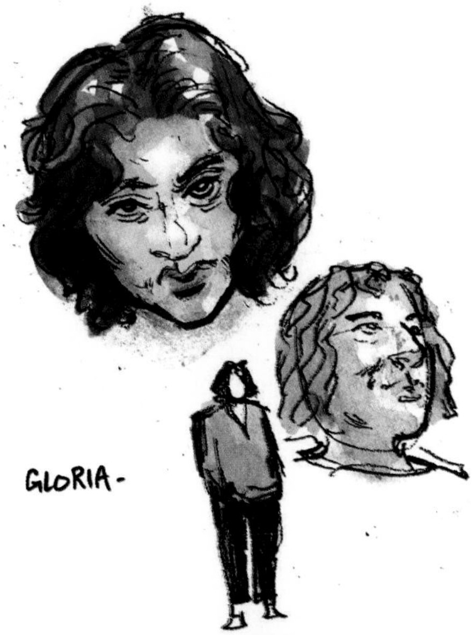
GLORIA-

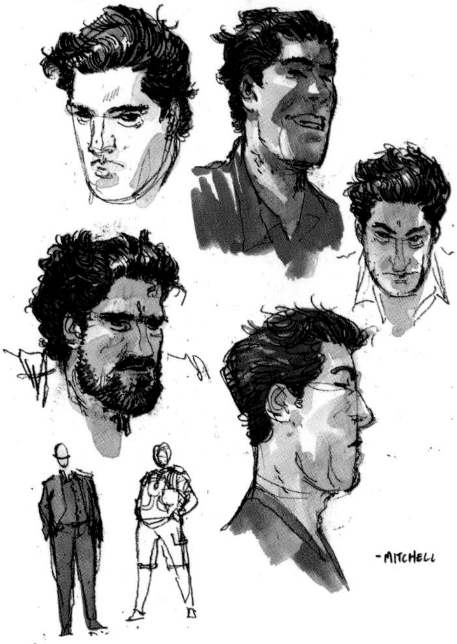
-MITCHELL

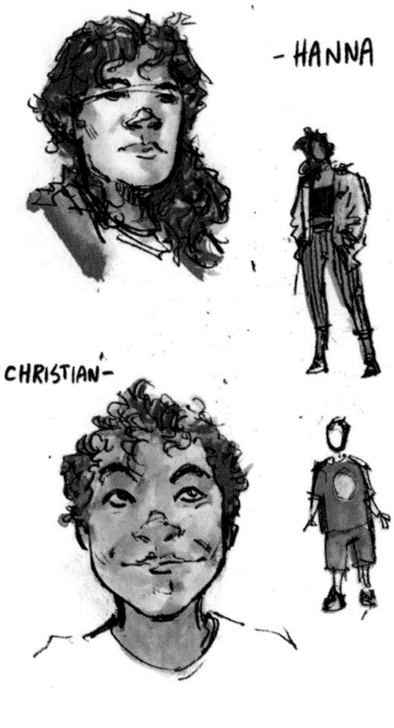
-HANNA
CHRISTIAN-

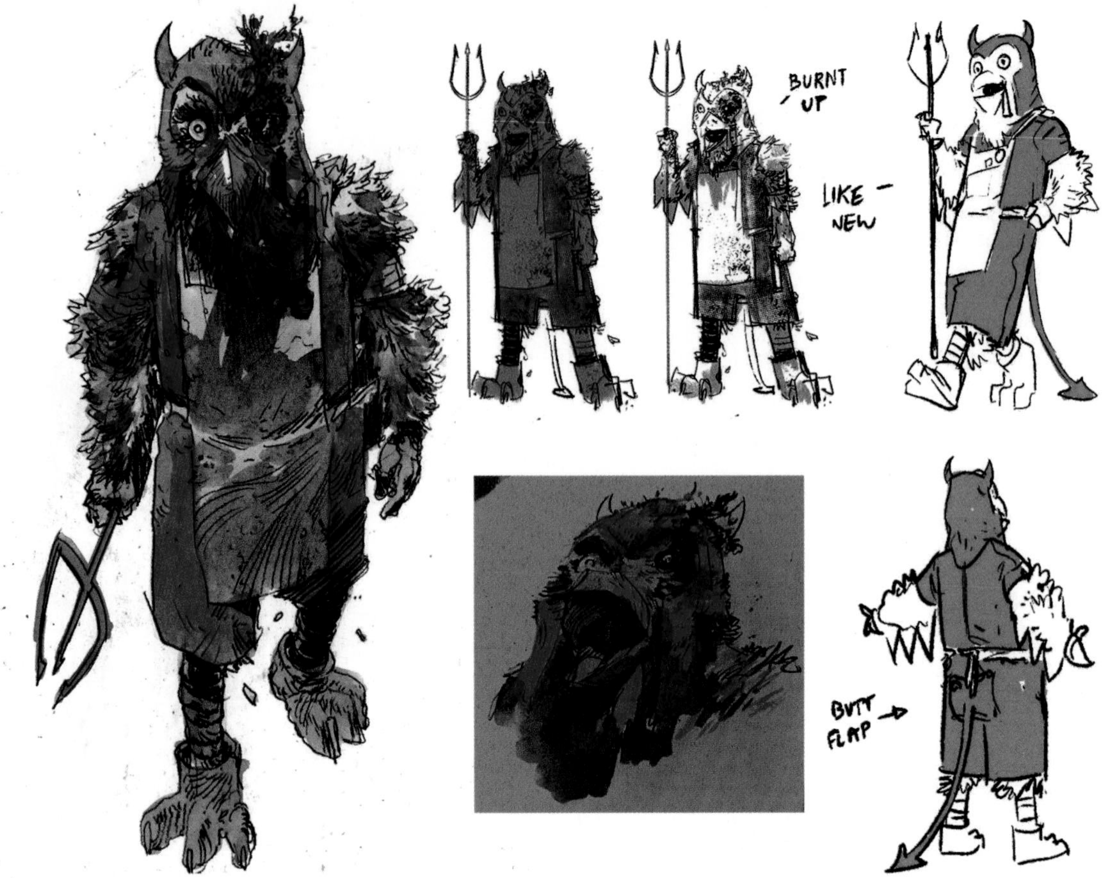
BURNT UP
LIKE NEW
BUTT FLAP

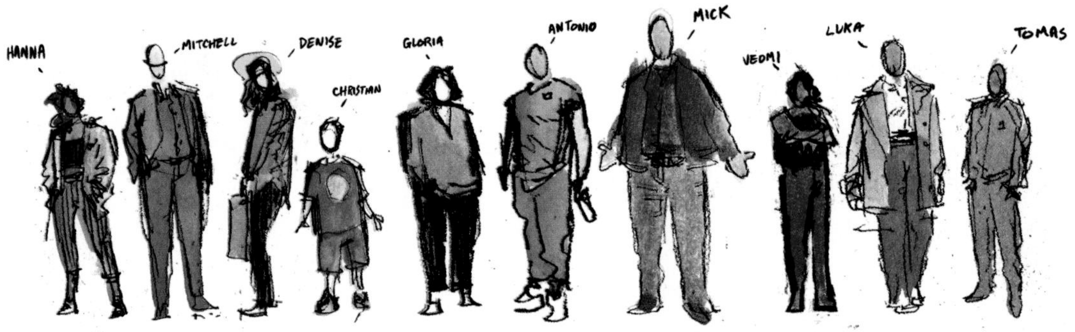
HANNA
MITCHELL
DENISE
CHRISTIAN
GLORIA
ANTONIO
MICK
NEOMI
LUKA
TOMAS

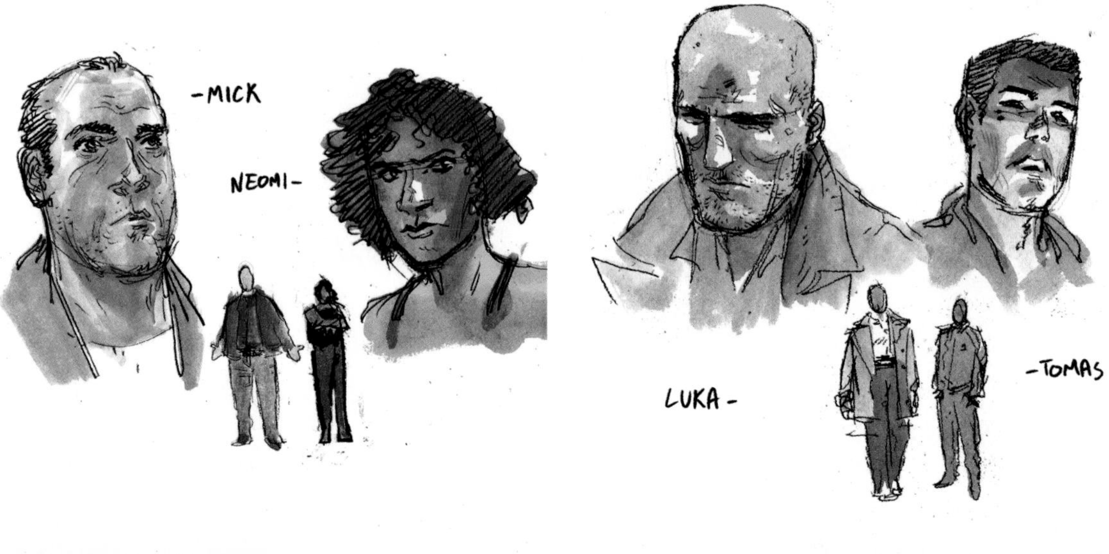
-MICK
NEOMI-
LUKA-
-TOMAS

THANK YOU

Order Up!

Well. That escalated quickly. Like fast food fast. We introduced Mitchell to the world and then turned his life upside down.

But truth be told, it took a little time to get the right ingredients together for this comic. Once we did, the book was off and running. And it's been a hell of a ride ever since. One that I'm incredibly proud of and thankful for.

It's hard to describe the surreal feeling of creating something with a bunch of words on a page and then watching as super-talented people bring it to life. I'm truly honored to be a part of the amazing team that hatched CHICKEN DEVIL into this world.

At poor Mitchell's expense.

Life gets complicated when you're just a guy who makes good chicken and someone murders your family. Especially when said family turns out not to be dead AFTER you've gone on a kill-crazy rampage. But, with apologies to Mitch, that was the point from the start. Not just to see what happens when a regular guy takes it upon himself to become a revenge killer...

...but to explore the question, how do you unbreak bad after you've crossed that line? Or, in Mitch's case, blown that line to smithereens with a proprietary chicken fryer.

To the readers, thank you for giving this book a shot and sticking with us. I really hope you've enjoyed the Moss family's ups and (mostly) downs, the dark humor, the death count and the meta-weirdness of this offbeat revenge tale. I didn't set out to create something different...just something that was closer to my own personal (albeit it odd) creative aesthetic.

For those of you that were expecting a traditional superhero tale, sorry. For those of you who picked up the book because of the amazing cover and super weird title, I hope it blew away expectations. And for those who understood what was on the menu and ordered it anyway...I hope you got a taste for it and want more.

A profuse thanks to Mike, Christina, Lee, Jon and the entire AfterShock team who have been a dream to collaborate with. And one last ultra-heartfelt thank you...to the Herculean efforts of Hayden Sherman, who did all of the heavy lifting to bring this weird hot chicken world to life in the most colorful way imaginable. Hayden's talent truly blows me away.

Like a proprietary pressure fryer in a ball pit.

Stay tuned...We've got more CHICKEN DEVIL cooking...!

Brian Buccellato
December 2021

CHICKEN DEVIL™

BRIAN BUCCELLATO *writer*
🐦 @BrianBooch

Brian Buccellato is a New York Times best-selling writer best known for his work on *Flash* and *Injustice* for DC Comics. Brian started in comics as a colorist, working on titles such as *The Uncanny X-Men*, *Superman*, *Witchblade* and *The Flash*. He started his comic writing career at Top Cow with *The Darkness* before teaming with Francis Manapul to co-write *The Flash* and *Detective Comics* at DC. He is the creator of *Foster*, *Sons of the Devil* and is the co-creator of *Cannibal* for Image Comics. His most recent work includes *Detective Pikachu* and *Lost in Space: Countdown to Danger* for Legendary. He is currently semi-quarantined in Cypress Park with his family and a very small cat.

HAYDEN SHERMAN *artist*
🐦 @Cleanlined

Hayden Sherman is an award-winning comic artist whose work includes *Wasted Space*, *The Few*, *Thumbs*, COLD WAR and MARY SHELLEY MONSTER HUNTER. They're a lover of fun, colorful fiction who has had the joy of illustrating for companies such as Marvel, Image, Dark Horse, Dynamite, AfterShock, Vault and BOOM! Studios. They currently reside in Boston, Massachusetts, where they share a home with their significant other and an increasingly dumb cat.

HASSAN OTSMANE-ELHAOU *letterer*
🐦 @HassanOE

Hassan Otsmane-Elhaou is a writer, editor and letterer. He's lettered comics like *Shanghai Red*, *Peter Cannon*, *Red Sonja*, *Lone Ranger* and more. He's also the editor behind the Eisner-winning publication, *PanelxPanel*, and is the host of the *Strip Panel Naked* YouTube series. You can usually find him explaining that comics are totally a real job to his parents.